A Pastor Preaching

Toward a Theology of the Proclaimed Word

William Powell Tuck

Copyright 2012 by William Tuck

Published in the United States by Nurturing Faith Inc., Macon GA, www.nurturingfaith.net.

Library of Congress Cataloging-in-Publication Data is available.

ISBN 978-1-938514-08-1

All rights reserved. Printed in the United States of America

Permissions:
A Child Is Born: Meditations for Advent and Christmas (Philadelphia: Westminster Press, 1988) used by permission of Westminster John Knox Press (www.wkjbooks.com). "Toward a Theology of the Proclaimed Word" first appeared in a slightly different format in *Review & Expositor*, vol. LXXXI, no. 2 (Spring 1984). "Exorcising Demons in the Modern World" first appeared in *The Twentieth Century Pulpit*, vol. II, ed. James W. Cox (Nashville: Abingdon Press, 1981).

Biblical translations consulted include: *Revised Standard Version* © 1946, 1952, 1971, 1973, Division of Christian Education of the National Council of the Churches of Christ in the USA; *New Revised Standard Version* © 1989, Division of Christian Education of the National Council of the Churches of Christ in the USA; *King James Version*, public domain; *New English Bible* © 1961, 1970, Delegates of Oxford University Press and Studies of Cambridge University Press; *New International Version* © 1973, Zondervan Bible Publishers; *Good News for Modern Man* © 1972, Thomas Nelson, Inc.; James Moffatt, *A New Translation of the Bible* © 1935, Harper & Brothers Publishers. Unless otherwise marked, Scripture quotations are the author's translations.

With appreciation

To my "mentors" in preaching:
J. P. Allen
Roy McLain
Harry Emerson Fosdick
Leslie Weatherhead
John Killinger

and

To my seminary students over the years from whom
I have continued to learn

Other Books by William Powell Tuck

Authentic Evangelism: Sharing the Good News with Sense and Sensitivity
The Bible as Our Guide for Spiritual Growth (editor)
Christmas Is for the Young ... Whatever Their Age
Facing Grief and Death
Getting Past the Pain: Making Sense of Life's Darkness
*A Glorious Vision: The Worship Symbols in the Sanctuary of the
     St. Matthews Baptist Church, Louisville, Kentucky*
Knowing God: Religious Knowledge in the Theology of John Baillie
Loving as a Way of Living
The Lord's Prayer Today
Ministry: An Ecumenical Challenge (editor)
Our Baptist Tradition
The Compelling Faces of Jesus
The Struggle for Meaning (editor)
Through the Eyes of a Child
The Way for All Seasons
The Left Behind Fantasy: The Theology Behind the Left Behind Tales
The Ten Commandments: Their Meaning Today
Facing Life's Ups and Downs: The Struggle To Be Whole
The Church in Today's World
The Church under the Cross
Modern Shapers of Baptist Thought in America
The Journey to the Undiscovered Country: What's Beyond Death?

Contents

Preface vii

Introduction 1
Toward a Theology of the Proclaimed Word
Sermon—Exorcising Demons in the Modern World

Part 1 29
Biblical Preaching: The Foundation of Proclamation
Sermon—Standing Up for the Kingdom: The Good Samaritan

Part 2 91
Seeing Inside the Listener's Head: Preaching to Human Needs
Sermon—The Wilderness Places of Life

Part 3 141
Pulpit and Pew Rediscovering Theology:
Preaching as a Ministry of the Word
Sermon—A Word on Behalf of Sin

Part 4 191
Confronting Our Culture Through Literature and the Arts:
Preaching and Christian Imagination
Sermon—A Ticket to Wherever It Is

"Clearly, William Tuck's antenna has been aimed toward God for years. In *A Pastor Preaching* he writes with the wisdom of a sage and the passion of a new believer. With words and stories that rise off the page, Tuck makes a fresh case for preaching that requires all of the biblical, pastoral, theological, and creative commitments in a pastor's mind and heart. This excellent book will appeal to veteran preachers and newbies alike."

Julie Pennington-Russell, Pastor
First Baptist Church
Decatur, Georgia

"From a preacher's preacher comes this deeply theological reflection on proclaiming, indeed, embodying the Word. WIlliam Tuck exemplifies what it means to be a scholar-practitioner, and this latest book helps those called to the perilous task of preaching to become more grounded in their encounter with the Holy One who beckons such vocation. Congruence between one's life, one's words, and the Living Word are essential for homiletical integrity, which Tuck richly illumines by his inclusion of thoughtful sermons. The author's capacity for critical interrogation of his own practice is a model for all of us who bear witness to God's self-disclosure in texts and the larger world."

Molly Marshall, President
Central Baptist Theological Seminary
Shawnee, Kansas

"Drawing from his wide reading and deep experience as both a professor and pastor-preacher, Bill Tuck shares with us the essential and enduring tools for the craft of preaching. His passion for theologically reflective and pastorally faithful sermons runs throughout the book."

Guy Sayles, Pastor
First Baptist Church
Asheville, North Carolina

Preface

Preaching has been both a joy and frustration through my years of ministry. It has been a joy to proclaim the good news of the gospel, but it has always been a frustrating experience to know how to do that proclamation effectively. I have always wanted to do it well, but was aware of how far short of my aspirations I usually fell after each sermon.

There are still some voices that speak of the decline of preaching. No doubt, preaching has undergone many facelifts in recent years. Sometimes it seems that preaching has been turned upside down. Some preachers call for the use of all kinds of technology, including screens, images, and sounds. Sermon outlines are projected on the screen or passed out for the parishioners to see. Casual dress such as jeans and polo shirts are replacing robes or suits. And, rather than proclaiming from behind a pulpit, some preachers prance back and forth in front of their congregation like attorneys before a jury. Whether these experimental attempts at preaching will last or are simply a passing fad, only time will tell.

The intent of this book is not to answer or cast a final or even a passing judgment on the "new" approaches to or styles of preaching, but to look seriously at what constitutes the content and background of authentic preaching.

I am convinced there is still a real interest in preaching, evidenced by the many new and varied books about preaching and the large number of preaching conferences and colloquiums on preaching. Pastor search committees still put preaching at the top of their list of the expectations they have of their prospective ministerial candidate. Most pastors with whom I have conversations indicate they have a genuine desire to be the best preachers they can be. I have spent a lifetime striving to improve my preaching skills and am still working on them today. I am still excited about preaching and believe that "good" preaching continues to communicate the good news of our faith.

This book is offered as one pastor and preaching professor's suggestions on how I have tried to share the gospel through my ministry both in the classroom and in the pulpit. I have been pastor of small and large congregations, rural and downtown urban churches, college and seminary congregations, healthy and troubled parishes. During my busy pastoral ministry with my congregations I have tried to share with them not only my verbal sermons from the pulpit, but also a written copy by the next Sunday. This has often been an exacting but rewarding discipline. It has pushed me for originality, careful craftsmanship, sound biblical exegesis, and the desire for clarity and to offer my best gifts. Being pastor in a college and seminary community has certainly heightened my awareness to offer my best all the time.

I know at times I have failed in all of these efforts, but I did reach for the heights. Falling short is no excuse for not trying to do one's best. The resources I mention in the following chapters are those books, magazines, and so on I have found helpful in my sermon study and preaching preparation. There are, of course, many other resources, some more contemporary, from which a preacher can draw.

The sermons in this volume include some I have preached in my local parishes, in pastors' schools, on preaching missions, and as a "traveling" preacher in various types of congregations. I offer them as one preacher's efforts to approximate the type of preaching delineated in the chapters before them. The chapters on preaching are drawn from lectures I have given at the Southern Baptist Theological Seminary in Louisville, Kentucky, where I served as professor of Christian preaching; at the Baptist Theological Seminary in Richmond, Virginia, where I have been an adjunct professor; and at the University of North Carolina at Pembroke, where I was a visiting professor. I delivered portions of these chapters as preaching lectures at Wake Forest University in Winston-Salem, North Carolina, and at various pastors' schools and preaching conferences.

I want to express my appreciation to Carolyn Stice, my secretary for ten years at St. Matthews Baptist Church in Louisville, Kentucky, who typed earlier parts of this manuscript, and to Barbara Nickel, my administrative assistant at First Baptist Church in Raleigh, North Carolina, who helped me get my manuscript in final shape for publication. They have given of their time faithfully and have helped to see this project, for which I have labored for many years, come to a conclusion. I also appreciate Molly Marshall, a noted preacher, seminary president, and theology professor, and James Cox and John Killinger, distinguished preachers and professors of preaching, for taking time to read the manuscript for me, and fellow ministers, Mike Clingenpeel, Julie Pennington-Russell, and Guy Sayles, for reading the material and sharing their positive support for my efforts. I also want to thank W. Rand Forder, my fellow pastor and friend, for his careful proofreading of the final manuscript and Jackie Riley for her thorough copyediting of the manuscript and for her helpful suggestions.

In an Advent meditation on how John the Baptist pointed beyond himself to Christ, J. Barrie Shepherd challenges every preacher of the gospel to follow the example of the Baptist and not draw attention to one's self when preaching, but to direct attention past one's self to Christ. His personal prayer should become the prayer of everyone who heralds the good news:

> Forgive me, Father, when my faith becomes a self-promoting thing, when my testimony speaks more of my own outstanding virtue and ability than it does of your great mercy and forgiveness. Deliver me from all the pompous posturing that lays its claim so swiftly and so sweetly on my soul. Let my life this day become a signpost, an arrow that points clear and true toward your Son, my Lord.[1]

In all of our studying about how to preach and in the preaching process itself, the ones proclaiming acknowledge that our best efforts feebly point to the wonder and mystery of the God who has come uniquely into our world through Jesus Christ and that it is about him we preach and to whom we call persons to commit their lives. In humility we affirm that the preaching task is not really about the preacher, but about the grace and love of God we are charged to herald.

Note

[1] J. Barrie Shepherd, *A Child Is Born* (Philadelphia: Westminster Press, 1988), 40.

Introduction
Toward a Theology of the Proclaimed Word

What can be more preposterous than a person claiming to speak in the name of God? Yet this is what preachers claim week after week. "The word which I received from the Lord," they say often without much timidity, "I declare unto you." In the preacher's lineage stand such impressive figures as Paul, Chrysostom, Augustine, Francis of Assisi, Martin Luther, John Wesley, Charles Spurgeon, Fredrick W. Robertson, and John Broadus. But the line continues with Phillips Brooks, Harry Emerson Fosdick, Martin Luther King, Jr., Billy Graham, Carlyle Marney, Ernest Campbell, John Claypool, Gardner Taylor, Peter Gomes, Elizabeth Achtemeier, Fred Craddock, William Willimon, Tom Long, Barbara Brown Taylor, John Killinger, and maybe you and maybe me.

How dare we, you, they, I make such a claim! Is it only our hot breath that keeps the words from freezing on our lips? Is it merely the moisture in our mouths that prevents the words from turning to dust through our teeth? What an absurdity it seems! How shameless is its claim! Even through our ministerial casualness with holy things, our sloppiness with the ordinances, and our careless sermon preparation, we claim his light still "shines in the darkness, and the darkness has not overcome it." "The obligation to speak of God," James C. Howell reminds us, "whether it feels like zealous passion or the numb inevitability of this week's calendar, is inextricably paired with an inability we all know too well."[1]

Sometimes it happens and words become Word to us, but more often they do not. Sometimes the words are more like "sounding brass or tinkling cymbal." The Word is obscured and hidden by tattered rags of outworn phrases and clichés or buried under alliterated glibness and decorative triteness. But sometimes it happens and there is *viva vox*, "a living voice," words through whom the Word penetrates to become an event once more.

From the beginning when Christianity witnessed to the event of the Incarnate One, its very witness became a part of the event itself. The

Gospels, as we have them, are the early church's preaching about the event. Emil Brunner underscored this emphasis when he declared: "The basic or primal function of the church is that of preaching, for it is this which establishes the church in every sense of the Word."[2] Jesus himself came preaching (Matt. 1:14-15). Luke 4:14-19 recounts the occasion when Jesus spoke in the synagogue at Nazareth. Jesus read from the prophet Isaiah and declared:

> "Today this scripture has been fulfilled in your hearing." The Spirit of the Lord is upon me, because he has anointed me to preach good news to the poor. He has sent me to proclaim release to the captives and recovering of sight to the blind, to set at liberty those who are oppressed, to proclaim the acceptable year of the Lord.

Jesus sent his disciples into the world and instructed them to preach (Mark 3:13-14, Matt. 19:7, Luke 9:2). He told his disciples, "He that hears you hears me" (Luke 10:10). Paul lifted his voice to sound this same refrain as he told Timothy, "Preach the word" (2 Tim. 4:2). Paul felt he had been set apart by God to preach (Gal. 1:15-16) and sighed, "Woe to me if I do not preach the gospel" (1 Cor. 9:16). And Paul listed preaching the Word of God as the supreme commission of the church (1 Cor. 12:31).

Luther affirmed the high view that Scripture gave to preaching. He openly preached Christ the Word, which he believed was the utterance of God's own heart. "When thou hearest the Word," Luther said, "then thou hearest God."[3] A marginal note in the Second Helvetic Confession states, "*La predication de la parole de Dieu, est parole de Die.*" ("The preaching of the word of God is the Word of God.").[4] It was an audacious claim, but other voices have joined these. Dietrich Bonhoeffer declared:

> The proclaimed Word is the Incarnate Christ himself. . . . He is the entrance to the historical Jesus. Therefore the proclaimed Word is not a medium of Expression for something else, something which lies behind it, but it is the Christ himself walking through his congregation as the Word.[5]

Listen to Rudolf Bultmann: "The salvation-occurrence is nowhere present except in the proclaiming, accosting, demanding, and promising word of preaching."⁶ "The crucified and resurrected Christ encounters us in the word of preaching, and never in any other way."⁷

Emil Brunner qualified his assurance only slightly: "Where there is true preaching, where, in the obedience of faith, the Word is proclaimed, there, in spite of all appearances to the contrary, the most important thing that ever happens upon this earth takes place."⁸ P. T. Forsyth made a similar claim: "With preaching, Christianity stands or falls because it is the declaration of a gospel. Nay more—far more—it is the gospel prolonging and declaring itself."⁹

The audacity of preaching is rooted in the boldness of Jesus himself, carried forward by the Gospels and Pauline traditions, and exposed by many theologians. The origin is found in God's Word. Even that awareness, however, does not lighten the awesome responsibility of speaking in the name of God; in fact, it may only heighten it. Barth puts his finger on the dilemma: Preaching is "an act of daring, and only the man who would rather not preach and cannot escape from it ought to ever attempt it."¹⁰ I don't know about you, but it has never been easy for me to be a "man (person) of the cloth." It goes against the fabric of my nature a little. There are times I would rather do other things, but a sense of compulsion has been laid upon me. I must proclaim the good news of the Word become flesh. My boldness and your boldness to declare this word does not rest in our strength, power, or fame but in the living Word of God. And preach I/we must!

Personal Encounter

Before we can proclaim the Word of God, we must first be addressed personally by its presence. No one can deliver a message from God that has not been received. How can anyone speak for God who has not heard God "speak"? It is essential to have a word from God before we speak it. Christianity cannot be described from without. Its reality is known from within as we have been grasped by the Word. There is a claim upon us that comes from beyond us. No second-hand knowledge about this Word is sufficient. Out of a first-hand, personal experience the Word becomes real to us. The First Epistle of John expresses it this way:

> That which was from the beginning, which we have heard, which we have seen with our eyes, which we have looked upon and touched with our hands, concerning the word of

life—the life was made manifest, and we saw it, and testify to it, and proclaim to you the eternal life which was with the Father and was made manifest with us—that which we have seen and heard we proclaim also to you . . . (1:1-3)

The early disciples bore witness to that which they had experienced personally. God to them was known not by argument but by encounter, not by influence but by a presence.

Throughout the Old Testament it is clear that no prophet or leader of Israel ever spoke for God without a powerful sense of the Word of the Lord coming to him. In many ways and places the Old Testament declares that "the word of the Lord came unto" Abram (Gen. 15:1), Ezekiel (Ezek. 1:3), Micah (Micah 1:1), Isaiah (Isaiah 6), Jeremiah (Jer. 1:4, 13; 2:1; 7:1), Hosea (Hosea 1:1), and others. In the Old Testament the phrase "the word of Yahweh" occurs more than 400 times and is the most common way in the Old Testament to describe God's revelation. The meaning of the phrase is not limited merely to words. Greek thought made a distinction between word and deed, between speech and action, but this is not true of the Hebrew concept. *Dabar* in Hebrew may be translated as an action or event. God's Word can bring about an action or deed. His Word may be "eventful" because God's fiat and effective action are one. This is seen in the creation story in Genesis 1 where God speaks and events become a reality. "And God said, 'Let there be light,' and there was light" (Gen 1:3). God's Word was proclaimed, and words became events. God spoke and something happened.

The Hebrew concept for the Word prepared the way for the New Testament declaration that "the Word became flesh." The "Word" of God is not limited to words or utterance, but is declared, by the Gospel of John, to be an event in the flesh and life of Jesus Christ. Words ring with reminders of Genesis 1: "And the Word became flesh and dwelt among us" (v. 14), or to use J. B. Phillips' translation, God "expressed himself." The incarnation became the fullest articulation, disclosure, or utterance possible to unveil the presence of God in a personal and historical way. The New Testament witness, then, was to bear testimony to what the disciples had seen and experienced in the Logos, God's communication of God's self through Jesus Christ. And so the witness is carried forward by us.

Most of us will admit that the Word of God came. We might acknowledge that it came to Moses while he was on a mountain side tending sheep. It came to Jacob with his head on a rock for a pillow. It came to

Isaiah when he was in the temple and saw the Lord high and lifted up. The Word broke in upon Jeremiah in a country village near Jerusalem. It came in a blinding light to Saul on the Damascus Road. It came here and there to others. But does it still come?

How can we preach if it does not? Dare we scale our own Sinai or Horeb to the point that we come face to face with the Holy One and bow before God to hear the divine Word until our face shines and we know it not? What stone will be your pillow and what awakening so startling that you will declare this is a new Bethel? "Surely the Lord was in this place and I knew it not." Can we ever really preach if we have not come to our own Jabbok and wrestled until the break of day and declared, "I will not let you go until you bless me"? Can we ever preach until we come to our temple worship and see the Lord high and lifted up? Who can preach effectively until she has cried from the bottom of the pits of life, "I sat alone" (Jer. 15:17), or cried from the agony of pain or grief, "Where now is my God" (Ps. 42:10)? Can we ever preach if we have not heard the still, small voice against the Ahabs and Jezebels of the world? Will our voice remain muted until we hear the click-clack of some branches of our sycamore tree assuring us of the presence of God sending us forth to speak in God's name? Will we stride prayerfully through the written Word and our theological tomes to the point that God's holy utterance empowers us with a genuine word from on high?

The Word of the Lord came unto . . . Does it not also come to us? Let us wait before God with expectancy. Let us wait before God with confidence. Let us pray and study the Scriptures with ears attuned to listen. If we have no word, let us be silent or remain till there is a word from God.

For too long many preachers have preached second-hand sermons, borrowed other preacher's experiences, recited someone else's beliefs, and glided along on the surface of religious convictions. Biblical preaching is not "Saturday night specials" made especially easy for lazy ministers. The Word of the Lord does not come as simple sermons from secondary sources for satisfied minds. It is dismal to be beggars for a gospel to proclaim because the gospel has not grasped us. We have surrendered the thunder of God's penetrating Word for the parrot's mechanical imitation. With King David we should vow: "I will not offer unto the Lord that which cost me nothing."

Authentic preaching is costly. Time, prayer, study, and listening will be demanded from us on the side of the mountain with God. Having been addressed by God, we preach because we must. God is known to us not by hearsay, but by personal encounter.

Our Lives

Words have never been enough, not even words about God. Words are difficult to understand apart from some embodiment of them. Even words such as faith, love, hope, and saintliness are difficult to comprehend without some personality to give them flesh and meaning. "How can we know what God is like?" people have asked through the centuries.

In Jesus Christ, God made the divine self known. Of Jesus it was said: "Emmanuel, God with us." The Word became flesh, not concept or proposition. "He that has seen me has seen the Father," said Jesus (John 14:9). God became incarnate to communicate love and grace to us. Jesus was the clearest and most visible utterance of God's nature. The medium became the message. Through his incarnation Jesus has provided us a model for preaching.

The Christian message cannot be proclaimed as though it were an objective bit of information unrelated to the person doing the preaching. The life of the one who dares to declare in God's name must not contradict her words by her life. It is necessary for the preacher to be in her speaking, but also essential for the authenticity of the preacher's life that the utterance she speaks is seen in her life. The preacher's life is intricately related to the Word that is proclaimed. The Word preached is not merely a subjective word of the preacher, nor is it totally an objective word separate from the preacher's life.

The gospel does not exist in a vacuum. It is made real, incarnate, in the life of a person. Phillips Brooks' definition of preaching as "truth through personality" moves in this direction. Jesus challenged his followers: "Be not speakers of the Word alone but doers of it." Preached words, without a life that corresponds to the high demands of the words, are like the empty and flat sounds of a plastic bell—motion without sound or meaning.

There is a maxim in philosophy that states "one's actions follow from one's being." What a person does and says arises out of the quality of one's character. Quintilian declared centuries ago that an orator is a "good man speaking well." The essential element he stressed was "the good man." How much more is this true for the preacher?

The preacher's personality is so linked to what he says and does that a weakness in character can damage the gospel message. We cannot say one thing and live out another. "Is preaching the art of making a sermon and delivering it?" He responds to his own question. "Preaching is the art of making a preacher and delivering that."[11] What kind of gospel does a preacher proclaim who never pays his debts, violates personal confidences, whose word cannot be trusted, and defames his marriage vows? What a preacher "is" reveals whether or not his message is credible. The question of credibility is of vital theological importance. If a preacher doesn't practice his faith, it really does make his words nonsense.

In the last century, Henry Ward Beecher rose to be one of the most famous ministers of his age. While he was pastor of the Plymouth Church in Brooklyn, New York, Beecher went on trial for adulterous behavior with Elizabeth Tilton. The trial lasted six months and received more space in the newspaper than any event since the Civil War. Although he was found innocent of the charge, many people and publications—including the historian Milton Rugoff and newspapers such *The New York Times* and the *Louisville Courier-Journal*—believed he was guilty of the charge and escaped only because of great wealth and powerful lawyers.[12]

Whether Beecher was guilty of the charge of adultery, it is difficult to determine at this date, but he was certainly guilty of serious acts of indiscretion and poor judgment. This scandal hurt the proclamation of Christ by widening the gap between religious words and everyday living.

Martin Luther was right. We are "little Christ" to others. The Apostle Paul declared, "It is on Christ's behalf we come; it is in Christ's stead we beseech you." It is an awesome role! We all have clay feet. Our humanity will always show through. None of us can walk on water. My wife likes to remind me of my humanity. She says: "The thing about being married to a minister is you have to live with him all during the week and then listen to him be the voice of God on Sunday."

The person of the preacher, however, cannot be separated from the event of proclaiming the message. Preaching is the conveying of the reality of the presence of God through human personality. Preaching is the medium through which the Word of God is transmitted through human words. The preacher is not the message, but is intimately involved with this message, and constantly struggles to understand how she can witness to the Word with her words and life without focusing attention upon the messenger and not the message. "I have been crucified with Christ," Paul states. "It is no longer I who live, but Christ who lives in me; and the life I now live in the flesh I live by faith in the Son of God who loved me and gave himself for me" (Gal. 2:20). But Paul also knows that "we have this treasure in earthen vessels, to show that the transcendent power belongs to God and not to us" (2 Cor. 4:7).

Several years ago when a church where I was pastor was looking for an assistant minister, we received the following letter of reference from one of a young man's former college professors:

> There is something wonderfully clean about this young man, and the reference there is to his mind as well as his physical being. He is unfailingly a gentleman. . . . He is loyal to the very highest ideals, and he has both the intelligence and the character to render estimable service to those ideals. I believe that if one word summarizes his many splendid qualities, it is integrity, and I like to think of the relationship of that word to integer. He is a "whole number," solid and sound and unblemished.

Obviously we called him. The preacher is first a good person proclaiming the good news. Dare we be less!

In *The Canterbury Tales*, Chaucer described a kindly person who traveled with some other companions. He concluded his description of him with these lines:

> Indeed I'm sure you could not find a minister more pure.
> He was a Christian both in deed and thought.
> He lived himself the Golden Rule he taught.[13]

Our Words

The Word, however, is proclaimed not only through our lives, but also through the preacher's words. Hear a word about words. More than 5,000,000 sermons are preached in the United States alone each year. In a typical ministry of 40 years a minister will speak about 3,750 words in a 25-minute Sunday morning sermon, if you calculate about 150 words a minute. Excluding vacation time and at least two other times away, a minister will speak about 172,500 words a year. Over a 40-year ministry that will total 6,900,000 words. Add Sunday night and it swells to 13,800,000. Add Wednesday night and it rises to 27,600,000. That is a lot of talk, and it doesn't include the other occasions we have to speak. Each of us will utter enough words in our lifetime to fill more than 500 books.

Preachers need a healthy respect for words, the tools of our trade. We are ministers of the Word and of words. Labor at the study and forge for the right words to communicate the good news. Our people deserve our best work with words so that they might hear and respond to the redeeming Word of God. Avoid dull, lifeless, and abstract words but struggle for powerful, sharp, incisive, and penetrating ones. Since the gospel has got to be told, learn to tell it well. Give careful attention not only to the content of your message, but also remember that the effective packaging of that message may enable the listener to be grasped more easily by the Eternal Word. But even our best polished words are fragmentary in disclosing the wonder of God's grace. Our words, of course, cannot be identified with the Word. The preacher's words point to the Word of God behind and within our faint pictures of it. Any inadequate word, however, is always ours and not God's.

For our words to reach the inner ears of our listeners in the pews, our hearers need to be convinced that the preacher knows their real needs. Biblical preaching is not merely expounding a passage of Scripture; it also takes seriously the concrete issues the text addressed originally, and then it seeks to show us how the text is released in our own day to address similar particular needs. If the preacher keeps the message only as an ancient event of the past, then the listener will not hear the word of address today. On the other hand, if the contemporary situation alone is addressed and the biblical event is ignored, then the listener will not hear the historic word of good news. Both are essential for proclaiming the Word of God. The preacher labors to master the Scriptures, but ministers among her people to know their needs. Phillips Brooks said in his Yale Lectures that "the work of the preacher and the pastor really belong together and ought not to be separated."[14]

When the preacher stands up to preach, the listener wants to feel that what the preacher is saying concerns him. One should be able to say: "I see myself in that image." "How did the preacher know how I felt?" "Why, that's me he's talking about." The *Sitz im Leben* of the Scriptures converges on the listener's contemporary situation. To do this effectively, the preacher engages in a continuous dialogue with his people. As he meets them on the street, converses with them in the hospital or their home, at work or play or the grocery store, he listens to hear their questions and confessions, their joys and griefs, their dreams and failures, their faith and disbelief. As Carlyle Marney once said: "If we have spent twenty hours listening to our people, then we can expect them to listen to us for twenty minutes on Sunday."

When we have walked with our people and have sat where they sat, our words then are authentic. We have struggled with our people, ached with them, wept with them, groaned with them, argued with them, laughed with them, and rejoiced with them. Our words from the pulpit sing with sighs from within; they march with motivation; they are charged with concern; they ring with the rhythm of life; they pulsate with power.

Our words reveal that our finger has felt the pulse beat of people's needs. Our words scratch where they really itch. We seek to address what Henry Mitchell has called the "transconscious level" within our listeners.[15] This is the inmost self, the existential self, the "gut level" self, the intuitive self, the self of our feelings and sensitivities, the self of our unconscious and subtle mentality. Too often our preaching has spoken only to the intellectual self and failed to communicate to the depths within. (And we wonder why people are unmoved by our preaching.) Transconscious preaching attempts to preach to the total person—the unconscious dimension as well as the intellect.

But we also look within our own lives and with our struggles with the faith and with life. All authentic preaching is autobiographical. There is *the gospel* but as Paul said, there is "my gospel." Where we have been most profoundly addressed, we can most clearly guide others. The "wounded healer" demonstrates that the sermon is her own and not another's. Our own experience can provide a deep pool from which to draw. Arthur John Gossip put it this way:

> Preach to your own heart, and many startled passers-by will stop to listen, feeling you are addressing them. Draw anonymously on the story of your life, and they will sit astonished in the pews asking, "Who has been telling him about me? . . . Beneath the skin, people are strangely much alike in every age, in every land.[16]

If the Word is to be proclaimed through our words, and if we are going to communicate with our congregation, then theological translation is a necessity for the preacher. I will spell this out more in a later chapter, but let me allude to it here.

Too many preachers preach behind biblical or theological words or images that are meaningless to their listeners. Every preacher is charged with the responsibility of conveying biblical, theological truths in ways the listeners can grasp and apply to their lives. Many listeners are turned off by preaching because he is talking in a language they do not understand or in a way they do not communicate. The gospel, when written originally, was in the language of the common people, and the preacher is charged with that demand every time he steps into the pulpit, or else he needs to forget about the congregation listening or understanding what the preacher is trying to say. This demands that the preacher labor hard to understand the biblical text he is to preach, but the preacher is also charged with conveying—translating—the text so it can be grasped by its hearers. Careless preparation, lazy study habits, impromptu messages, and inadequate translating of the texts will all lead to a closed mind on the part of the listeners and soon will result in empty pews. No one is going to come for long and listen to sermons that show sloppy preparation and fuzzy thinking and are layered with theological jargon or what seems like pious nonsense to the listeners.

As I will expound later, this does not mean we are to discard all the great biblical and theological words of the Christian vocabulary. We need to interpret, paraphrase, and translate them but not reject them completely. Whatever our new theological words are, they must know and build on the old categories. P. T. Forsyth spoke of this danger:

> I cannot conceive a Christianity to hold the future without words like grace, sin, judgment, repentance, incarnation, atonement, redemption, justification, sacrifice, faith and eternal life. No words of less volume than these can do justice to the meaning of God, however easy their access to minds of modern men.[17]

Since Bonhoeffer declared several decades ago that the preacher had to learn to speak in a "secular way" about God, our society has become even more secular. Scientific and technological advances have been sweeping. The "Greek" mindset of contemporary society finds the gospel story a greater "foolishness" today than centuries ago. Modern society is boisterous in its assertion that everything is natural, biological, social, scientific, technological, clinical, revolutionary, or theoretical. The church often is viewed as a fossil left over from past archaeological digs—interesting but often unrelated to modern culture. How does the preacher understand the modern world, much less preach to it?

Barth's image of the Bible in one hand and today's newspaper in the other hand speaks to this dilemma. The preacher who starts in the Bible and stays in the Bible is not doing biblical preaching. To be biblical, the sermon must also address people today in their culture. The biblical message must come alive today as a contemporary event.

The preacher is often isolated from much of the real world. Indeed, we see the pain, grief, and joy of a selected group of people. But these are mostly those within the church, and they reveal only a dim or partial image of the secular world. Contemporary literature offers one of the clearest windows into the modern world today. I will focus on this more acutely in another chapter, but a brief word here might be appropriate.

Literature will lift the preacher out of his cloistered cell of ministerial isolation and open his eyes to the world outside. "Authentic preaching," Charles Rice observed, "is worldly because it is grounded in biblical faith; it is truly biblical only when it is worldly."[18] The preacher will be reminded constantly of the world where real people live with their precarious and mysterious position in the universe. Modern literature often struggles with many questions and issues years before theologians do. The preacher who reads contemporary literature will be able to use Paul Tillich's method of correlation: "It tries to correlate the questions implied in the situation with the answer implied in the message."[19] The preacher cannot give answers to questions he has not heard. Literature offers him an ear to the sounds of the modern world.

Literature reflects and echoes the discord and alarm in our world today. Through Eugene O'Neill's *Long Day's Journey into Night*, one can experience alienation and isolation. Eugene Ionesco's *Rhinoceros* uncovers the struggle with freedom and conformity. The value of human relationships and the problems of pain, injustice, and suffering meet us in Alan Paton's *Cry, the Beloved Country*. The search for meaning in an alienated society leaps at the reader from Walker Percy's *Love in the Ruins*. Graham Greene's whisky priest provides an unlikely hero in *The Power and the Glory*. John Updike's "Rabbit" books about Harry Angstrom reveal a side of the middle-class life many preachers ignore. And the list goes on and on.

Study the lives of great preachers such as George Buttrick, Paul Scherer, Harry Emerson Fosdick, Arthur John Gossip, and Charles Spurgeon and you will find they were wide readers of contemporary literature, both novels and plays. They were constantly picking the pockets of great and less significant writers. The many references, illusions, and quotes from literature in the sermons of these preachers not only revealed that they probably knew more effectively the contemporary conditions, but also their own sermon style was enriched by their constant exposure to creative writing, poetic images, metaphors, narrative style, vivid picture words, and simple, colloquial language. If we want to improve our preaching, then we must drink deeply from the fountain of contemporary literature. Our language will become more vivid, our style more oral, and our sermons more understandable to the ears of laypersons.

Of course, literature provides only one avenue of acquaintance with modern society. The preacher must confront its problems and needs personally. Literature may provide for some an escape instead of an avenue for meeting issues. The problems in our own homes, down the street, across the railroad track, in the ghetto one block away, or the poverty, hunger, prejudice, disease, suffering, and war near and far challenge us. Whether the sins are personal or collective, sandpaper rough or velvety smooth, the preacher must be a voice letting modern society know there is a word from God. The church, to use Harvey Cox's phrase, is "the cultural exorcist" challenging the powers of evil and darkness in modern society.[20]

The preacher's words to society should reflect God's Word within us. The Lord we follow was constantly challenging social and religious traditions and orthodoxies. God's Word addresses both the church and the world. We acknowledge that nothing we say or do is immune to corruption. Thus we attend to the voice of God. Voices have always tried to reverse the words of Jesus and have tried to use words—religious words—to imprison others in a newly founded orthodoxy. Jesus said, "If the Son makes you free, you are free indeed." No one else's creedal words have the power to define or confine the fiery nature of the preacher's prophetic voice. The Word of the Lord came; we listened and obeyed. And sometimes, like our Lord, the Word leads us to a place of suffering and rejection.

Loren Eiseley recounted the words a black girl once said to him in Bimini, on the Old Spanish Main: "Those as hunts treasure must go alone, at night, and when they find it they have to leave a little of their blood behind them."[21] There has never been a finer estimate of "the price of prophetic preaching" to the modern world. The prophetic word is indeed a treasure for which we always leave behind some blood: toil, pain, time, misunderstanding, and much more.

Our Silence

Speak in the name of God, we must. It is a divine compulsion. Sometimes, however, our words get in the way. They are too small, too feeble, too puny to speak of the unimaginable majesty of God and his love. When I attempt to describe the Word of God in Christ, I feel like a small boy trying to look with one eye through a knot hole in a wooden fence to see the world on the other side. Oh, my vision is so narrow, so limited. When I have said all I can discern from the Scriptures about the incarnate Word, I must bow before the mystery that is beyond me. Sometimes I am mute in the wonder of God's love. Oh, tell it I must, and will. But my telling of it is always so inadequate. And so is yours.

To say that one can never put on God's glasses and look at the world from the divine perspective is not necessary, or is it? I remember hearing Bob Soileau at New Orleans Baptist Theological Seminary relate once an experience that took place in one of his classes in theology. Dr. Soileau had been giving his interpretation of a certain theological area, and when he paused for comment, one of the students declared quite sincerely: "Well, Dr. Soileau, we have listened to your interpretation; let's look at it now from God's viewpoint." But isn't that always our problem? We simply can never know absolutely what is God's perspective.

We have the Scriptures and also hints and whispers within nature. Nevertheless, eternal truth is always read with misty eyes or through a glass darkened by ignorance, superstition, or religious, economic, and cultural mores. Our theological puddings are also flavored with spices of nonsense, prejudice, fear, and mythology. The best of our theological systems still smacks of the comic book level when we think of the mystery of God. We attempt to make sense out of nonsense, draw light from darkness, refine knowledge from ignorance, cultivate faith from agnosticism, and sow seeds of hope in fields of despair.

We always know less than we think—and yet more. We define faith in terms that are less than it is, and yet more than we can understand. We stumble in our articulation of the realities that exist; yet, we are aware that our words conceal as much as they reveal. Then we wonder why we must think of our faith in symbolical and paradoxical terms.

A few sentences ago I advised you to be theological translators. We need to make our words about the Word plain and simple. But I quickly flash a caution light here to warn you not to be too simple. R. E. C. Browne states it forcibly:

> Never get things too clear. Religion can't be clear. In this mixed-up life there is always an element of unclearness . . . If I could understand religion as I understand that two and two make four, it would not be worth understanding. Religion can't be clear if it is worth having. To me, if I can see things through, I get uneasy—I feel it's a fake. I know I have left something out. I've made some mistake.[22]

None of us ever see the whole of truth, especially religious truth. Who dares to state that she can explain the problem of evil and suffering or the mystery of goodness? Whose mind or limited words can explain all about God's creation of the universe, the Incarnation, the Atonement, the Resurrection, or eschatology? We cannot capture God or these great theological themes in a tiny web of words. They will always break under the movement of such thoughts. Even the best of our words fail to describe fully the mystery of God's love. For the sake of simplicity we cannot surrender all of our metaphors, paradoxes, and symbols. So, I return again and again to the biblical words and shout and whisper them about the God I have known through his word, Christ.

But words are not the only way we can express ourselves. Conversation is an intimate means of communion, but it is not the only means, nor was it the first. Men and women had communion with one another before speech was developed. Even today with speech, communion can be established by a nod, a gesture, a glance, a smile, a touch, a facial motion, or a body motion. Communion can be established in a vital way without a verbal word passing. In my former church in Bristol, Virginia, our deaf choir would sometimes "sing" by sign language. Their gestures were breathtaking at times, and were expressed without a verbal sound. We can speak with our eyes, our hands, our face, our gestures, and our touch. In so many ways we can speak without talking.

In some of our deepest experiences, words are inadequate. When we have lost a loved one or have had a bitter disappointment or have felt rejected, words cannot address our deep need. Nevertheless, a touch or an embrace by someone who understands us and loves us can strengthen us without a verbal word passing between us. And that is a powerful language.

Centuries ago King Zedekiah asked the prophet Jeremiah: "Is there any word from the Lord?" And the question is addressed to us again today. Yes, the Word has come, but will we be able to hear it coming now? We cannot hear God's Word if we do not listen. The Word of God came, but it was not verbal. It does not continue to come just as words. Only when we pause and listen will we hear.

Jesus said the first and greatest commandment began with the call to listen. "Hear, O Israel." On many occasions Jesus warned his followers: "He that hath ears to hear, let him hear." The Apostle Paul directed the church to remember that "faith cometh by hearing." When we listen, we will hear the Word of God. As the Psalmist has reminded us, "Be still and know that I am God." When the prophet Elijah sought to find the Lord, he did not find him in the noise of the wind, earthquake, or fire. He heard "a still small voice." This verse might be translated more closely to the original text as "a sound of gentle stillness." Apart from and within the rush, noise, and hectic pace of our lives comes "a sound of gentle stillness." The sound of God's eternal Word comes to interpret the silence.

In that silence I simply bow before God and remain silent before God's silence. Sometimes God speaks in the silence before my words, at other times between the pauses in my words, and again after my words have been said. In the silence, God has taught me that the divine Word goes forth even when I am mute or my words fail or are inadequate. God's Word is still proclaimed.

The sound that comes to interpret the silence is not found in the noise of words, written or verbal, but is heard in the Living Word. We read in the Vulgate: *In principio erat verbum et verbum erat epud Deum, et Deus erat verbum . . . Et verbum caro factum est.* "In the beginning was the Word, and the Word was with God, and the Word was God . . . And the Word became flesh" (John 1:1, 14). Is there any word from the Lord? Yes. The Incarnate Word has come from the depths of the very being of God to interpret the sounds of silence. So, go preach. Proclaim his word, knowing that in our words and in our silence, God continues to speak the divine Word.

Notes

[1] James C. Howell, *The Beauty of the Word: The Challenge and Wonder of Preaching* (Louisville: Westminster John Knox Press, 2011), 3.

[2] Emil Brunner, *Revelation and Reason* (Philadelphia: Westminster Press, 1946), 142.

[3] Martin Luther, *Werke*, quoted in Philip S. Watson. *Let God Be God: An Interpretation of the Theology of Martin Luther* (Philadelphia: Muhlenberg Press, 1947), 152.

[4] See *La Confession Helve`tique Poste`tieure* (Texte Francais de 1566) (Neuchatel: Delachaux Niestle A. A., 1944), 42.

⁵Dietrich Bonhoeffer, *Gesammelte Schriften*, ed. Eberhard Bethge (Munich: Chr. Kaiser Verlag, 1961), 4:240. Quoted in Clyde Fant, *Preaching for Today* (New York: Harper & Row, 1975), 22.

⁶Rudolf Bultmann, *Theology of the New Testament*, vol. 1, (New York: Charles Scribner's Sons, 1951), 302.

⁷Rudolf Bultmann, *Offenbarung und Heilsgeschelhen*, vol. 7, of *Beitrage zur evangelischen Theologie*, ed. E. Wolfe (Munic: Evangelischer Verlag, Albert Lempp, 1941), 66. Quoted in Fant, *Preaching for Today*, 21.

⁸Brunner, *Revelation and Reason*, 142.

⁹P. T. Forsyth, *Positive Preaching and the Modern Mind* (London: Independent Press, 1907), 3

¹⁰Karl Barth and Eduard Thurneysen, *Come Holy Spirit* (Grand Rapids: William B. Eerdmans Co., 1978), ii.

¹¹William A. Quayle, *The Pastor-Preacher*, ed. Warren W. Wiersbe (Grand Rapids: Baker Book House, 1979), 27.

¹²Milton Rugoff, *The Beechers: An American Family in the Nineteenth Century* (New York: Harper & Row, 1981), 449-503.

¹³See the General Prologue, Geoffrey Chaucer, *The Canterbury Tales* in *The Poetical Works of Chaucer*, ed. F. N. Robinson (Boston: Houghton Mifflin Company, 1933), 24.

¹⁴Phillips Brooks, *Lectures on Preaching* (New York: Seabury Press, 1964), 75.

¹⁵Henry Mitchell, *The Recovery of Preaching* (San Francisco: Harper and Row, 1977), 12ff.

¹⁶Arthur J. Gossip, *In Christ's Stead* (Grand Rapids: Baker Book House, 1968), 83.

¹⁷Forsyth, *Positive Preaching and the Modern Mind*, 197.

¹⁸Charles L. Rice, *Interpretation and Imagination: The Preacher and Contemporary Literature* (Philadelphia: Fortress Press, 1970), 41.

¹⁹Paul Tillich, *Systematic Theology* (Chicago: University of Chicago Press, 1951), 1:8.

²⁰Harvey Cox, *The Secular City* (New York: Macmillan, Co., 1965), 149.

²¹Loren Eiseley, *The Night Country* (New York: Charles Scribner's Sons, 1971), 224.

²²R. E. C. Browne, *The Ministry of the Word* (Philadelphia: Fortress Press, 1976), 58.

Sermon

Exorcising Demons in the Modern World
Mark 5:1-20

The eyes of the demonic seem to be burning brighter again with the appearance of movies and novels such as the earlier *Rosemary's Baby* and *The Exorcist* and more recently *The Exorcism of Emily Rose*. Although the world is in a scientific and technological revolution, the impact of the occult with its astrology, séances, Satan cults, witches, horoscopes, and drugs reveals an emerging force that must be confronted in the Age of Aquarius and especially in the twenty-first century. In this sense, then, the story of Jesus and the demoniac from the fifth chapter of Mark's Gospel, while sounding a bit like a tale of Edgar Allan Poe, does have a faint contemporary ring.

A Frightening Story

The disciples never forgot the experience with the demoniac of Gadara. So vivid was it in their minds that all three of the Synoptic Gospels record it. After an exhausting day, Jesus and his disciples took a small boat across the Sea of Galilee. The tiny craft was caught in a sudden storm whose fury became so intense that it lashed fear into all the disciples, even the experienced fishermen. The strained nerves of the disciples found strength in the words from Christ: "Peace, be still." As suddenly as it had arisen, the storm subsided. But the stillness of this peace was short-lived. A fury as wild and uncontrollable as the wind and the sea was about to confront them.

As soon as the vessel touched the southern shore of the Sea of Galilee, Jesus and his disciples, with their nerves already on edge, began to climb slowly up the weird, steep gorge to the bluff above. Suddenly out of the darkness of the mountain graveyard leaped a screaming, naked, hideous creature dragging and clanging the chains that were supposed to restrain him. His eyes were wide with derangement, his body was covered with huge bloody welts, his arms were waving wildly, his long hair was entangled in a mass of twisted knots, and his movement seemed to indicate he possessed superhuman strength. With hair standing on end, knees knocking, cold shivers running up and down their spines, and their eyes bulging, the disciples must have been terrified at this breathtaking collision.

While the disciples were frozen with fear, the tormented creature threw himself at the feet of Jesus. With quiet confidence and the serene assurance of a man who seemed always ready for such an emergency, Jesus responded to the man's need instead of allowing appearances to frighten him so he could not act. Jesus the Master of the unexpected had already been saying to the man: "Come out of him, evil spirit."

In Jesus' words to the demoniac the tense is important. From the moment of his encounter with the demoniac, Jesus had repeatedly ordered the demons to be exorcised, but his first efforts were unsuccessful. Then Jesus asked what might sound like a strange inquiry to us: "What is your name?" You might ask, what importance could that possibly have? In an age when the belief in demon possession was prevalent, the knowledge of a demon's name gave the exorcists power over him. Instead of giving his name, the demons replied with a number. We are six thousand. This was the number of soldiers in a Roman regiment. There are many of us; we are a mob; we are Legion.

The herd of swine on the slopes nearby indicated Jesus and his disciples were in pagan country. No Jewish man would raise pigs. They were considered religiously unclean animals. The strange request by Legion to enter the hogs, if the demons were to be cheated out of a human habitat, was an attempt to avoid the abyss of the deep sea waters, where it was commonly thought in biblical times to be the final area of destruction for all evil spirits. Ironically, the force of the demonic entrance into the pigs was severe enough to send the whole herd of two thousand plunging dramatically to their deaths off the precipice into the depths of the sea.

The Epilogue

Notice the epilogue. When the pig herdsmen rushed into the city and brought back the owners, did they rejoice at the great miracle they had seen? They saw the demoniac sane, clothed, calm, and talking normally with Jesus. Instead of celebrating in the wonder of the redemption the demoniac received, however, the people feared Jesus, the exorcist, and asked him to leave. The demoniac was alone in expressing gratitude and asked Jesus to let him go with him. But Jesus sent him home and urged him to tell his friends about the power of God's gift of healing.

A Meaning for Today

Now what are we to make of such a story today?[1] Do we merely reject it as an ancient folk tale, reflecting the superstition and demonology of its time, with notions of magic and the occult?

Some people approach the problem of demonology as an ancient way of expressing what is called in contemporary society by psychiatric nomenclature. Biblical references to demon possession are seen as ancient descriptions of epilepsy, schizophrenia, or various forms of insanity. Without question there is much truth in this approach. Jesus himself did not attribute all illness to demon possession. The blind man, Jairus' daughter, the woman with the hemorrhage, the paralytic, and the centurion's servant were all cases where Jesus did not associate these diseases with evil spirits. In some instances the healings of Jesus are clearly evidence that the person was either an epileptic or suffered from some kind of psychological disturbance. But the problem of demon possession in the New Testament cannot be solved that easily.

It is apparent from a reading of the Gospels that Jesus not only spoke about the power of demons, but he also exorcised them and commanded his disciples to cast them out in his name. Though it may seem embarrassing to a church that feels it has "come of age" and functions in a scientific age, the power to cast out demons was central to the ministry of Jesus. Harvey Cox noted this attitude when he declared that "most of us would prefer to forget that for many of his contemporaries Jesus' exorcism was in no way peripheral, but stood at the heart of his work."[2] The late Paul Tillich, in an address to the graduating students at Union Theological Seminary, affirmed that preaching Christ as the power to conquer the demonic forces that control our lives, mind and body, will prove to be the most adequate way to communicate the message of Christ for the people of our time.[3]

The Reality of Demons

Can this possibly be true? How can this demonic imagery be meaningful to us today? The answer lies in breaking through the pre-scientific images of demons and evil spirits to the reality to which they attest. The New Testament acknowledges vividly the awesome power of evil in such images as "principalities and powers," "messengers of Satan," "rulers of darkness," "Satan, the father of lies and deception," "the Anti-Christ," "the Evil One," "the Adversary," and "the Destroyer." "Principalities and powers," a phrase that recurs frequently in the writings of Paul, was a common New Testament conception of the cosmic dimension of the power of evil.

Modern persons like to laugh at the old Cornish prayer: "From Ghoulies and Ghosties, and long-leggity Beasties, and all things that go bump in the night, Good Lord deliver us." We assert ourselves as too modern for that. We prefer "From systems, and ologies and isms, Good Lord free us." Evil becomes more comfortable for us when it is abstract and impersonal. Challenging this comfortable approach, Colin Morris, in a recent book, stated: "I make no apology for calling evil by that old-fashioned, personal name, the Devil. It is a good way of keeping us alert to the fact there is about the operation of evil the subtlety of a malevolent personality rather than the crudity of a blind, irrational force."[4]

The Awesome Reality of Evil

You do not think evil is real? Can we possibly believe that the depths and the dimensions of the kingdom of evil in the world are merely illusions of the mind? Tell the relatives of the six million Jews who were annihilated by the Nazis that there is no evidence of demonic power in the world. Tell the onlooking villagers at Mai Lai who were staggered by the mountain of bodies of civilian men, women, and children that evil is an illusion. Tell the thousands of children fathered by American soldiers and deserted in Vietnam that there is no evidence of the power of evil. Tell the families of those who died with AIDS in Africa that evil is an illusion. Tell the families of those who were victims of genocide in Ghana and Rwanda that evil does not really exist. Tell the child born blind because of syphilis contracted from a prostitute mother that demonic power does not exist. Tell the relatives who lost loved ones in the 9/11 terrorists' attacks that evil is not real. Tell Sam Jones, who lost his left leg in Iraq, that evil is abstract. Tell Mrs. Rush, who lost her son in Afghanistan, that evil has no personal demonic dimension to it. Tell it to the parents whose son jumped from the twelfth story of a building after an overdose of LSD.

Are we really so civilized that we cannot see the awesome power of evil? We no longer throw ink wells at the devil as Martin Luther once did. We are too civilized for that, too mature. Yet one of the most civilized nations in the world exterminated six million humans of one race. Let us be honest and admit it openly and forcefully, as did the early New Testament Christians: evil is real, and it is demonic. Somewhere we have lost the New Testament urgency of the unseen warfare. Without hesitation the New Testament senses a mighty contradiction at the heart of the universe. The New Testament writers pictured the Christian engaged in combat with the forces of evil; but they shouted a ringing affirmation that in Jesus Christ, God has unleashed victory over sin, death, and the principalities and the powers.

A Mirror for Us Today

Almost without exception, the commentaries I examined indicated that the demoniac passage was clearly one without any realistic theological or moral value for modern man. Without question, to my mind, this man Legion, the demoniac, rather than being out of focus for today's man and woman, is symbolic of modern humanity. He is contemporary man/woman, come of age. He is each of us. Legion refuses to allow us to be mere spectators in this story. We are participants. The demoniac becomes our mirror.

What Is Your Name?

Jesus says, "What is your name?" "My name is Legion." I am many; I am a mob. I do not know who I am. There are many selves within me, and I am torn and pulled in every direction, seeking to find myself. How often we say: "I don't feel like myself today." "I was nearly out of my mind." "I said to myself. 'pull yourself together'." "Excuse my action; I just was not myself the other day." "I am ashamed of myself." "I forgot myself for the moment." "I just hate myself for doing that." Each of us is rarely a unity; each of us is constantly at civil war within.

In Arthur Miller's play *The Death of a Salesman*, the younger son, Biff, stands by his father's grave and reflects: "He never knew who he was."[5] But who does? Who are you? Who am I? Is our name really not Legion? There are many selves within each of us. We hide behind many masks from one another. Sometimes our masks are peeled back like layers of skin on an onion and reveal so often that we are hollow at the center. Was T. S. Eliot correct? Are we merely "the hollow men, the stuffed men, leaning together, headpiece filled with straw?"[6] Without a polestar, without a center of gravity, without knowledge of who we are, we are Legion—our nature is that of the demoniac.

The Wilderness Within

We are, in Carl Sandburg's words, a menagerie. Within the wilderness inside each of us is a wolf, a fox, a hog, a fish, a baboon, an eagle, and other creatures. We are indeed paradoxical creatures. We are loving and hateful, harmful and saving, educating and destroying, wise and foolish, visionary and shortsighted. Each of us is the "keeper of the zoo." We may deny it, but we cannot hide it. There is a wilderness in every person. Here is the Legion element of our inner struggle that can be calmed only by the power and strength of the re-creative spirit of Christ.

Listen to Jesus when he cried out to Legion, "Come out of him!" But Legion responded: "What have you to do with me, Jesus, Son of the Most High God?" He sounds like today's crowd. It is contemporary man's reaction to the Christ. What have you to do with me, Jesus Christ? Leave me undisturbed, unchanged, uncommitted, uninvolved. Before Christ can cast any evil spirit out of a person's life, he comes first as tormentor. He comes as disturber. When we are initially confronted by Christ, he comes in judgment. A single life standing in the light of the judgment of his presence sees the dimension of the wilderness within, the immensity of the force of Legion within, which divides and perplexes one's personality. He will not leave our prejudices unchallenged or our attitudes rigid. Lesser values cannot remain when higher ones are possible. Brokenness is molded into wholeness. Depravity is overpowered by redeeming grace. The status quo is constantly moving toward renewal.

In *The Brothers Karamazov*, Dostoevsky tells a striking tale of the return of Christ to Seville, where he performs many wonderful acts of healing before he is arrested and thrown in prison by the Grand Inquisitor. Later the Grand Inquisitor confronts Jesus and inquires why he had to return at the present time and disturb the life and teachings of the church. Without a word, Jesus accepts all the abuse directed at him. Finally, without a comment, Christ leans over and kisses the blood-drained lips of the religious leader. The Grand Inquisitor, unable to stand in the presence of Christ, opens the prison door and shouts: "Go, and come no more! Come not at all, never, never."[7]

Christ is the great disturber. No life can remain the same when confronted by his presence. Alfred North Whitehead once pictured our human reaction to the divine this way: "Religion is the transition from God the void to God the enemy, and from God the enemy to God the companion."[8] First we pass through the door of Christ's judgment before he brings a center into our divided lives.

The Wholeness of Redemption

Legion's cry, then, was real, and it is the cry of every person: "What have you to do with me, Jesus, Son of the Most High God? I beseech you, do not torment me." But redemption did come to this disturbed man. His torn personality found wholeness through the power of Christ. "Come out of the man, you unclean spirit!" Here is the act of redemption, freeing a man's spirit from chaos to unity, conflict to peace, bondage to freedom, despair to hope, fragmentation to oneness. Jesus Christ offers to each of us the unification and integration of personality. He calls a truce to the internal civil war and furnishes wholeness and stability.

If Jesus' exorcism is viewed merely as a healing, the deep implications of the cosmic dimension of salvation are minimized. It is clear from the Gospel accounts that Jesus wanted to avoid the reputation of simply being a healer. There was a cosmic element to his healings. The salvation of Jesus is concerned with the total person, not just the physical self or the moral or spiritual side, but the whole person and his other interrelatedness. Redemption is concerned with overcoming everyone's estrangement from himself, others, and God.

The Power of Collective Evil

The mighty contradiction we sense in the universe goes beyond our need merely for redemption of individual sins; we experience the power of collective evil. The modern demons that threaten to destroy us are more than just the sum of individual evil acts. Exorcizing demons modern style will involve redeeming not only individuals, but also the systems that have enslaved them.

The evil forces that crucified Christ are representative of the corporate aspect of evil. The collective evil that destroyed the life of Christ is ever present. Look at this evil: religious intolerance, commercial graft, political corruption, injustice, the mob mentality, public apathy, militarism, and the class system. These are evil forces deeply rooted within our social systems. Jesus was crucified by a system that allowed him to be executed although he was found innocent. As a member of the lower class, he was not given representation or defense. But corporate evil is not confined to the first century.

Confronting the collective power of evil is the modern equivalent of exorcising demons. The church, as Walter Rauschenbusch said more than ninety years ago, is the social factor of salvation.[9] The church is the social force in the world that challenges the collective powers of evil. At least it should be! The church, to use Harvey Cox's phrase, is "the cultural exorcist." The church is the social force that says, for example, not only do we seek to challenge and overcome racial prejudice, but we also shall strive to help minority groups attain their own sense of personal respect and dignity.

Some voices say all we need to do is get persons to make a personal commitment to Christ and the problem with society will be solved. I wish it were so! In a community in the South a young minister attempted to relate the gospel to include persons of all races. He was told he could not enter the pulpit again, and he, his wife, and five children were put out of their home within a week. Was that church, where individuals had made "commitments" to Christ, free from the demonic power of evil? Deeper dimensions of redemption and healing were needed. Sometimes, instead of being the force to change society, the church is perpetuating the very evil from which it needs deliverance. But the challenge remains: the church is called today to be the exorcist, the healer, and the deliverer from the demonic forces in society.

A Contemporary Response

Notice again the epilogue of the story. After the demoniac had received redemption, the townspeople did not respond very well. They were terrified by a man who had such powers, and seemed little concerned with the change in Legion. The owners of the pigs were also greatly disturbed at their loss. They appeared more upset about the loss of the pigs than the cure of the man. How contemporary can a story be?

Pigs are more important than people, they are saying. Property rights are more important than human rights. The mirror is before us as we sense modern man and woman's reaction to war, environmental issues, open housing, racial desegregation, poverty, and the ghettos. Property, wealth, and security are more important than people. Here is a demonic force whose power is so intense that it is incessantly moving us closer to chaos. Cured and sane, Legion desired to follow Jesus. But Jesus instructed him to go to the toughest territory of all for him to demonstrate his wholeness: Go home. Go home and show your family and friends the wholeness and unity God has given you—no easy task for anyone.

T. H. White, in a modern fantasy titled *The Sword and the Stone*, depicts a contest between Merlin the magician and the evil witch, Madame Mim. It is a contest to the death, each using his or her greatest skill and powers. Madame Mim assumes many horrible and deadly shapes, but each time Merlin meets her with one better until finally the witch is annihilated.

Through the centuries evil has assumed many forms, shapes, and disguises. It has come in all kinds of clothing, manners, and descriptions. Sometimes it was recognized in the form of one nation enslaving another, or a small group of men crushing anything in the way of their self-appointed goal, or one individual demanding absolute obedience to his fanatical wishes.

An Ongoing Struggle

Whatever shape evil may take, the Christian must never lose sight of the fact that she is indeed engaged in a conflict, "an unseen warfare," with the "principalities and powers." But the Christian engages in this struggle with the assurance of victory. Through Jesus Christ we find inner courage and strength, "having done all, to stand." The Christian is aware, though she may stumble under the impact of the demonic power, that ultimately evil will be defeated. In hope and anticipation, we shout in the face of evil the words from the Apostle Paul:

> If God is on our side, who is against us? . . . And yet, in spite of all, overwhelming victory is ours through him who loved us. For I am convinced that there is nothing in death or life, in the realm of spirits or superhuman powers, in the world as it is or the world as it shall be, in the forces of the universe, in heights or depths—nothing in all creation that can separate us from the love of God in Christ Jesus our lord. (Rom. 8:31, 37-39 NEB)

Notes

[1] Some scholars treat exorcism as a literal reality. See, for example, Leslie Weatherhead, "The Problem of Demon Possession," in *Psychology, Religion and Healing* (New York: Abingdon Press, 1962), 89ff; Leslie Weatherhead, *Wounded Spirits: Case Histories of Spiritual and Physical Healing* (New York: Abingdon Press, 1962); M. Scott Peck, *People of the Lie: The Hope for Healing Human Evil* (New York: Simon & Schuster, 1985). For some who interpret exorcism as figurative or parabolic rather than literally true, see Paul Simmons, *Faith and Health: Religion, Science and Public Policy* (Macon, GA: Mercer University Press, 2008), 235ff; Carl Sagan, *The Demon-Haunted World: Science as a Candle in the Dark* (New York: Random House, 1996); and Paul Tillich, *The Eternal Now* (New York: Charles Scribner's and Sons, 1963).

[2] Harvey Cox, *The Secular City* (New York: Macmillan Co., 1965), 149.

³Paul Tillich, *The Eternal Now* (New York: Charles Scribner's Sons, 1963), 60.
⁴Colin Morris, *Mankind My Church* (Nashville: Abingdon Press, 1971), 11.
⁵Arthur Miller, *The Death of a Salesman* (New York: The Viking Press, 1958), 138.
⁶Carl Sandburg, "The Wilderness," in *Complete Poems of Carl Sandburg* (New York: Harcourt, Brace & World, Inc., 1950), 100-101.
⁷Fyodor Dostoevsky, *The Brothers Karamazov* (Garden City, NJ: International Collectors Library, n. d.), 230.
⁸Alfred North Whitehead, *Religion in the Making* (New York: The Macmillan Co., 1938), 16-17.
⁹Walter Rauschenbusch, *The Theology for the Social Gospel* (New York: The Macmillan Co., 1917).

Part 1
Biblical Preaching:
The Foundation of Proclamation

On most pulpits in this country and abroad, a Bible lies open before the preacher. Whatever else the open Bible symbolizes, surely it denotes that the preacher is the person who has been given the chief responsibility to be the interpreter of the written Word. In some traditions an open Bible lies on a table in front of the pulpit before the congregation. Is the symbolism here that the preacher works with the congregation in determining the meaning of the Scripture? He is engaged with the congregation in a dialogue to explore the depths of the Bible and discover together an authentic word from God. In either case the end is to encounter the living God through the written Word. Both the preacher and the congregation affirm the significance of the Bible in disclosing the God to whom the Scriptures reveal.

In spite of many strange interpretations and nonsensical beliefs some people have drawn from the Bible over the centuries, the Bible continues to be the chief source of authority for the church. Through its pages many people have experienced the message of God's love, grace, and redemption. As persons have read the pages of Scripture, they have met not abstract speculation about God and the meaning of life but real people, who out of their struggles and stories direct us to the God they encountered. The Bible speaks to us today because it came into existence out of life itself. It records the beginning of life, the story of men and women searching for and being found by God; the struggle of a people under the bondage of slavery and the birth of the nation Israel and their journey to become the people of God. The Bible discloses the defeats and the victories of Israel in seeking to follow God's leadership. Finally the Scriptures reveal the coming of the one called Christ, God's redeeming love revealed through him, and the founding of the church following his resurrection.

The Bible as Primary Source for Preaching

For many people today the Bible is an unknown book. So why should anyone suggest that preachers draw from it as the primary source for preaching? Although most homes have a copy of the Bible, it is seldom read. Often the Bible has pressed between its pages clippings, roses, and pictures of children or grandchildren or other family members. Some people have confessed that they have tried to read the Bible but found it dull and hard to understand. The stories about a scarlet woman, a great beast, a talking snake, and a talking ass and the discussion about ancient tribal rights, sacrificial systems, and "who begat whom" often leave the reader perplexed, confused, and disinterested.

In spite of the Bible being a neglected and misunderstood book, it is still our chief source for understanding God's involvement in the lives of people, especially a group called Israel, and the coming of Jesus and our basic Christian doctrines. The Scriptures provide the primary reservoir for our religious knowledge. To neglect them is to ignore the foundation of our faith. A sermon cannot truly be a sermon that is not biblical.

Humanity's Story

We should preach from the Bible because it reveals humanity's story. The stories of many of the characters within its pages are mirrors of our own stories. The struggles, failures, victories, faith, hopes, and dreams of the men and women in the Bible reflect in kind those of every man and woman. Everywhere you open the Bible it reverberates with life. It sobs with the pain of Job, the rejection of Jeremiah, the depression of Elijah, the frustration of Jonah, and the grief of David. It affirms the hope of Isaiah and the bigoted hatred of a psalmist while denoting the security of another psalmist. It heralds the courage of Queen Esther, the challenge of Amos, the weakness of Samson, the devotion of Ruth, and the love of Jacob. It acknowledges the doubt of Thomas, the failure and forgiveness of Peter, the promise of John, the faith of Paul, the friendship of Andrew, the loyalty of Timothy, the generosity of Phoebe, and the teaching gifts of Priscilla.

The Bible records the story of men and women as they seek to find meaning and purpose in their lives and as they strive to relate to others and to God. The Bible enriches our life today because it came to birth out of the life of people. It addresses personal and family conflicts in addition to national and supernatural struggles. Almost every known human story is depicted in the Bible. Its primary concern is not with abstract speculation or obscure thinking, but with life itself. Although the people within its pages lived thousands of years ago in a different time, place, and culture, they reflect universal patterns of thought and behavior. Like an old family album, the Bible reveals our family tree and how we are offshoots of those ancient roots. Its story is our story. When we read the Bible we cannot miss seeing our own faces in its pools of reflection.

The Church's Story

Another reason to preach from the Bible is that it is the church's story. The Bible contains the record of God's revelation to men and women. For centuries the Bible has nurtured and guided the church in our understanding of God, creation, providence, sin, redemption, grace, eternal life, and other matters of faith. It is our primary source for understanding Christ, his church, the history of Israel, and our Christian doctrines. No other book contains this unique record.

The great themes of the sixty-six books of the Bible—thirty-nine in the Old Testament and twenty-seven in the New Testament—are an integral part of the language, devotion, liturgy, art, literature, music, theology, speech, and practices of the Christian community. The early church drew upon the Old Testament, Jesus' bible, and made it a part of its canon. Like our master teacher, we continue to draw water from that ancient well to quench our spiritual thirst and satisfy our quest to understand how persons in the past encountered God and were led by God to new paths of insight and fresh awakenings of religious awareness of God and the meaning of life.

Touch the stories almost any place within the Bible and they pulsate with a story similar to many of our own. We overhear our stories as we seek to encounter God; struggle with moral and ethical decision-making; long for encouragement and support; strive to follow Christ even with our doubts, uncertainties, and questions; hunger for a deeper sense of God's presence and the assurance of God's forgiving grace and the hope of life everlasting in the constant face of suffering, pain, and grief. "The Bible becomes the authority for the church," Elizabeth Achtemeier affirmed, "because the church learned, over decades of worship and practice, that the biblical story was the one story that created and sustained its life."[1]

The Bible records the early church's story as it came into being and struggled with Judaizers who wanted to contain the new movement within the restraints of its ancient Jewish traditions and the church's debate with the heresy of Gnosticism that freely acknowledged Jesus was divine but denied his humanity. The New Testament unveils Paul's missionary journeys and the churches he founded and their struggles to understand and put into practice the meaning of the life, death, resurrection, and teachings of Christ. Paul's letters to these young churches reflect not only the ancient church's struggle with this gospel message, but also serve as a mirror to reflect our continued strife today.

Although the images, metaphors, and illustrations may have changed from the early church's conflict or quest for understanding how to be the church of Christ, our own strivings, endeavors, and efforts run a parallel or analogous course as we seek to be Christ's church in the world today. The similarity astounds us. We continue to struggle to understand the meaning of Christ's death on the cross, atonement, resurrection, ascension, and second coming. And how do we understand the meaning of, much less put into practice, such teachings as "love your enemies," "forgive those who have sinned against us," "turn the other cheek," "blessed are the peacemakers," "take up your cross and follow me," "he or she that does not forsake father and mother is not worthy of me," "eat my flesh and drink my blood," and countless other sayings and parables? The early church's story is not only an ancient tale, but also our story today. The Bible continues to read us as we read it.

The Word of God

We preach from the Bible because it is a word from God to us and for us. It is not only humanity's story and the church's story, but it is also the story of God's activity revealed to us. As the record of God's revelation, the Bible becomes the preacher's ultimate source of authority. The church congregation longs to hear not just some word from the preacher but "a word from God." The preacher, of course, must always be careful not to assume her words are "God's words" but rather to draw from the Bible, to the best of her spiritual insight and quest, a word from the Lord. Should not all of our preaching be a quest to communicate to our listeners a word from God where they can overhear some enlightenment, hope, guidance, comfort, challenge, and inspiration or possibly have a genuine encounter with God?

The purpose of the written Word is to direct or point us to the "Living Word." As a record of God's revelation, the Bible has become authoritative to the church for matters of belief and practice. We affirm that God's presence has been revealed through the Bible. For twenty centuries, men and women have sensed the presence and power of God within the Bible. Through passages such as Psalm 23, Romans 8, and John 14, persons have encountered a word from God. To be authoritative, however, the Bible does not have to be understood as infallible or inerrant. To make such an assertion does not strengthen the authority of the Bible, but actually renders harm.

God inspires people, not books, and the writings of the Bible clearly reveal that God inspired persons from many cultural, intellectual, and scholarly levels. The Bible is both divine and human. The humanity of the Bible reminds us that God communicates his divine message through ordinary people, warts and all. The Bible is divine because it is inspired (God-breathed) by God and reveals God's message through some human instrument. God did not control or destroy the personality or ability of the one who was inspired. That individual used the resources he had, weak or strong, to communicate what he had sensed about God. Through ordinary persons, God's word was originally communicated to humanity, and God continues to use ordinary persons, like you and me, to communicate the divine message of redeeming love to others today. The ancient writers of the Bible were not infallible; neither are you and I infallible or inerrant today as we proclaim once again that ancient gospel.

Inappropriate Practices of Biblical Preaching

Before we examine various forms of biblical preaching, let us begin with a negative perspective and seek to set aside inappropriate practices that some people want to call biblical preaching. These practices should not be considered as authentic biblical preaching but probably render much negative reaction from anyone who hears them used in the name of preaching. If we are honest, we will have to say that not only have we heard all or many of these practices, but we ourselves also may be guilty of using one or two of them.

Compiling Numerous Biblical Texts

A biblical sermon is not merely the compilation of various proof texts or the copious citations of other biblical passages to prove some point. The mere quotation or reference to a large number of Scriptures does not constitute a biblical sermon. Some preachers seem to have the naïve notion that if their sermons contain a lot of scriptural references, it will guarantee they are biblical. So the preacher fires off one after another like a repeating rifle. He cites proof texts with no target in mind and without regard for the context of the situation it originally addressed. I have seen sermon outlines such as the following that the preacher assumed was a string of pearls, but more likely represented a knotted cord:

Jesus Is God
    1. And the Word was God (John 1:1b).
    2. I and the Father are one (John 10:30).
    3. Whoever has seen me has seen the Father (John 14:9).

In addition to these texts, the sermon was filled with dozens of other Scripture quotations that "proved" Jesus was God. All of these references are taken out of context, and consider neither the writer's intent nor the relation to the person hearing the sermon. The texts are used almost like weapons to force the listener to accept the conclusion of the preacher. Unlike Harry Emerson Fosdick who preached a sermon on "The Divinity of Jesus" and acknowledged that many did not always find this an easy tenet to affirm, the sermon mentioned above allowed no possibility that someone might find this creedal statement hard to affirm.[2] The preacher of this sermon could have made this theme workable by considering objections, nurturing the listener along a spiritual pathway, affirming both the humanity and divinity of Jesus, carefully focusing on the intent of John's Gospel, and allowing the listener to "enter" the sermon where she was "comfortable."

Presenting a Research Project

A biblical sermon is not an essay or a research project on some antique idea or pretty gems from favorite biblical texts. Some preachers do a marvelous job of researching a biblical passage or theme. They gather all kinds of "interesting" information; data; exegesis; descriptions of persons, places, or events; quotations; and so on from commentaries, Bible dictionaries, computer websites, and/or noted scholars or preachers. They may engage in a great deal of study and investigation and compile a mountain of information on a biblical text or theme, but a recitation of those findings is not biblical preaching. Some of it may indeed be useful in preparing a sermon that can be biblical, but research is not an end in itself. It is a means to reaching a higher goal: an effective and meaningful sermon that shares a word from God.

Viewing All Scripture Alike

Biblical preaching does not present all Scripture as being on the same level. For example, no preacher should place the words of the Psalmist, "Happy shall he be who takes your little ones (referring to the Babylonian captors) and dashes them against the rock" (Ps. 137:9), on the same level with the words of Jesus, "You are to love your enemies" (Matt. 5:44) and "Blessed are the peacemakers" (Matt. 5:9). Likewise, no preacher should put the "begat" passage of Genesis 10 or 1 Chronicles 1-9 or the Israel census passages (Numbers 26, for example) or some of the ancient restrictions recorded in Deuteronomy 14-18 on the same theological or preaching plain as the Beatitudes, 1 Corinthians 13, or Romans 8.

    All Scripture is measured by Jesus Christ, the Lord of all Scripture. He did not hesitate to challenge or refute some of the ancient traditions, rituals, ceremonial laws, and teachings. Matthew notes six references from Jesus where he declared boldly: "It has been said unto you, but now I say unto you" (Matt. 5:21-22, 27-28, 31-34, 38-39, 43-44). If some passage from the Old Testament or from any book seems to have a depiction of God or a level of morality or ethics that is sub-Christian, the preacher measures that teaching by the higher revelation we have in Christ. Don't fall into a trap of trying to justify, explain, or preach from passages that are clearly not ones our Lord would confirm. Ronald Allen reminds us that "some parts of the Bible do not articulate the gospel. In fact, some passages are anti-gospel."[3] The passage where the prophet Elisha curses children and watches as bears kill them (2 Kgs. 2:23-25) cannot be placed on a Christian level or equated with our Lord's words, "Blessed are the merciful, for they will receive mercy" (Matt. 5:7). All Scripture is judged by the highest revelation we have in Jesus Christ.

Taking All Scripture Literally

Neither should we assume that in biblical preaching all Scripture should be interpreted literally. Surely no one thinks Jesus' reference to being "the Good Shepherd" means he is literally a shepherd herding sheep or his reference to "I am the door" or "the light" means he is literally a door or a real lamp. All of these are metaphors or images that point to a descriptive meaning. The preacher should try to determine what kind of literature the biblical passage is before interpreting it. Some of the biblical passage may be poetry, drama, saga, allegory, history, letter, biography, parable, prophecy, narrative, sermon, folklore or myth, apocalyptic, or some other type. One needs to interpret the passage and preach it in a way that does justice to its type of literature. Trying to press stories such as the creation accounts, Baalam's talking ass, and Joshua causing the sun to stand still into a rigid literal interpretation does an injustice not only to the literature genre, but also creates an impossible task for the preacher to communicate with an educated and thinking congregation.

Marcus Borg has stated that in the twenty-first century the older lenses of literalism and infallibility need to be replaced with new lenses as the old have become for most people incredible and irrelevant. He argues for a new reading that "is about a deepening relationship with the God to whom the Bible points, lived within the Christian tradition as a sacrament of the sacred."[4]

Try not to press all Scripture into a one-size-fits-all literalistic mold. Much rich preaching can be found in some of these strange texts and other difficult passages. Probe the deep meaning of Jesus' teachings, for example, "if your right hand causes you to sin, cut if off and throw it away" or "if your right eye causes you to sin, tear it out and throw it away" (Matt. 5:29-30). To be honest, I have not seen too many one-eyed and one-armed men and women in church who have taken this passage literally. These and other startling hyperboles of Jesus offer challenging preaching when the preacher exerts study and effort to ascertain what such teachings can possibly mean if not taken literally. Genuine biblical preaching does not assume that all Scripture needs to be taken literally.

Peter Gomes urged his readers to take the Bible seriously but not literally. "The language of the Bible is meant always to point us to a truth beyond the text, a meaning that transcends the particular and imperfectly understood context of the original writers, and our own prejudices and parochialisms that we bring to the text," Gomes argued. "Literalism is not part of the solution to this problem," he asserted. "Literalism is the problem."[5]

Ignoring Critical Biblical Scholarship

A preacher will not do meaningful biblical preaching if she ignores or denies the importance of utilizing the best available scholarly tools she can find. Critical scholarship has discovered new manuscripts of the Bible and provided meaningful tools to help unravel the ancient texts. A personal knowledge of Greek and Hebrew will greatly enrich any preacher's grasp of a biblical passage. Every preacher should consult new Bible dictionaries, commentaries, and biblical studies written by the finest contemporary scholars. Drawing your understanding of a passage from some scholar who wrote in the late 1800s, for example, may provide you with colorful images but not the best of modern scholarship. Refusing to draw from the rich resources of modern scholarship may close the door that could usher you into a deeper and more vivid realization of the original meaning of why a passage was written and the author's original intention. This insight might enable you to preach the text with greater clarity and come closer to the biblical writer's original purpose for writing.

I remember hearing a sermon on "The Christian Family" based on Colossians 3:18-4:1. It was outlined as follows:

1. Wives, submit yourselves to your husbands.
2. Husbands love your wives.
3. Children, obey your parents.
4. Servants, obey your masters.

This sermon seemed to be drawn directly from the passage, but it failed to use critical scholarship related to these points:

- the nature of Greek marriage and family life in that time, especially at Colossae
- the likelihood of household slaves or servants in our day
- Paul's understanding of marriage in the culture of his day
- Paul's statement that "in Christ there is neither male or female"
- the inclusive love expressed in the teachings of Jesus

The preacher tried to press on his listeners a rigid moralism of another day and age that would not fit in our contemporary world. Ignoring the cultural and social differences from a first-century Greek community and trying to press that image of submission and obedience on women and children today open one to ridicule, scorn, and rejection.

Biblical preaching on a text such as the Colossians passage cannot ignore the cultural differences, the social settings out of which it arose, and the intention behind Paul's lesson and how that message of family love, support, encouragement, and devotion might strengthen a family's relationship. Even the preacher's clear struggle with Paul's view of marriage might draw the listener into the sermon as she hears honest appraisal of how Paul's understanding of family life, marriage, and slavery were conditioned by his own cultural perspective. The preacher should feel free to acknowledge that this may not be the highest Christian insight into marriage or the best insight even Paul has to offer.

Taking Biblical Side Streets

Biblical preaching is not turning down some side street to explore a theme, certain details, or a topic that may cause the central thrust of the sermon to get lost in the minutiae of unimportant material the preacher may want to unload on the listener. Consider the following examples:

A preacher might preach a sermon based on Psalm 23 and spend endless time describing the kinds of sheep, their wool and mating and gazing habits, clothes and tents made from their skins, the kind of sheepfolds or shepherds in biblical times, but never focus on the meaning of the psalm. Another preacher might refer to Paul's missionary journeys and focus on the kinds of Roman and Greek ships that existed then, but never discuss his missionary efforts. Still another could preach about Jesus asleep in the boat with his disciples when a storm arose and then discuss at length what boats were like in biblical times, but fail to deal with the real meaning of the text. Likewise, a preacher might spend most of the sermon discussing what clothes were like in the days of Jesus when the Scriptures refer to the woman with an issue of blood who touched the edge of Jesus' outer garment and was healed, but fail to relate the importance of the miracle performed or the woman's faith.

Marginal matters do not direct the attention of the listeners in the proper direction. I call these dead-end side streets, because they carry the listener's attention away from the main intention of the text.

Another side street for some preachers is turning almost every biblical passage into a proof text for some favorite theme. Too many preachers ride the same hobbyhorse almost every Sunday. I knew one preacher whose favorite one was apostasy. There are numerous passages that obviously teach the possibility of apostasy, but this preacher would find it in unlikely and improbable sources simply because he wanted to and not because that particular text addressed it. Any mention of water, whatever it was about—a cup of water, a boat on a lake, disciples fishing, the flood—reminded a certain preacher of the importance of baptism, and he would launch into that theme. A preacher needs to avoid preaching on pet themes or texts all the time and assuming this is real biblical preaching.

Remaining in the Text of the Past

Some preachers believe that biblical preaching keeps them in the text. They focus on the significance and meaning of the text, but never take the sermon beyond the text itself. If the preacher remains only in the past—with the ancient text—and never shows its relevance for today or does not allow the listeners to overhear its meaning for them, then it is not genuine biblical preaching.

Biblical preaching does not trap the listener in the past without giving her the opportunity to identify with the writer's original intention for that passage. Authentic preaching seeks to move the event from the past where it is recurring in the listener today in some similar sense. The existential event is a continuous unfolding of the revelation of Christ in one's present life. To retain it only in a museum of the past does not allow it to be a timely or timeless word from God for this moment. The text has to be liberated and released into the modern-day world in a way that allows the listener to experience its purpose for having been written.

It is not sufficient to ask what a particular text meant to Moses, David, Isaiah, a psalmist, Peter, Mary, or Paul. Ask instead: How is its meaning relevant for you today? In what sense is this event transforming in your life or is a witness to an event or an experience in your own journey? No biblical text that is isolated in a past event—no matter how significant that event is—without disclosing its relationship to one's life today or allowing one to discern the word from God to us today, can really be called biblical preaching.

Barbara K. Lundblad, in a moving sermon preached in the chapel at Union Seminary in New York City only two days after 9/11, drew on John's account of the feeding of the five thousand and heard the detail of "fragments" in a different way because of the events of that week. She affirmed that although the meaning might elude us in this moment, God might create "something we cannot yet hear or even imagine."[6] She read the biblical text as it addressed not only the ancient world in the day of Jesus, but also the world in which she and her fellow students lived.

Biblical preaching will always seek to nourish persons and the life of the church today as it affirms the reality of the resurrection of Christ and the possibility of change or a new beginning in Christ.

Focusing on the Future

Some preachers view biblical preaching as chiefly prophecy about the future. These preachers see the Bible as predicting global catastrophes and significant events that point to the Rapture, the Second Coming, and the Glorious Appearing of Christ. Preachers such as John Nelson Darby, John Walvoord, Cyrus Scofield, Hal Lindsey, Tim LaHaye, and other dispensational pre-millennialists have used the Scriptures to prove their theories about the end times. They all predict that the end is "near," but seldom set an exact timetable. They draw deeply from Daniel and the Book of Revelation for their predictions.

Tim LaHaye and Jerry Jenkins have produced sixteen novels built around the theme of the Rapture that have sold more than sixty million copies. In these novels they have turned the Scriptures primarily to focus on the end of the world. They seek to find a "futuristic" text under every passage they examine. This approach ignores the kind of literature it is, especially apocalyptic literature, and fails to interpret it appropriately. Based on my examination of Scripture, most of their interpretations are an abuse of the best of biblical scholarship.[7]

Without question, prophecy is a part of Scripture. Most prophecy, however, is not foretelling the future; rather it is the biblical writer's way of "telling forth" the power and presence of Christ in the life of individual Christians or in the life and ministry of the church. The writer of the Book of Revelation, for example, was not seeking to write some message for Christians thousands of years later, but was writing about God's presence and ultimate triumph over the forces of evil in his own day. Readers from later generations find meaning in the Revelation today when they sense how it addresses similar situations or crises in their lives or in the church's struggle with the powers of the world. Authentic biblical preaching will strive to discern what the writer was addressing in his own day before looking to the present or the future.

Ignoring the Listener

Biblical preaching is not concerned chiefly with a text or a passage of Scripture, but with communicating a message or allowing the listener to overhear her own story in the one preached. Our goal is not to communicate a text but to address a person with the text. The text is not important if it does not address someone in the congregation or if someone cannot identify with the biblical story's intention. Don't get lost in the text and forget to make contact with the people to whom you are preaching. Our goal is to enable our listeners to sense that God not only communicated with Abraham, Moses, Isaiah, Jonah, John, Mary, Lydia, or Paul in the past but also addresses us today. We "listen" to discern God's Word for us. We do not simply read a text; we are read by it.

Harry Emerson Fosdick, probably the greatest preacher in the first half of the twentieth century, used a method in sermon preparation he called "project preaching" or "project method." Rather than focusing on an expository or a topical sermon, Fosdick saw that the goal of a sermon was to address or solve some problem the listener found puzzling, distracting, burdening, important, or personal. He reminded the preacher that she was challenged not with a "subject to be elucidated" but with "an object to be achieved."[8]

He confronted the listeners and engaged them with his preaching. He sought to address their hopes and fears, doubts and belief, questions and struggles, assurances and objections. The focus was on them—not just a subject. Through illustrations, repetition, restatements, an oral style, and inviting the hearers to journey with him in his thinking and method of engaging the problem in a textual theme under consideration, Fosdick sought not "to debate the meaning and possibility of Christian faith, but to produce Christian faith in the lives of his listeners . . ."[9] He directed his sermons to people—not to biblical texts.

The texts are a means of inviting the listeners to find their own word from God. The purpose of the Word is to inspire those who hear it to respond to it.

The Meaning of Biblical Preaching

Now that we have noted some inappropriate approaches to biblical preaching, we turn our attention to the meaning, forms, and best practices of biblical preaching. Some preachers want to confine biblical preaching to expository preaching. Many, who espouse this view, limit biblical preaching to an examination of a line-by-line or word-by-word interpretation of the text. This is not a good definition of expository preaching and should not be maintained as an understanding of biblical preaching. Rather, biblical preaching could result from one of several approaches. For example, the preacher could:

- Center on a particular text or selected verses in a text (ex.: a parable of Jesus or one of Paul's theological studies).
- Focus on a biblical theme (ex.: grace, faith, salvation).
- Draw on the theme of a particular passage (ex.: love, hope, sinfulness).
- Relate a lengthy passage to our situation today (ex.: Old Testament characters or Jesus' life, crucifixion, and resurrection).
- Apply a one-verse text or a biblical story to our story (ex.: the mighty acts of God in human history).

Biblical preaching can have endless possibilities or forms. The Bible should relate to the life of the listener in a way that bears some similarity to the way it touched the life or lives of the persons to whom it was addressed originally. Just as the writer of a biblical text directed that passage to meet a particular need in ancient times, so a sermon is biblical when it is released today to address an issue or need in a similar way. "The impact of the Bible on preaching should result in making its words and themes increasingly accessible to the needs of people living today," James Cox observes. "If this does not happen," he continues, "something is amiss in our preaching and must be set right.[10]

Forms of Biblical Preaching

Through the centuries biblical preaching has taken many shapes and forms. Deductive preaching is a movement that sets forth a general thesis, propositional, or truth and breaks that truth into particular subheadings and applies that truth to the specific needs of the listeners. This was the basic method of preaching for centuries.

Under the influence of Fred Craddock, an approach called "inductive preaching" was introduced. This method begins with a particular human situation and moves forward, allowing the hearers to determine truths for themselves as they actively participate with the preacher in the movement of the sermon. Narrative preaching presents a story plot by indirection that invites the hearers to overhear their own stories. Inductive preaching, narrative or another form, not only delays a conclusion to the sermon, but also invites the listeners to arrive at their own conclusions.

Experimental preaching utilizes various artistic or innovative means to express the gospel. Sometimes these sermons might take the shape of a dramatic monologue, dialogue, mime, multimedia presentation, or other expression. But they still seek to convey a gospel message.

In confessional preaching, heralded by John Claypool, the preacher is put in the center of the sermon to convey his own struggle or dilemma to communicate the gospel story. Whether the preaching is called doctrinal, life situation, expository, or something else, the intent of the preacher is to share a word from God—to be biblical.

A Definition of Biblical Preaching

Several decades ago, Leander Keck, a renowned New Testament scholar, called for a renewal of biblical preaching in the pulpit. His definition is still helpful today. He attests that preaching is biblical when it has two foci: "(a) the Bible governs the content of the sermon and when (b) the function of the sermon is analogous to that of the text."[11] This approach challenges the preacher to determine what the biblical text is actually saying and then to decide how to appropriate that message so the hearer can identify with the biblical writer's intent in writing this text.

For example, in hearing about the personal struggles of Jeremiah or Jonah's flight away from God's will for his life or Job's suffering or Martha's questions about her brother's death or Thomas' doubts about Jesus' resurrection, the listener identifies with the person with a clear acknowledgment: "That's my pilgrimage, too!" This sense of "equilibrancy" makes the ancient event meaningful to persons today. The preacher strives to help the hearer make the story of the Bible her own story.

Biblical preaching affirms two essential features: (1) what the biblical text meant originally and (2) what it means today. Whatever the biblical event was in the past is now preached in a way that enables that past event to happen again in a similar way in the life of the hearer today. In this sense, Karl Barth was correct: the preached Word conveys the Word of God—the spoken Word.[12]

The preached Word conveys the living Word of God in a continuously new way, patterned after the way the original Word was lived and communicated before. The task of the church, the preacher, is to allow the spirit to keep that Word fresh and lively as it ushers in newness and renewed freshness of life. This is what Barbara Lundblad calls "preaching the biblical stories in present tense." She challenges the preacher to remember that "marking time" includes two intertwined realities: (1) Our time marks the text, and (2) the text marks our time. Both must be remembered and honored, she asserts. We cannot read the text authentically by trying to bend it to say something against its will. The text has a voice that continues to speak across the ages. Our task, she claims, is not to update the Bible, but to open up a space in which time and text are in lively conversation with each other.[13]

The story of "Legion," the man out of whom Jesus cast unclean spirits (Mark 4:35-5:1-20), is dismissed by many as a story trapped in time by an ancient understanding of demon possession and having no relevancy for today. To me, I find this a powerful story about the fragmented nature of contemporary men and women who need the wholeness Jesus can bring to the legions of modern demons that pull us in all directions. Mark told that story to affirm Jesus' power to set us free from the destructive forces of evil, and as we identify with "Legion," we can discover the healing power of Jesus to bring salvation (wholeness) to our broken and fragmented spirit. That ancient event can become an event in a similar way for us when we discern it as a word from God that continues to bring healing and wholeness to us.

The Danish philosopher, Søren Kierkegaard, has reminded us that the Scriptures are "a letter from God with your personal name on it." As we read the Scriptures, they read us and hold a mirror up before us so we can see ourselves in its reflection.

How the Bible Tells Its Story

As we try to discern the message or story of an ancient book such as the Bible, we have to ask how that book conveyed its own story. The Bible, of course, does not have only one way of communicating its message but instead various mediums. It is filled with history, legends, myths, stories, drama, poetry, proverbs, biography, prophecy, parables, allegory, letters, sermons, songs, narratives, and other types of literature. These stories were addressed to particular communities: the Old Testament to Israel and the New Testament to the young church. They were addressed to each of these communities to meet particular historical or theological needs. These stories sought to remind these communities of faith of the abiding presence, power, and ultimate triumph of God. The Bible's stories, images, and pictures gave witness to God's activity as individuals—warts and all—responded to that revelation. Frail humans reacted to God as they understood that encounter, and the Bible did not attempt to disguise or ignore their inadequacies. In reality, because of its humanity, the Bible is more likely to connect with humans today than when it is made into a book without blemish or blur and is infallible or inerrant. Authentic biblical preaching will not deny these flaws, but rather will affirm their humanity.

Failures or inadequacies in the lives of some of the "giants" in the Kingdom give us hope today as sinful persons. Abraham's lying about his wife, Jacob's betrayal of his brother, David's adultery, Elijah's depression, Job's suffering, Peter's denial of Jesus, Thomas' doubts, Paul's mistrust of Mark—all reveal characteristics with which we can identify. We can see ourselves in the Bible through their stories and in countless others. The parables of Jesus invite us to enter the story and find the place where we connect. Even the Book of Revelation can become the story of brave Christians suffering under oppression, whether it comes from governments that oppress or from oppression because of race, economic condition, class, gender, or sex. Whenever preaching helps the listener to hear his own story in the ancient story and the Word of God that addresses that story, then preaching becomes biblical. "Biblical preaching happens when a preacher prayerfully goes to listen to the Bible on behalf of the people," Tom Long argues "and then speaks on Christ's behalf what he or she hears there."[14]

If we are going to preach the ancient biblical texts, then we have to understand their meaning. We first seek to discern the meaning of the ancient event before we can understand it as a contemporary event. We have to hear the "good news" before we see its relationship to our contemporary situation. The preacher will be challenged to a lifelong pattern of biblical study. No one can be an effective biblical preacher without diligent, critical Bible study. This requires time and dedication on the part of the preacher. Both the preacher and the congregation will be rewarded by the faithfulness to this important responsibility. Let me suggest some approaches to Bible study that have been helpful to me as I have prepared sermons.

Markers on the Trail of Biblical Preaching

I have found the following markers or steps as helpful procedures in doing powerful biblical preaching. If a preacher will observe these steps carefully, her effectiveness in preaching the Bible will be greatly enhanced.

Continuous Study

Effective preachers will continuously read in a wide field of thought. I have made it a practice every week to read or listen to recorded books in the areas of novels, short stories, or drama. I also keep before me various books in the areas of theology, ethics, biblical studies, and practical pastoral matters, along with some light or humorous reading. I also select TV shows, movies, and videos or DVDs that I can watch occasionally. This wide variety of reading/listening helps me keep my finger on the theological pulse of the day. Novels and popular literature help me sense the field of the layperson's perspective on life. Literature and TV or the movies may help us grasp the questions arising out of society faster than any place else. I keep a notebook to record my thoughts or quotes from what I read or hear.

The sermon may actually find its launching pad coming from the questions, issues, or problems from the society in which we live rather than first arising out of the Scriptures themselves. When that happens to me, I turn to the Scriptures to see if I can find an "answer" that responds to that particular need. If the preacher is reading and studying daily the Scriptures, the biblical response will often leap out at you. I sometimes feel there are several passages that would be appropriate, but I have to decide which one seems to be more focused. On some occasions I begin with the biblical text, and then some incident or happening from the news, my reading, or personal experience will enrich my reactions to the text either directly or illustratively.

Reflecting on the Text

After arriving at a text, simply read it and brood over it for several days. Like a cow chewing its cud, chew over the text in your mind thoughtfully before you consult commentaries or Bible dictionaries or other helps. Use your imagination to try to get inside the theme or meaning of the text or passage. See if you can put yourself in the story, whether you literally can be one of those to whom it was addressed, as you try the text on for size. Look inside and under every facet of the text. Hold it up as a mirror in which you examine your own reflection and see the summons it directs to you.

I usually make notes on a legal pad of ideas or impressions that come to me as I read. I simply record them in whatever order or form they come. If I see a pattern, I put them down in the format that emerges or leave them as isolated thoughts or images until later. If key words or phrases come to me, I note them. At times, something from my reading or personal experience is triggered by these random, rambling thoughts, and I make a note alongside that thought so I can draw on it later. I also try to write my own paraphrase of the text before I consult other translations.

I usually do this kind of meditative reflection over several days while I am walking, jogging, cutting the grass, driving to the hospital, or going on other pastoral calls. I usually have a small notebook with me, so I can record any thought that might come to me. Early on Monday or Tuesday I spend several hours reading the text in various translations to see if they offer any new perspective. I sometimes find that the sermon seems to have a plot or form emerging even before I have done my major critical study.

This freestyle approach may help you put your stamp of originality on the sermon rather than allowing someone else's ideas to direct your thinking before you have done any study.

Investigating the Text

After you have reflected on the text on your own, then turn to the tools of critical scholarship and consult commentaries, Bible dictionaries, lexicons, and other resources to help you understand the original meaning of the text. This will involve creative exegesis. If you can read the Greek and Hebrew languages, then examine the text in its original language and see if you get a different perspective on its meaning. It would be helpful to write your own paraphrase of the text from this study. Your effort is to determine what the writer was trying to say to the people to whom he wrote. Ask yourself some questions:

- Who was the writer? Was it Hosea, Isaiah, a psalmist, Paul, or one of the Gospel writers?

- When did the writer pen or preach his message? Was it a thousand years before Christ or in the middle of the first century? What was the historical situation?

- Where may the writing have originated? Was it, for example, while Israel was in captivity in Babylon or while John was on Patmos or while Paul was in jail?

- What shape or medium did the writer use? Was it poetry, prose, drama, proverb, song, letter, narrative, or something else?

- What is the clear message the writer was seeking to deliver to his day? Does that message have meaning for us today? If so, how?

- What theme does the text address: love, grace, atonement, worship, eschatology, providence, etc.? What is the theological message?

- Are there any exegetical problems in the text that might cause it to be interpreted in several ways? How can I help focus it for my hearers today?

- Is the theme of this text in balance with the highest insight we have from the teachings of Jesus, or does it need to be corrected by the higher revelation? (You would not want to preach on some Old Testament legalism or ethical theme that might be out of accord with the teachings of Christ. For example, Jesus did not teach us to stone women who committed adultery, but rather to acknowledge our own sinfulness and affirm God's forgiveness as we seek to follow God and not continue sinning.)

- Are there practical demands of the text that can be implemented, or would they be disruptive in a negative way in the life of those who try to respond to the text?

- How have other scholars treated this text? Have they found it to be a genuine part of Scripture and translated correctly?

- Are there other Scripture texts or passages that affirm a similar meaning to what this text counsels, or does its truth seem to stand alone?

- Is the real meaning of the text obvious? Is "reading into" (eisegesis) the text necessary instead of "bringing out" (exegesis) the real meaning of the text?

- Are there ways to allegorize the texts as Origen did in the third century? Are there "hidden" or "spiritual" meanings instead of denoting the original meaning? (For example, the gifted Scottish preacher James Stewart used allegory liberally from Acts 27:29 in a sermon built around the theme, "Anchors of the Soul," when Paul's ship was crossing the Adrian Sea and let down four anchors. Stewart labeled these four anchors as Hope, Duty, Prayer, and the Cross of Christ.[15] In no way can these thoughts be drawn from that text except by allegorizing the text to find whatever hidden meaning the preacher may want to find there. This kind of preaching can cause our biblical scholarship to be suspect.)

- Have I placed the text in its rightful context and examined its significance in the rest of the chapter of the Bible where it is found? Have I taken it out of context and allowed it to stand in isolation to its larger passage? (When a text is isolated from it basis pericope, it can then be made to mean whatever the interpreter wants. For example, Psalm 53:1 reads, "There is no God." The preface, however, reads: "The fool has said in his heart." Always note the connections and examine the whole text in order to glean the full meaning of a passage.)

In his book, *Between the Bible and the Church*, David L. Bartlett challenges the preacher to use the latest methods of biblical and narrative criticism. "Do not tell us what the passage says, . . . say the new critics, show us what the passage does."[16] For example, is the text singing, explaining, warning, directing, recounting, informing, exhorting, or summoning? To do this, he proposes that the preacher examine three areas:

1. the world in front of the text
2. the world behind the text
3. our world and the text

According to Bartlett, the preacher needs to draw upon literary and canonical critics, social and social scientific scholars of the Bible, and liberation perspectives such as the Latin American, feminine, African American, or other multiple readings of the Scriptures. Bartlett reminds the preacher that investigation through the historical-critical approach enriches preaching by enabling the preacher to understand the authentic meaning of the Scriptures and therefore make genuine connections between the text and the preacher, connections between the text and the lives of the people, and sometimes connections between the text and the social and political movements of our time.

"It is by the ongoing enterprise of religious and scholarly communities that the text lingers over time in available ways. Out of that lingering, however, from time to time, words of the text characteristically erupt into new usage," Walter Brueggemann notes. "They are seized upon by someone in the community with daring. Or perhaps better, the words of the text seize someone in the community who is a candidate for daring."[17]

"Listening to the Bible" demands the use of the best critical tools the preacher can draw upon to interpret the text if she seeks to provide an occasion for one to be "seized" for "daring" by the text. I encourage you to draw upon and use the best critical scholarship available to you today. It will help make your preaching research more current, honest, insightful, and useful. I often consult a dozen or more commentaries for each sermon and draw upon word studies, Bible dictionaries, and various books.[18]

There are, of course, many online resources for sermon preparation. Some of these sources present the preacher "ready-made" sermons, and others provide avenues to commentaries, Hebrew and Greek lexicons, Bible dictionaries, and other helpful resources. Some of them, for example, Logos, offer classic studies by Luther, Calvin, and Spurgeon. *Ipreach* by Cokesbury offers helpful resources for preaching. The preacher will need to be selective in the choice of online and other reference materials to avoid becoming a slave to someone else's interpretation and sermon suggestions.

Interpreting the Text

Having investigated the text, the preacher then seeks to "listen" to the text to determine what the text meant originally and then what it means in the present. Does the text have a valid word from God for us today? It is not enough to know what the text may have meant two thousand years ago to those to whom it was written. Is there eternal good news that addresses contemporary men and women? The preacher obviously would make notes from investigation of the text and then formulate some sense of movement, form, or outline of the text—or at least a rough idea in your mind. Look over the key words, ideas, phrases, or themes you have jotted down as you examined the pericope. Focus on how the text can make a claim on the listener now. True biblical preaching will build a bridge from the text to the life of the congregation.

Good biblical preaching is not a focus on the distant past, but on what difference that ancient word makes in our lives today. Our investigative task is not primarily to garner ideas or theological thoughts, but to listen to what the text can produce or achieve in us. The text is purpose driven. Its end goal is to make a difference in the lives of those who read or hear it. The interpreter seeks to lift the ancient word out of the dust of the past to plant it in fertile soil where it can be enlivened, grow, and produce fruit once again. To be meaningful beyond scholarly knowledge, investigation moves to interpretation—the good news in this text for modern persons. The bridge built by the preacher's interpretation will bear the load of intention that resides within the text. That intention has to be translated—communicated—in some way so it is discernible to the hearer.

Older homiletic textbooks urged preachers to consider carefully the purpose in their sermon. Was the purpose to convert, inspire, inform, challenge, etc.? Surely even preachers should have some sense of direction, intention, or purpose that arises from the text in the widest sense of that word. "Every sermon," David Buttrick reminds us, "will involve an intending *to do*."[19] If the sermon does not say something for a purpose, we might note, does it have any purpose in being said? The sermon should knock at the listener's door and, by the presence of its summons, be invited in to present its claim on the hearer. This is the hardest challenge for the preacher. What the text says can be fairly easily expounded after careful study. But the real challenge is the summons to move the listener to where he meets the original intention of the writer and experiences that challenge—summons—again.

Identifying with the Intent of the Text

The last stage for preaching on a text is moving from study, reflection, investigation, and interpretation that transports the hearer to the place of identifying with the original intention of the text. The purpose of a sermon is not to give a lecture but to let the text live again today. Having discerned the truth of the original text, the preacher now attempts to move the timeless message into our own time. Most congregations are concerned not only with what the Lord may have said at one time through some distant biblical messenger, but they also await a fresh word from God. "God kept on talking after his book went to press," Paul Scherer wrote.[20] The preacher's challenge is to let us hear God's Word in a new translation that is clear and precise.

Carol Marie Noren, professor of preaching at North Park Seminary in Chicago, notes the relevance of the story recorded in Mark 4:35-41 for her listening audience in a sermon titled the "Storm at Sea." Follow her sermon movement below:

1. We claim our identity with the fear of those disciples in our own personal turmoil.
2. The storm story reminded the disciples and us today that our worst fears are not caused by storms, but by forgetting what God has promised and done in the past.
3. The good news is that even our failures in faith can be used by God to proclaim the gospel.
4. The episode about the boat caught in the storm shows us the sovereign nature of Jesus Christ, who does not abandon his disciples because of their unbelief. No storm has the last word.[21]

In some sense of the word the hearer is invited to enter into the sermon, overhear the message, sense the plot, be engaged by the communication, respond to the summons, or visualize the Spirit's direction. The preacher has to visualize the congregation when she prepares the sermon with the needs and expectations of the people clearly in mind. This means the preacher knows the people in the congregation or has at one time "sat where they sit." Through oral communication directed to the ear and with vivid images drawn from the text that summon the listener to travel with the preacher on this sermonic journey, the congregation may indeed be engaged with the teller of the tale to follow the plot laid before them until they do identify with the intent of the text.

In the parable of the good Samaritan, for example, the listener may be drawn into the story to identify with the man who was robbed, the priest, the Levite, the Good Samaritan, the innkeeper, or an unknown observer. From this perspective the story, plot, and meaning touch the life of the listener and presents one's own understanding, purpose, and conclusion in how we might indeed be a neighbor to another. In this telling there is not one interpretation of the parable or only one meaning, but rather a variety—depending on where and how we have connected with the story. But wasn't that the way Jesus often told a story as he began "once upon a time," and before the listener realized it, it was his time in the story and a summons to respond.

Variety in Biblical Preaching

When it comes to preaching biblically, the preacher is not confined to just one way. Some identify biblical preaching with expository preaching, but that is only one instrument in the orchestra on which the preacher can play the gospel message. To confine preaching to one method is like playing with only one string on a violin. Effective biblical preaching will try to use a variety of approaches to communicate the good news. Forthcoming are a few examples the preacher might want to consider.

The Lectionary

Many church traditions, such as Roman Catholic, Episcopal, Lutheran, Presbyterian, and United Church of Christ, follow a three-year series of chosen biblical lessons for each Sunday of the year. Beginning with Advent, there is one lesson from the Old Testament and two from the New Testament. Over a three-year cycle—with the first, second, and third years identified with the letters A, B, and C respectively—the series surveys a comprehensive portion of the Bible. There are some clear advantages to using the lectionary, for example:

- The lectionary has several designated texts for each Sunday, so the preacher does not have to wonder what to preach.
- By using the lectionary, the preacher joins many others, both Protestant and Catholic, who will be preaching on the same pericope.
- There are standard lectionary helps in books and magazines and on the Internet to assist in sermon preparation. Many of these offer exegesis, sermon digests, outlines, reflections on the text, illustrations from life and literature, prayers, and responsive readings.[22]
- The lectionary helps prevent the minister from preaching on a favorite theme.
- The lectionary forces the minister to preach on passages he would likely never address.
- The lectionary allows the preacher to cover more of the Bible over a three-year period than if she were selecting a pericope on her own.
- The lectionary forces the preacher to confront the biblical text and not engage in topical preaching.
- The lectionary is a useful resource for beginning preachers because it provides particular guidance for preaching weekly.

There are also disadvantages to following the lectionary. Here are a few:

- The preacher is "forced" to select one of the given texts each week.
- Some preachers feel that much of the Scripture is not considered in the lectionary readings.
- Except for Advent/Christmas and Lent/Easter, on most holidays and other special days the sermon has nothing to do with that particular holiday. This is true of New Year's Day, Mother's Day, Memorial Day, Father's Day, Fourth of July, Labor Day, Thanksgiving, and so on.
- It might be hard to relate a national event or special tragedy, for example the 9/11 attacks, to the Sunday's text without distorting its real intent.
- The preacher would not be free to preach a special series of sermons he feels would be helpful for the spiritual growth of the congregation.

- Some preachers find the lectionary too restricting on their sense of following the leadership of God's Spirit in confronting social injustice, world issues, or particular human needs.
- Some preachers use the lectionary as a crutch and rely on the insights of others by drawing their material from the lectionary resources and conducting little research and biblical study on their own.

The following points shared by Elizabeth Achtemeier illustrate one approach to sermon preparation using the lectionary. Preaching on an Ascension Day, her sermon titled "What's Left Behind?" and based on Luke 24:44-53 and Acts 1:1-11 addressed the significance of Christ's departure for us today. In asking what's left behind, Achtemeier suggested the following:

1. Today we join the 120 ordinary people who were originally left behind.
2. Later this ordinary group received power from on high.
3. They now had power to forgive those who had wronged them.
4. The love poured out upon them by Jesus kept them from being ordinary again.
5. They also received power over death.
6. They also received an unquenchable hope in Christ's coming again and of God's ultimate reign on earth.
7. In the light of what Christ has left his followers, "O let us never ever be content to be ordinary people again."[23]

Personally, I have found it useful to follow the lectionary for portions of a year, but I have wanted freedom to address special national holidays and to develop series of sermons as I found they were needed. The preacher can choose to follow the lectionary occasionally and still preach on other texts on other Sundays.

Sermon Series

One of the ways I have done biblical preaching over the years is through sermon series. Working on a series helped me to focus on selected biblical texts or themes and concentrate my study on that series for an extended period of time instead of jumping around with isolated passages or a different text or themes each week. By determining what particular series I would preach on six months to a year in advance, I could purchase books I needed for the series or obtain them from the library. The series also helped the congregation to focus on a theological, biblical, personal, or spiritual issue or need. Many preachers have also found this kind of preaching is an effective way to lay the foundation for books they would later publish.

Several of John Killinger's books came out of his preaching various sermon series. In particular one might note his books on the Beatitudes, *Letting God Bless You*; the Lord's Prayer, *The God Named Hallowed*; the Apostles' Creed, *You Are What You Believe*; and the Ten Commandments, *The Ten Commandments for Today*. *Be My People* by Ross W. Mann is based on a sermon series on the Ten Commandments he preached at First United Methodist Church in Bloomington, Indiana. Through the years I have preached many series of sermons. Here are only a few:

- The Signs in the Gospel of John (ten sermons)
- Inspiration from the Psalms (two series, separated by several years)
- The Parables (several series)
- The Seven Words from the Cross
- The Beatitudes
  (later published as *The Way for All Seasons*)
- Questions about the Dark
  (later published as *Getting Past the Pain*)
- The Ten Commandments
  (later published as *The Ten Commandments: Their Meaning Today*)
- The Lord's Prayer
  (later published as *The Lord's Prayer Today*)
- Jesus' Journey to the Cross
- The Difficult Sayings of Jesus
- On Christian Love: A Pattern for Living
  (later published as *Love as a Way of Living*)

In addition to using biblical commentaries to prepare sermon series, I also read books, particularly theological, topical, and sermon collections on the series theme. I took notes and worked on the series months in advance, before focusing in each week on the particular pericope for that sermon. I always found it a rewarding, inspiring, and educational process. Most ministers of music are also appreciative of receiving sermon topics long in advance so they can plan carefully their anthems and other music to coordinate the worship service.

Storytelling

Narrative preaching or preaching as a story is another avenue to utilize for biblical preaching. Much of the Bible is presented in story form, and narrative preaching is simply a way of reaching back to the biblical writing style. Since much of society today has been oriented to think in stories by radio, television, and movies, this medium can be a popular one. Much of Garrison Keillor's *A Prairie Home Companion* revolves around his telling of "the news from Lake Wobegon." All children love stories, both those from written sources and those their parents may compose. My small children loved to hear about the "magic airplane" that took them to their grandparents' home and to other wonderful places of adventure and surprise.

The Old Testament records the stories of Abraham, Isaac, Jacob, Joseph, Moses, Elijah, Rebecca, Ruth, and countless others. The Gospels tell the story of Jesus, while Jesus' main method of preaching was by stories (parables). Much of Acts is the story of Paul and the early church. The Epistles arose out of the efforts of Paul and others to spread that story about God's good news. In many places the Bible message is a summons to remember the story of God's deliverance and grace.

Lloyd John Ogilvie, former pastor of the First Presbyterian Church of Hollywood, California, and chaplain of the United States Senate, used the following movement of thought to preach on the Old Testament character, Joseph. "As we follow Joseph's pilgrimage carefully," Ogilvie suggests, "five powerful guidelines for disappointed dreamers emerge."[24]

1. Let God be God of your dreams.
2. Let God be God when circumstances seem to contradict your dream.
3. Let God be God in the successes of life.
4. Let God be God over the failures of others who have frustrated your dreams.
5. Let God be God of the future as he works out his greater purpose in history.[25]

Every preacher needs to develop the ability to tell a story well. People love a good story, and if the preacher communicates well the ancient biblical stories, that telling will help draw people to listen to "the old, old story" of God's love and grace. Homileticians such as Eugene Lowry have challenged the preacher to develop plots rather than points in their sermons. Fred Craddock and others have challenged the preacher to let persons "overhear" the good news rather than state it as abstract truths to be gathered in and acknowledged. His inductive approach has suggested also stories or sermons that are "open-ended," where the listener can arrive at his own conclusion while listening to the story.

Well-known preacher John Claypool published a book of sermons based on seventeen biblical characters, men and women in the Old Testament who are our spiritual ancestors. The book is titled *Glad Reunion*, and its subtitle suggests the goal of these sermons: *Meeting Ourselves in the Lives of Bible Men and Women.* "Memory," Claypool asserted, "is a crucial component of identity."[26]

The ancient scrapbook of biblical memory summons us to remember who we are or can be as we hear or rehear the stories of others meeting with God and their response to these encounters. We are pulled back into these ancient roots to discover our own stories. And that is one of the challenges of narrative preaching.

In one of my efforts in preaching on biblical characters, a series on Old Testament Heroes of the Faith, I told the following stories:

- "Abraham: A Journey of Faith"
- "Jacob: Wrestling to Find His Place"
- "Moses: Responding to God"
- "David: The Lamb and Lion of Israel"
- "Elijah: From Mountain to the Valley"
- "Jeremiah: When Life Crashes In"
- "Ruth: The Bond of Loyalty"

Jesus often used metaphors to describe what the kingdom of God was like. In Matthew 13:44, he stated that "the kingdom of heaven is like treasure hidden in a field, which someone found hid; then in his joy he goes and sells all he has and buys that field." The preacher might bring that metaphor to life for the contemporary listener by telling the story in an imaginary way. Here is an attempt I used once in a sermon on that text:

> The hot sun was beating down upon his neck. He could feel the redness of it from the heat of the day and the hot breeze blowing in off the sea nearby. He was tired of his difficult labor already.

"Oh, I'll never amount to much," he thought to himself. "I have to rent somebody else's land and work it like a dog; I own almost nothing. I just can't amount to much at all."

Suddenly his plow hit something in the ground where he was plowing.

"Not another rock," he exclaimed aloud. "I have already removed so many today."

He stopped his oxen, bent down to remove the plow from the ground to discover it was not a rock but a box he had hit, and it was partially opened. He caught a glimpse of the inside of the box and saw that it was filled with gold coins and jewels.

He looked around to see if anyone else had seen his discovery. No one was around. He covered up the hole quickly and pondered on the teaching of the Talmud that in essence states, "finders keepers." He knew that sometimes people buried their possessions in the ground to hide them. After all, there were no banks, no attics, and no basements in which one could hide his valuables. Sometimes a person would hear that an enemy army was coming and he would hide his treasure in the ground. That person might be carried off into captivity and never return or, if he did return, forget where he had hidden the treasury. He knew that he did not dare try to carry the box away at that moment.

He pondered to himself, "What can I do?" "Ah, I know," he reflected to himself. "I will buy this piece of land, and this box will be mine without any questions asked."

He rushed home and told his wife: "Gather up everything we've got. I want the candlesticks, your few jewels, any books I have. I want everything!"

"Have you gone mad?" his wife asked.

"I want everything we've got; give it to me now," he urged. "Put it in this bag," he exclaimed as he extended a cloth-patched sack toward her.

Quickly he rushed off to see a friend from whom he believed he could borrow some money.

"I need to exchange these items for some money," he declared breathlessly. "Lend me enough money to buy the field I have been plowing for several years now. I want to buy it. I have already sold everything I own. I'll pay you back tomorrow."

He took the money he had received from selling all he owned and purchased the field because of the treasure buried there. His purchase made him a wealthy man indeed! For the sheer joy of his discovery, he sold all he had to buy the field where he found the fortune.

This is the kind of joy one has when he or she sacrifices all to be a part of the kingdom of God that Jesus proclaimed.

This brief story attempted to "flesh out" the metaphor from this teaching of Jesus. Use your imagination to help your hearers visualize the story. Do not be afraid to use that wonderful gift! In a later chapter I will draw on one of Jesus' parables and put it in contemporary garb to try and make it more understandable to the modern mind.

Draw on your imagination to read between the lines and help reweave the old stories into contemporary clothing so they may be more familiar to your hearers. Use humor, exaggeration, color, and overstatements to adorn your tale. Be willing to be daring to communicate your message. Remember: You have good news. Share it joyfully.[27]

Dramatic Monologue

If a preacher wants to be innovative and present a biblical story from a first-person perspective, a dramatic monologue can be effective. Through this medium the preacher can present an eyewitness account of a particular story. I have found it most effective to dress the part of the person I am seeking to represent. I wear a robe that looks like what we think a biblical one was like, adorn a long beard and wig, and put on scandals. Sometimes a staff is necessary. For many sermons on Children's Day I have dressed the part to tell the story of Noah, Jonah, Elijah, John the Baptist, or another biblical character. I tell the story without notes or a manuscript so that I can be a real storyteller. And, if I am claiming this is my story, I should not need props or notes anyway.

Try to follow the plot of the biblical story by seeing it in scenes in your mind's eye and guiding your listeners with you as you move through the story. Try to be true to the biblical text, but feel free to use your imagination and color the tale enough to make it understandable to a contemporary congregation. Sometimes I do not dress as the character but simply identify who I am and tell the story. I told the story of Ruth one time as an observer who was an onlooker and relayed that tale to another. Dressing for the part helps to make the storytelling more realistic, however.

Alton H. McEachern, former pastor of First Baptist Church, Greensboro, North Carolina, was a pioneer in monologue preaching. He researched well his story and then dressed for the storytelling and communicated it well. In a book of monologue sermons, he introduced his sermon on Hosea with the title "A Broken Home Provides a Gospel" this way:

> My name is Hosea. I am a prophet of the Lord God, Yahweh. My preaching ministry overlapped that of Amos in Israel, the Northern Kingdom. Amos' name means "burden," for he carried the weight of the sins of his people. I was influenced by Amos' message, and certainly my early prophesying contained a strong note of judgment. I preached against sin and warned of the peril at hand, unless the people repented and returned to the Lord.
>
> For nearly half a century our country enjoyed a political golden age. It was an era of peace. King Uzziah was the king of Judah in the south, and Jeroboam II ruled in Israel. The two of them were in power for almost forty years. This gave our countries a time of political stability. Another factor that certainly contributed to peace was the fact that no great power was dominating the politics of our region. Egypt was dreaming of glories past; and Assyria, a sleeping giant, was not yet aware of its might.

He concluded the sermon this way:

> Now I can preach grace and God's suffering love. I learned much through heartbreak. I learned something of how God feels toward his erring children. He, too, is heartbroken by our sin but loves us still. I also learned that all sin is really against covenant love and that the root of sin is deserting God for something or someone less.
>
> I loved Gomer in spite of all she did wrong. *How much more* does God love us?
>
> My message is simple, "Repent, return, come home to the God who loves you enough to make you and then buy you back."[28]

If the preacher is a bit of an actor, or can at least try to act, the sermon will be more realistic and cause the people to want to listen. Do not be afraid to be a little dramatic; after all, this is a dramatic monologue. To tell the story well, the preacher needs to do careful research and interpretation by perusing Bible dictionaries and commentaries.[29]

I suggest you write out your drama in an oral style to be spoken. Weave the historical and background information into the story in a way that it doesn't distract from the story but sets it firmly in time. Don't just rehash a known story, but read between the lines and make it come alive for your hearers.

Dialogue

Another innovative approach to biblical preaching might be in the form of a dialogue. This would obviously require another person to assist the preacher in this effort. A layperson or another minister could work on the presentation of this type of sermon. A dialogue sermon could be depicted as a conversation between Jesus and Nicodemus, Jacob and Esau, Ruth and Naomi, Moses and Pharaoh, Jesus and Peter, Jesus and Thomas, Jesus and John the Baptist, Paul and Agrippa, Martha and Jesus, or any choices one might want to make—presented complete with costumes if they could be arranged.

The script should be carefully drawn from the text. Imagination could fill in the blanks with dialogue to help set the stage or to clarify the situation. It would be helpful for the two preachers to practice their exchanges to determine their clues and proper timing. Remember the goal is to communicate the good news of the gospel in a way that touches the life of the hearers and does not simply entertain them. Some dramatic presentation could enliven the sermon and pull the listeners in more effectively. Do not be afraid to express your acting gifts. All preachers have this gift to some extent, I suspect.[30]

Another form of dialogue might happen in "talk-back" sessions the pastor has with the congregation. The preacher delivers the sermon on Sunday morning and has a "talk-back" time on Sunday night or Wednesday night with laypersons. This session is spontaneous and not rehearsed, but can be refreshing and enlightening to the pastor and the congregation. In many predominantly African-American congregations, "dialogue" between the preacher and the hearers is a natural and expected happening. The minister often calls to the congregation to "come on up" with their response to his preaching. The preaching in that context is enriched by the congregational response in a very verbal way.

The Great Texts

There is an old fifteen-volume set of books called *The Great Texts of the Bible*, edited by James Hastings, that offers many wonderful examples, models, and research on how a preacher can preach endlessly on nothing but the great texts of the Bible. How can a preacher exhaust the birth stories in Matthew and Luke or texts such as Psalm 23 and 100, John 1 or 3 or 14, Romans 8, 1 Corinthians 13, Ephesians 4, Philippians 2:5-11, Colossians 3:1-17, Hebrews 11, 1 John, and countless others? Examine the sermons of outstanding preachers such as Harry Emerson Fosdick, George Buttrick, John Killinger, Peter Gomes, and Barbara Brown Taylor and note how they often preach on the great texts.

The preacher could select her own "great" texts or ask the congregation to suggest their own and then compose a list for preaching. Prepare a series of sermons on these texts. Like all of your preaching, this type will require reflection, investigation, interpretation, and identifying the intention of the pericope. Persons in the congregation can have a real sense of involvement if they suggest the texts and if you also allow for some sessions to receive their input on the texts. This might focus on their understanding of the meaning of the texts, why they chose them, or how they feel they relate to their lives. I have always found congregations willing to give me feedback and up-front suggestions on what they would like to hear preached or what their "needs" are. This can make your preaching timely, lively, and exciting for your people and hopefully for the preacher as well.

Individual Texts

There are occasions where the preacher can draw on a single verse to expound on a powerful message about God's love, grace, or the call to discipleship. The preacher needs to be certain that the usage of the passage is not taken out of its context and misused, however. Examining the context and intent of the passage is essential. All the scholarly tools used in any sermon preparation are still required. There are many marvelous texts that can enrich our preaching and inspire our hearers. Again, the pastor might want to ask members of the congregation to share their favorite verses and plan a series based on the list. Many verses will make that list. Some of them will probably include the following ones:

- "For God so loved the world that he gave his only Son, so that everyone who believes in him, may not perish but may have eternal life." (John 3:16)
- "For by grace you have been saved through faith, and this is not your own doing; it is the gift of God." (Eph. 2:8)
- "I can do all things through him (Christ) who strengthens me." (Phil. 4:13)
- "We know that all things work together for good for those who love God, who are called according to his purpose." (Rom. 8:28)
- "And the Word became flesh and lived among us, and we have seen his glory, the glory as the father's only son, full of grace and truth." (John 1:14)
- "The Lord is my shepherd, I shall not want." (Ps. 23:1)

In a personally moving sermon, Barbara Brown Taylor draws on one verse from John 8:25: "They said to him, 'Who are you?' Jesus said to them, 'Why do I speak to you at all?'" She relates it to its context and wider biblical theme to summons the hearer (reader) to the one who is the "I am." Karl Barth has a sermon that draws on the powerful words from Ephesians 2:8. His movement is simple and advances a word at the time.

1. **By grace** you have been saved.
2. By grace *you* have been saved.
3. By grace you **have been saved.** [31]

Try to determine the theme of each phrase in the verse as you seek to preach it. For example, John 3:16 might take the following movement:

1. The source of love: "For God"
2. The extent of love: "so loved the world"
3. The sacrifice of love: "that he gave his only Son"
4. The inclusive nature of God's love: "so that everyone"
5. The response of faith to God's love: "who believes in him"
6. The eternal nature of God's love: "may not perish but have eternal life."

Paul's letter to the Romans offers a powerful verse for proclamation: "For I am not ashamed of the gospel; it is the power of God for salvation to everyone who has faith, to the Jew first and also to the Greek" (1:16). In a sermon titled "Christians Unashamed," here is how I made my movement through that text:

1. No stranger to shame
2. Not ashamed of the gospel
3. The power of God
4. Power of God for salvation
5. A gift for everyone

The challenge I felt was not only to understand Paul's "pride" in the gospel, but also to "overhear" or sense Paul's intention for his day and how that intention translates into our contemporary setting. Instead of being timid Christians, we are called to let the flag of faith wave proudly in our world and follow Christ with enthusiasm and a sense of joy as we affirm Paul's words in Romans 1:16. I, too, am not ashamed of the gospel but am proud of its power in the lives of people today.

Bible Books

Probably one of the more difficult kinds of biblical preaching is a Bible book sermon. The preacher will attempt in a sermon or, more likely, in a series of sermons to focus on a particular book of the Bible. This bird's-eye view of a book will require the preacher to do all of the scholarly research and exegetical investigation for not only a selected pericope of a book, but also eventually for the whole book. Some preachers have attempted to start with Genesis and go through all of the books to Revelation. If the preacher took one book a Sunday, that would take almost a year and a half. People would probably get tired of that approach before the preacher arrived at the conclusion of his study. It would probably be more helpful to take the study by types of books and break them down into the following sections.

1. Pentateuch—Genesis, Exodus, Leviticus, Numbers, Deuteronomy
2. History—Joshua, Judges, Ruth, 1 Samuel, 2 Samuel, 1 Kings, 2 Kings, 1 Chronicles, 2 Chronicles, Ezra, Nehemiah, Esther
3. Poetry—Job, Psalms, Proverbs, Ecclesiastes, Song of Songs
4. Major Prophets—Isaiah, Jeremiah, Lamentations, Ezekiel, David, Hosea, Amos
5. Minor Prophets—Joel, Obadiah, Jonah, Micah, Nahum, Habakkuk, Zephaniah, Haggai, Zephaniah, Malachi
6. Gospels—Matthew, Mark, Luke, John
7. New Testament History-Acts
8. Pauline Epistles—Romans, 1 Corinthians, 2 Corinthians, Galatians, Ephesians, Philippians, Colossians, 1 Thessalonians, 2 Thessalonians, 1 Timothy, 2 Timothy, Titus, Philemon
9. Hebrews and General Epistles—Hebrews, James, 1 Peter, 2 Peter, 1 John, 2 John, 3 John, Jude
10. Eschatology—Revelation

The preacher could do a series on a particular type for several months, for example, the Pentateuch, and then follow the Lectionary for several months or preach on selected passages and return to another book type later in the year for several months. Some of the sections, such as Paul's letters, may need to be divided because of their length.

I have attempted several of these studies over the years, particularly in Romans, Ephesians, 1 Corinthians, Ruth, and Jeremiah. In a series of sermons I preached on 1 Corinthians, I addressed the following themes or issues:

"The Gospel Address to a City"	(1:1-3)
"Quarrels in the Church"	(1:10-18)
"Being Moral in an Immoral World"	(6:9-10)
"The Illusion of Freedom"	(9:1-23)
"Modern Idolatry"	(10:12-33)
"Women in Ministry"	(11:2-16)

"The Lord's Supper"	(11:23-34)
"Spiritual Gifts"	(12:1-26)
"The Greatest of All: Love"	(ch. 13)
"Speaking a Distinct Word"	(14:1-19)
"Now Concerning the Offering"	(16:1-3)
"The Assurance of Christ's Resurrection"	(15:3-56)
"Giving Thanks"	(1:4-9)

Even in thirteen sermons I could not cover the whole epistle. But I tried to deal with most of the major themes in the book. Someone else might approach the letter differently. I personally felt it was too difficult to try to deal with a Bible book in one sermon.

In examining a book of the Bible to preach, state the kind of literature it is—for example, poetry, an epistle, a gospel—describe its historical setting, and give an overview of its contents. In other words, try to tell briefly its story and then note the relevant message of the book for our day or suggest the listener try to determine if there is an abiding message for her. Every preacher should test his own gifts and scholarship to try this kind of challenge.[32]

Multimedia

Some preachers choose to augment their verbal words with various usages of multimedia. While Power Point presentations can be effective, these can be easily overdone and the preacher can rely too much on the internet for resources. A computer might feed information to a projector that sets an outline of the sermon on a large screen before the congregation. Other projectors may show pictures of an ocean, if there is a Scripture reference to the sea, or an image of a ship on the sea or a fisherman casting a net by the sea. Images on a screen may be used to augment or reinforce the Scripture lesson for the day. The sound of music or the ocean or other kinds of sounds might also be utilized. Rather than just hearing a passage read and expounded, visual and oral images may be synchronized to enhance the message or make it clear. Images of maps, roads, people, children, animals, farms, or houses from the first century might be used to add authenticity to the spoken word or simply to heighten the congregation's sensitivity. Some churches have budgets that include a large amount for technological equipment, including computers, projectors, DVDs, microphones, audio and video cameras, and so on.

When pop/folk singers Simon and Garfunkel were at their height of popularity, I preached a sermon using as the title of my sermon one of their famous hits, "The Sounds of Silence." Before preaching that sermon, I let the congregation listen to a recording of the song. That was my first introduction to the use of media in preaching.

Test your congregation's response. Many listeners find this type of approach more effective in contemporary worship services where the congregation likes and expects innovations. Remember not to lose your biblical message in all the media presentation, however. I have heard some church members complain that their preacher seems to get his sermons off the Internet and gives them back via the computer. Remember you are preaching a sermon, not performing a concert or putting on a show. Preach the Word whatever medium you use.[33]

Expository Preaching

Some homileticians and preachers believe that all authentic biblical preaching is expository preaching. As I indicated earlier, I believe this is a limited perspective. Expository preaching is one among many ways to preach biblically. Only a few preachers have done this kind of preaching effectively in the past or are doing it well today. It is challenging and requires careful biblical exegesis and investigation and the ability to relate one's findings in a meaningful way to the life of the listener. Before we examine this type of preaching further, however, let's establish what expository preaching is not.

- Expository preaching is not simply running comments or platitudes about the verses a preacher has just read.

- Expository preaching is not a lecture about a particular passage of Scripture with quotations and citations from various commentaries and biblical dictionaries and other sources.

- Expository preaching is not merely reporting a word study conducted on the Greek or Hebrew text.

- Expository preaching is not an occasion where a preacher presents a laborious display of her exegesis of the passage.

- Expository preaching is not a method of proof texting a passage of Scripture so the preacher can find whatever he wants by abusing the text.

- Expository preaching is not just "moralizing on a text," as Leander Keck says,[34] in an effort to relate it to the present, whether the texts actually indicate that moralizing or not.

- Expository preaching is not merely a reporting of what the biblical passage says or means.

- Expository preaching is not a means of sermonizing that affords the preacher special authority or insight into the passage that makes his interpretation the only correct one or that gives him the right to draw moral, ethical, social, or political judgments that do not originate with the text.

- Expository preaching is not meant to be a launching pad for the preacher to go in any direction she desires. It should not provide the occasion, means, or excuse to preach on a theological hobby horse, pet peeve, or whatever current social issue the preacher supports or opposes.

Now that we have determined what expository preaching is not, let's look at various definitions of it as offered by different preachers and homileticians.

Some have defined textual preaching and expository preaching as different, while others have described them as similar or the same. Andrew Blackwood, who taught homiletics at Princeton Theological Seminary several generations ago and was considered by many as the dean of homiletics professors, stated that "expository preaching means that the light for any sermon comes mainly from a Bible passage longer than two or three consecutive verses."[35] F. B. Meyer defined expository preaching as "the consecutive treatment of some book or extended portion of Scripture on which the preacher has concentrated . . . until it has yielded up its inner secret and the spirit of it has passed into his spirit."[36] A contemporary professor of preaching, John S. McClure, gives the following definition in the *Concise Encyclopedia of Preaching*: "The expository sermon is a sermon which faithfully brings a message out of Scripture and makes that message accessible to contemporary hearers."[37]

Although many variations of expository preaching are practical, I choose to limit it to a larger passage of Scripture rather than restricting it to a verse or two. To me, that type of preaching is textual preaching or simply preaching on an individual verse. Although some preachers have expounded effectively on only one verse, it takes real skill to make it an expository sermon. I envision expository preaching as a sermon that draws on the theme of a biblical passage and follows the textual movement of that portion of Scripture to determine the sermon movement, and either the preacher deduces the application from the text or allows the hearers to sense their own story in the text that is preached. I would identify the following guidelines for expository preaching:

- Expository preaching requires careful reflection, investigation, interpretation, and exegesis that reveal the original intention of the passage. Read the text in the original language and various translations and paraphrases to get inside the clear meaning of the text.

- The expository sermon will focus on the major theme or themes of the passage. Once this legitimate theme is acknowledged, the sermon may develop in whatever way the theme can be best communicated. The preacher will seek to cull out the minor themes and concentrate on the major details. I believe this can best be done with a pericope rather than with an isolated verse or two. Textual preaching, without question, can be a form of expository preaching, but a longer pericope should be preferred, if appropriate.

- The movement or development of the expository sermon will follow the movement of the Scripture passage itself. Try to determine the focus, rhythm, or function of the thematic movements and let that direct the shape or form of the sermon. If the sermon follows a deductive approach, the major movement or outline (ideas) may be broken down into subheads or smaller components. If the sermon were to be inductive and presented as a story or a narrative, then make note of the sermon's plot and the various "acts" in the story as it unfolds. Whether it is acts or parts, some form is essential to construct and preach an expository sermon or any kind of sermon.

- It is helpful if the expository sermon is consistent with the type of structure of the text. If the form is a story, a parable, or a narrative, it would be natural to follow the same form and preach the sermon in a narrative style. If the format is a discourse, teaching, or sermon by Jesus or a letter by Paul, then the sermonic approach allows a greater freedom of approach, depending on the theme of the passage.

- The interpretation of the intent of the theme of the passage may be essential to understanding the real meaning of the text and how it can be made accessible today. For example, do we follow Paul's advice that "wives are to obey their husbands"? Or do we see that wisdom as restricted by its own time in its understanding of family relationships and not necessarily transferable to us today, while hearing his "intent" to instruct Christian husbands and wives to be loving, respectful, and faithful to each other in Christian marriage? We need to get inside the text to determine its intention if we are to determine its modern application.

- If the sermon is an inductive message, after having determined the theme of the passage, the movement of the text, and the intent of the pericope, expound the passage so the listeners will overhear the message for them or be pulled into the sermon to reach their own conclusion or application. If it is a deductive sermon, suggest a human need or challenge that addresses the listener in a meaningful way. The sermon will not be truly biblical, no matter how much Scripture is quoted or explained or expounded, if the message in some way is not relevant to those hearing it today.

- If the preacher is going to insist on the authority of the Scripture, then the preacher is obligated to respect the context out of which the pericope comes and honor it and not exploit it to preach personal prejudices or theological agendas. Be true to the text. Misusing the text for any purpose other than the one it was originally meant to have is poor biblical preaching.

- Expository preaching should be expounded in a way that is clear and understandable. It is essential that the biblical message of the passage be communicated so the listeners will want to listen and can see the relevancy of the passage for their own lives. Many expository preachers believe this can be done through deductive preaching where the preacher through context, argument, logic, example, illustration, and persuasion cause the listener to respond to the sermon. This may be one effective means, but narrative, confessional, or other forms of inductive preaching may be as effective or more so.

- Often the best place to begin an expository sermon is with a human need the preacher is aware of in his own congregation or personal life. From the awareness of that need, the preacher will then select a passage that will enable him to meet that need. I find it helpful to keep a notebook and write down biblical themes, human needs, personal experiences, and stories I hear from church members and others that might suggest expository sermon topics.

- Be prepared to find the good news in the text that exalts Christ or points to his redeeming love and grace. We should seek to preach Christ and his power of redemption.

The best examples of expository preaching reach back to the nineteenth century and the early part of the twentieth century in the preaching of ministers such as F. W. Robertson of Brighton, England; Alexander Maclaren of Manchester, England; and Charles Spurgeon of London, England. All of these preachers were different theologically, by their education, personalities, and styles. But they were all masters of the expository style and are still good models for preachers today. Helmut Thielicke, the former professor of systematic theology at the University of Hamburg, Germany, advised preachers to "sell all that you have (not the least of all some of your stock of current sermonic literature) and buy Spurgeon."[38]

Many of Robertson's sermons were textual, focusing on a verse or two and then considering two contrasting truths. A sermon on the "Parable of the Sower" from Matthew 13:1-9, is a good example of his expository style. Here is his simple movement:

Introduction
I. The Cause of Failure
    1. The want of spiritual perception (some fell by the wayside)
    2. The want of depth of character (some fell on stony ground)
    3. Subjected to dissipating influence (some fell among thorns)
II. The Permanence of Religious Impressions
    1. An honest and good heart (some fell on good ground)
    2. Meditation (they keep the word they have heard)
    3. Endurance (they bring forth fruit with patience)[39]

Alexander Maclaren (1826-1910) was an excellent student and scholar of the Bible, who always began his study of a passage with the original language. His sermons are found in several collections, including a twenty-volume collection called *Exposition of Holy Scripture*. Here is a sample from Psalm 23:

Introduction – The experience of David as a shepherd
I. The Divine Shepherd and his leading of his flock (vv. 1-4)
    A. God leads his sheep into rest.
    B. He also leads us into work.
    C. He leads us through sorrow.
II. The Divine Host and the guests at his table (vv. 5-6)
    A. God supplies our wants in the midst of strife.
    B. He cares for our needs in this life.
    C. He brings us hope for the life to come.
Conclusion – Take this psalm as your own, by faith.[40]

Charles Haddon Spurgeon (1834-1892) was a child prodigy when he began as a preacher. He had no formal training but was self-taught and greatly disciplined. His disciplined ways, powerful preaching style, clear, resonant voice, and provocative sermons drew thousands to hear him preach in the Metropolitan Tabernacle in London. He saw the importance of founding a Pastors College in 1857. Thielicke observed that "by plunging with his message into the world and emerging in its climate, Spurgeon was fulfilling the original intention of the gospel to meet man where he is."[41] Based on John 10:15-17, Spurgeon preached a sermon titled "Other Sheep and One Flock," with "four things" he notes in the text and several minor movements under each of these four. I will note only the four major headings. This outline cannot begin to show how Spurgeon moved through the text with insight and clarity:

1. Our Lord Jesus Christ Had a People Under the Worst Circumstances.
2. Our Lord Hath Other Sheep Not Yet Known to Us.
3. Our Lord Must Bring or Lead Those Other Sheep.
4. Our Lord Guarantees the Unity of His Church.[42]

Sometimes I have preached expository sermons on some of the psalms or parables, the difficult sayings of Jesus, the signs in John's Gospel, 1 Corinthians 13, and other passages. It has not been my favorite form of preaching, but it has been a challenging one. Here are a couple of examples from my preaching notes where I have tried to focus on the major themes of the passage.

"God's Unfailing Mercy"
Psalm 138
1. The Psalmist begins with adoration.
2. He moves to acknowledge the attribute of mercy as lovingkindness, which is the root of praise.
3. The Psalmist concludes his call to praise with assurance.

"The Greatest of These Is Love"
1 Corinthians 13:1-13
1. Introduction
2. The Young Church in Corinth
3. The Love Hymn
4. The Greatest Gift in the Church
5. Love Contrasted with Other Gifts (vv. 1-3)
6. The Characteristics of Love (vv. 4-7)
7. The Permanence of Love (vv. 8-13)

In an expository sermon based on Acts 3:1-10 where Peter and John healed the lame man at the gate of the temple, I introduced the sermon in story form:

> A beggar routinely went to the temple each day in ancient Jerusalem. After all, he had been going there for many years. He had been lame since birth, and at forty years old, he had begged either at this place or some other spot all of his life. He didn't come to the temple with any great expectations, but he did hope that someone would notice him that day and give him some small alms.
>
> He sat outside the temple gate at the mid-afternoon time of prayer. He saw two strangers walking toward him. As he saw these men approaching him, he may have hoped that these two might give him some small contribution. So he began to beg more loudly. Peter and John walked up and stopped in front of the man. The beggar must have continued to beg from others who passed by, because Peter called out to the beggar: "Look at us!"
>
> The beggar turned and looked up at them with anticipation and hoped he would receive something from them.

"I have no silver and gold," Peter said.

At those words the beggar's hope may have faded.

"But what I have I give to you," Peter continued. "In the name of Jesus Christ of Nazareth, stand up and walk."

Peter reached down and took the man by his hand and pulled him up. The beggar discovered his feet and ankle bones were healed.

The words used here to describe his feet and ankle bones are technical medical phrases not used any other place in the New Testament. They are special to Dr. Luke.

After being healed, the beggar walked with Peter and John into the temple and began to leap into the air and praise God. The crowd marveled at the miracle they had just seen.

After noting that this was the first miracle performed by any of the disciples after the resurrection of Jesus and following Pentecost, I then raised a question to my hearers:

Who does this beggar represent today? Who is the beggar that sits at the church's gate today?

There are many persons who sit at the gate of the churches who suffer from cancer, heart trouble, Alzheimer's disease, and other illnesses who are waiting for someone to reach out to minister to them in the name of Jesus Christ.

Who does this paralyzed beggar represent to you? Does he represent those who are paralyzed by their sins and are unable to find freedom from them, because they are caught in bad habits, routines, and wiles that have led them down dead-end streets? Does this man at the gate represent those who are paralyzed by their loneliness, depression, anxieties, or fears?

Whoever these people are who are sitting at the gate today, Christ is sending you and me, who claim to be his disciples, to reach out to them and bring them healing, wholeness, and salvation.

Even in the introduction I attempted to summon the listener to examine how this text relates to our world today and where she fit in.

Let me share three sermons that are contemporary examples of expository preaching. The first one was delivered at Christ Church in Alexandria, Virginia, on Good Friday of 1998 by Ellen F. Davis, professor of Bible and practical theology at Duke Divinity School. Davis declares that she always preaches exegetically because she believes people are interested in what the text says. Is there a clear distinction between an exegetical and expository sermon? They are similar, I think. Here are the movements from one of her sermons whose approach to the text is "reading it from the inside."

Psalm 22
1. Horrible cries of pain and accusation are directed against God.
2. A reversal in mid-verse moves the writer from lament to praise as he appeals to the God whom he just called his enemy.
3. This contradictory psalm ends with praise as extravagant as the accusations were fierce earlier.
4. The Psalmist shows us that faithful suffering leads us into the depths to discover, beyond all logic, that we fall beyond the reach of God's love and power to save. Out of this certainty we discover our boundless capacity for praise.
5. Jesus' forsaken cry on the cross led him and fellow sufferers sometimes to the bottom of despair that lies within the heart of God.
6. The way of the cross traces a different route in each person's life, but in the midst of our pain—whatever it may be—one senses the mark of the crucified Savior.[43]

Another example can be found in the following sermon by Peter J. Gomes, the late minister of Harvard Memorial Church and the Plummer Professor of Christian Morals at Harvard University in Boston, Massachusetts. He delivered this sermon in the chapel at Duke University on February 19, 1995.

An Impossible Ethic
Genesis 45:8, Matthew 5:1-14
 1. Joseph was one of the more obnoxious figures in all of Scripture.
 2. My sympathy is with the brothers.
 3. Let us slay this dreamer and then see what will become of his dreams.
 4. The proximity of the family unity often stimulates perversity.
 5. The sign of God's providence is revealed.
 6. Joseph acts contrary to human instinct.
 7. What has this impossible ethic to do with us?
 8. This impossible ethic is the only one that counts.[44]

The next example is from a sermon by John Killinger, who has served as both a pastor and a seminary professor. This sermon is taken from a series on the Beatitudes in his book, *Letting God Bless You*.

Blessed Are Those Who Mourn
Matthew 5:4
 1. Most of us know a bit about mourning.
 2. Grief is a time of finiteness.
 3. Are there people who do not mourn or are seldom afflicted by sadness and despair?
    a. Was this directed to the Pharisees, the ultra-righteous people?
    b. Does this group include vain, ego-centered, and self-serving persons who are the "scrooges" of our time?
 4. Maybe Jesus was not isolating persons called mourners, but describing the coming kingdom in which all pain and grief would be banished. Examples:
    a. A new heaven and earth in the Book of Revelation (21:4)
    b. Jesus raising persons from the dead may have depicted a foretaste of what the reign of God is about.
 5. Those who mourn will be comforted.
    a. The Comforter (Paraclete) is the one who comforts.
    b. God, the source of all comfort, is already overcoming evil.
    c. The Holy Spirit, who is the Comforter, was given to Christ's followers after his death and resurrection.[45]

The Importance of Biblical Preaching

John Killinger reminds us that "the greatest preachers have always been lovers of the Bible . . . The ones who built their sermons on great biblical ideas and passages have lingered in our memories."[46] "There is always anguish in the preparation of sermons. Here comes Sunday again and what can I preach?" the pastor asks. The Bible contains an endless reservoir from which we can draw spiritual water to refresh our congregations and enrich our own spiritual growth. Every preacher should, if she does not already, love the Bible and devote her life to studying it and seeking to understand it and communicate its message to others. I express my confidence in the Bible in the words I wrote previously:

> The Bible has withstood kings, popes, agnostics, atheists, various interpretations—including heresy, translations, mistranslations, and controversy. It has withstood rejection, abandonment, desertion, liberalism, modernism, fundamentalism, hatred, evil, ridicule, and even preaching! But for people, the Bible is a cup of fresh water for a thirsty spirit. The Bible is rain on parched soil. It has provided directions down the path of life. It offers help through the valley of the shadow of death. It is light on the darkest of days. It is guidance in defeat and despair. It is a word among words. It is a song in the night. It is life to the dead. It gives us the pulse beat of God, the embrace of God's presence. Its words guide us to the Word.[47]

The Bible affords those of us who preach a resource like no other. It will touch the needs of our congregation and direct them to a source that will meet their needs in the most profound sense of the meaning—even to redemption and new birth. "Each renewal of preaching," Leander Keck declares, "in turn, has rediscovered biblical preaching."[48] "The biblical texts must be preached—under all circumstances at any costs," Gerhard Von Rad proclaims. "The people for whom we each have a responsibility need them for living (and for dying)."[49]

Whether you begin with the Scripture or end with it, every message should be biblical. How can it be otherwise if the Scriptures are indeed our ultimate source for our religious knowledge? "For all the human handiwork it displays, the Bible remains a peculiarly holy book," Barbara Brown

Taylor observes. "I cannot think of any other text that has such authority over me, interpreting me faster than I can interpret it."[50] We acknowledge the authority of the Bible first over our own lives, and then as it reads us we discover it has not only our own address but also the addresses of others. How can we not share that message? Tom Long in his book, *The Witness of Preaching*, states that biblical preaching is "the form regularly and urgently needed by the community of faith."[51] As a preacher I want to equip myself, prepare myself, and be continuously studying the Scriptures to listen for the Word of God, first for myself and then for the message I am challenged to witness to others.[52]

Notes

[1] Elizabeth Achtemeier, *Creative Preaching: Finding the Words* (Nashville: Abingdon Press, 1980), 19.

[2] Harry Emerson Fosdick, "The Divinity of Jesus," *A Preaching Ministry*, ed. David Pultz (New York City: First Presbyterian Church, 2000), 235f.

[3] Ronald Allen, "Why Preach from Passages in the Bible?" *Preaching as a Theological Task*, ed. Thomas G. Long and Edward Farley (Louisville: Westminster John Knox Press, 1996), 177.

[4] Marcus J. Borg, *Reading the Bible Again for the First Time* (New York: HarperCollins, 2001), 18.

[5] Peter J. Gomes, *The Good Book: Reading the Bible with Mind and Heart* (New York: William Morrow and Co., 1996), 46

[6] Barbara K. Lundbald, *Marking Time: Preaching Biblical Stories in Present Tense* (Nashville: Abingdon Press, 2007), 82.

[7] See my book, *The Left Behind Fantasy: The Theology Behind the Left Behind Tales* (Eugene, OR: Wipf and Stock, 2010).

[8] Harry Emerson Fosdick, *The Living of These Days* (New York: Harper and Brothers, 1956), 99.

[9] Ibid.

[10] James W. Cox, ed., *Biblical Preaching: An Expositor's Treasury* (Philadelphia: Westminster Press, 1983), 14.

[11] Leander E. Keck, *The Bible in the Pulpit: The Renewal of Biblical Preaching* (Nashville: Abingdon Press, 1978), 106.

[12] Karl Barth, *The Preaching of the Gospel*, trans. B. E. Hooke, (Philadelphia: Westminster Press, 1963), 12 ff.

[13] Lundblad, *Marking Time*, 71-75.

[14] Thomas G. Long, *The Witness of Preaching* (Louisville: Westminster/John Knox Press, 1989), 48.

[15] James S. Stewart, *The Gates of New Life* (New York: Charles Scribner's Sons, 1940), 102ff.

[16] David L Bartlett, *Between the Bible and the Church: New Methods for Biblical Preaching* (Nashville: Abingdon Press, 1999), 43.

[17] Walter Brueggemann, *Texts That Linger, Words That Explode: Listening to Prophetic Voices* (Minneapolis: Fortress Press, 2000), 1.

[18]I often consult a dozen or more commentaries for each sermon and draw upon word studies such as those found in Kiddle's *Dictionary of the Bible* and Robertson's *Word Studies of the New Testament*. Good Bible dictionaries such as those published by Harper, Mercer, and Eerdmans are essential. I have found, for the most part, it is still best to buy individual commentaries rather than whole sets of commentaries. For sets I would recommend those in *The New Interpreter's Bible, Interpretation: A Bible Commentary for Teaching and Preaching*, William Barclay's commentaries, and *The Daily Study Guides*. For preaching on the Book of Revelation I would suggest *Revelation* by Ben Witherington; *Revelation* by Mitchell G. Reddish; *Of Angels, Beasts and Plagues* by Kenneth H. Maahs; *Revelation: Vision of a Just World* by Elisabeth Schussler Fiorenza; *Revelation* by James L. Blevins; *Revelation* by M. Eugene Boring; the Revelation commentary in *The New Interpreter's Bible*; and several older ones such as the *International Critical Commentary* and ones by George Beasley-Murray, C. B. Caird, Martin Kiddle, and others. Some new commentaries, such as *The New Interpreter's Bible* and the Smyth and Helwys series, provide supplementary CDs.

[19]David Buttrick, *Homiletic: Moves and Structures* (Philadelphia: Fortress Press, 1987), 298.

[20]Paul Scherer, *The Word God Sent* (New York: Harper and Row, 1965), 26.

[21]Carol Marie Noren, "Storm at Sea" in *Sermons from Duke Chapel*, ed. William H. Willimon (Durham: Duke University Press, 2005), 304-308.

[22]Examples can be found in *Lectionary Homiletics*, ed. David B. Howell and others; *The Minister's Manual*, ed. Lee McGlone; *Preaching the Letters Without Dismissing the Law: A Lectionary Commentary*, ed. Ronald J. Allen and Clark M. Williamson; *Feasting on the Word: Preaching the Revised Common Lectionary*, ed. David L. Bartlett and Barbara Brown Taylor.

[23]Elizabeth Achtemeier, "What's Left Behind?" in *And Blessed Is She: Sermons by Women*, ed. David Albert Farmer and Edwina Hunter (San Francisco: Harper and Row Publishers, 1990), 98-105.

[24]Lloyd John Ogilvie, *Lord of the Impossible* (Nashville: Abingdon Press, 1984), 44.

[25]Ibid., 43-55.

[26]John Claypool, *Glad Reunion: Meeting Ourselves in the Lives of Bible Men and Women* (Waco: Word Books, 1985), 11.

[27]It would be helpful to consult works such as Claypool's mentioned above and Elie Wiesel, *Messengers of God*; Frederick Buechner, *Peculiar Treasure: A Biblical Who's Who*; William Barclay, *The Master's Men*; Frederick Speakman, *God and Jack Wilson*; G. Avery Lee, *Great Men of the Bible and the Women in their Lives*; Clovis Chappell, *Sermons on Biblical Characters*; George Matheson, *The Representative Men of the Bible*; J. Barrie Shepherd, *Faces at the Manger;* Leonard Griffith, *Gospel Characters: The Personalities Around Jesus*.

[28]Alton H. McEachern, *Dramatic Monologue Preaching* (Nashville: Broadman Press, 1984), 105ff.

[29]The following books are out of print but can likely be found in seminary libraries, through used book stores, or on the internet: Alton McEachern, *Dramatic Monologue Preaching*; John Calvin Reid, *We Knew Jesus*; and Raymond Bailey and James L. Blevins, *Dramatic Monologues: Making the Bible Come Alive*. More recent books on this theme include David P. Polk, *If Only I Had Known: Dramatic Monologues for Advent and Lent*; Stephen M. Crotts, *Heroes of the Faith Speak: Seven Monologues*; and Edward W. Thorn, *Hoof's Mouth Disease: Biblical Monologues and How to Do Them*.

[30]For help with the dialogical sermon, consult William D. Thompson and Gordon C. Bennett, *Dialogue Preaching*; George Swank, *Dialogic Style in Preaching*; John Killinger, The *11 O'Clock News and Other Experimental Sermons*; Thomas Troeger, *Ten Strategies for Preaching*

in a MultiMedia Culture; Reuel L. Howe, *The Miracle of Dialogue*; and Harold Freeman, *Variety in Biblical Preaching.*

[31] Karl Barth, *Deliverance to the Captives* (New York: Harper and Row, Publisher, 1961), 35ff.

[32] The following resources may be helpful: *Biblical Preaching: An Expositor's Treasury*, ed. James W. Cox; *A Handbook of Contemporary Preaching*, Michael Duduit, ed.

[33] Helpful resources may include Thomas Troeger, *Ten Strategies for Preaching in a MultiMedia Culture*, and Richard A. Jensen, *Envisioning the Word: The Use of Visual Images in Preaching with CD-Rom.*

[34] Keck, *The Bible in the Pulpit*, 100ff.

[35] Andrew W. Blackwood, *Expository Preaching for Today* (New York: Abingdon Press, 1953), 13.

[36] F. B. Myers, *Expository Preaching: Plans and Methods* (London: Hodder and Stoughton, 1912), 29.

[37] John H. McClure, "Expository Preaching," *Concise Encyclopedia of Preaching*, ed. William H. Willimon and Richard Lischner (Louisville: Westminster John Knox Press, 1995), 131.

[38] Helmut Thielicke, *Encounter with Spurgeon* (Philadelphia: Fortress Press, 1963), 45.

[39] Frederick W. Robertson, *Sermons Preached at Brighton* (New York: Harper and Brothers, n.d.), 33ff.

[40] Alexander Maclaren, *Expositions of Holy Scripture* (Grand Rapids: Wm. B. Eerdmans, 1942),

[41] Thielicke, *Encounter with Spurgeon*, 29.

[42] Charles Haddon Spurgeon, *Treasury of the Bible* (Grand Rapids: Baker Book House, 1988), 438-443.

[43] Ellen F. Davis, *Wondrous Depth: Preaching the Old Testament* (Louisville: Westminster John Knox Press, 2005), 152-158.

[44] Peter J. Gomes, "An Impossible Ethic," *Sermons from Duke Chapel*, ed. William H. Willimon (Durham: Duke University Press, 2005, 2005), 41-55.

[45] John Killinger, *Letting God Bless You* (Nashville: Abingdon Press, 1992), 41-55.

[46] John Killinger, *Fundamentals of Preaching*, 2nd ed. (Minneapolis: Fortress Press, 1996), 13.

[47] William Powell Tuck, *Our Baptist Tradition* (Macon, GA: Smyth and Helwys, 2005), 43.

[48] Keck, *The Bible in the Pulpit*, 11.

[49] Gerhard Von Rad, *Biblical Interpretations in Preaching* (Nashville: Abingdon Press, 1977), 11.

[50] Barbara Brown Taylor, *The Preaching Life* (Cambridge: Cowley Publications, 1993), 52.

[51] Long, *The Witness of Preaching*, 50.

[52] Helpful resources in this area include Leander E. Keck, *The Bible in the Pulpit*; James Cox, ed., *Biblical Preaching: An Expositor's Treasury*; Reginald H. Fuller, *The Use of the Bible in Preaching*; Elizabeth Achtemeier, *The Old Testament and the Proclamation of the Gospel*; Donald Gowan, *Reclaiming the Old Testament for the Christian Pulpit*; Grame Goldsworthy, *Preaching the Whole Bible as Christian Scripture: The Application of Biblical Theology to Expository Preaching*; John Stott, *Biblical Preaching Today*; Paul Scott Wilson, *The Four Pages of the Sermon: A Guide to Biblical Preaching*; and William Tuck, ed., *The Bible as a Spiritual Guide.*

Sermon

Standing Up for the Kingdom:
The Good Samaritan
Micah 6:6-8; Luke 10:25-37

An American couple had planned for many years to go to Australia. Finally, they saved enough money to take the trip. They enjoyed visiting some of the larger cities such as Melbourne, but they decided one day to visit a remote section in the back country. They rented a jeep and started down one of the roads. They had driven several hundred miles into the back country when suddenly their jeep began to sputter and finally stopped. The husband got out of the jeep to see if he could find out what was wrong. While he was working on the jeep, he noticed a car coming down the road toward him. "Ah," he thought, "maybe this is someone who can help us." But a man jumped out of the car with a gun in his hand and demanded all the money the tourist and his wife had. The American resisted at first, and when he did, the robbers began to beat him. They knocked him down, broke his arm, and left him lying wounded on the side of the road. They not only took the travelers' money, but also stole everything of any value that was in the jeep. The man lay bleeding and hurt on the road, while his wife tried to give him whatever assistance she could.

Soon they saw a jeep approaching with several men in it. They recognized a noted American preacher. His face was seen every week on television. They knew they would get help now. The car pulled up, and the preacher asked them what had happened. They explained what their problem was. "I wish I could help," he said, "but I have a TV appearance in Melbourne, and I simply can't stop. If I do, I will be late. We will let somebody know you are here. We will call for help." And he sped down the road.

Several hours later another car approached. This time it was a group of missionaries to Australia. They stopped and asked what had happened. The woman explained. One of the missionaries said, "I wish . . . I wish we could give you assistance, but we have to attend our annual missionary conference where we have to give a report of our work. If we don't get there in time to tell about what we are doing in our mission work here, our funds will be cut off. We must go on. We will let somebody know and send help back." They, too, went on down the road.

The sun was beginning to set and the wife was wringing her hands in desperation when suddenly another car came over the hill. This time a car stopped and a group of men got out. She could hear them speaking in a language that was unfamiliar to her. Then one of them, who could speak English, explained that he was a Russian. They were a group of Russian delegates who had come to Australia to arrange some cultural exchanges. Realizing the American was hurt, they came over and began to give assistance. They bandaged some of his wounds, placed a splint on his arm, and then lifted him into their car. They drove back to the nearest city, found a hospital, and explained to the doctors in the emergency room what had happened. "Whatever the cost is," they exclaimed, "we will pay for it." Then they drove off.

The story I just told is, of course, fictitious. But do you get the point of it? Do you understand the reason you felt the way you did toward the people who did not help this American couple, whom you thought should have helped, and the unexpected persons who became the heroes? The parable Jesus told two thousand years ago was probably even more dramatic than this story.

A Dramatic Parable

Jesus may have been sitting very close to or beside the Jericho Road when he told this parable. A crowd of people sat around him listening as he taught. After Jesus had been teaching for a while, a man stood up, which was the customary way a student asked a question of a teacher in that day. As he stood to ask his question, he also addressed Jesus as "Teacher" out of respect. Everyone knew immediately who this man was. All you had to do was to look at his robe. He wore a traditional lawyer's robe. They recognized him and were surprised that he would ask a question.

Around his forehead he wore a small calfskin box bound to his head with a leather thong. This small leather box was called a phylactery, which contained certain Scripture quotations. It symbolized his orthodoxy. The box likely contained quotes from Deuteronomy 6:4-5 and Leviticus 19:18: "Hear, O Israel. The Lord is our God, and the Lord is one. Thou shalt love the Lord thy God with all thy heart, mind, soul, and spirit, and your neighbor as yourself." He touched the small box when he left in the morning and touched it when he came in at night. He was a lawyer of the Mosaic law—a religious scribe.

"Teacher," he asked Jesus. "What must I do to inherit eternal life?" Jesus looked at him and said, "It is right there," pointing to his phylactery. "You know the answer. Why are you asking me that kind of question? You already know. You are a scribe, a keeper of the law. You know the answer to your own question. What does the law say?" "The answer," Jesus was saying in essence, "is bound around your forehead and you repeat it each day. You shall love the Lord your God with all your heart, soul, mind, spirit, and your neighbor as yourself." Then Jesus noted, "You do this and you will live."

The lawyer knew he had not communicated very clearly the question on his mind. He had not come across well. He realized that he of all people should have already known the answer to the question he asked. Trying to justify himself, he asked: "Who is my neighbor?" That question is familiar, isn't it? You know that lawyer, don't you? Yes, you know him. You see him all the time. Sometimes the lawyer is a banker, a carpenter, a doctor, a teacher, a secretary, a homemaker, or an accountant. You know this lawyer. You sometimes see him in the mirror. He is that person who thinks religion is primarily for discussion. If you talk about religion enough, you have done it, he thinks. "Who is my neighbor?" he asked. He wanted to know the limitations of his neighborhood. What are the restrictions? How far do I have to go in being a neighbor? What is necessary to be respectable? What is my duty?

In response to that question, Jesus told a parable about a man who traveled from Jerusalem down the Jericho Road and was attacked by robbers and left bleeding and dying. Along this same road came a priest and a Levi. They passed by on the other side. The Good Samaritan came along and gave him assistance.

Attitudes Toward Life

The story of the Good Samaritan describes at least three attitudes toward life I want you to note.

Taking from Others

The first attitude is "I'll take from others." This was the attitude of the robber. "I will take whatever I want. It doesn't make any difference who has it." The Jericho Road is about twenty-two miles long. When Jesus said the traveler went down from Jerusalem on the Jericho Road, that description is literally true. The road from Jerusalem to Jericho descends 3,500 feet in those twenty-two miles. The road leads through rough terrain, with desert on both sides of the road that is intercepted with gorges and wadies. Robbers would often hide behind rocks and in the wadies along the way. This road has been called the "Bloody Way." Many people were often robbed along this road.

You and I know the robbers of life. They declare in veiled ways: "I will take whatever I want from you. It doesn't make any difference how it affects you or how it hurts you. I will get my way. You are simply a means to an end for me. I manipulate, abuse, use people, cheat, steal, or lie. It doesn't make any difference what happens to others as long as I get what I want. I will take from you and anybody else." This is a philosophy we see too often in life.

This attitude was illustrated some time ago in the comic strip, "Crock." Two soldiers are standing on a balcony overlooking a desert. A lieutenant speaks to his captain: "Sir, how do we know what's right and wrong in life?" The captain responds, "There's only a right and wrong if you get caught."

Too often people follow this kind of philosophy through life. You do whatever you want to do as long as you can get by with it. It doesn't make any difference to you if you inflict hurt and pain on someone else. That is irrelevant to you. Your selfish end goal is all that is important. The robbers did not mind giving pain to the man on the Jericho Road. They beat him and left him for dead. Many of those who inflict pain are unconcerned about their actions. You and I may be victims in life of their abuse. We simply get in their way, and they run over us or around us in any way they desire to get ahead or get their way. The pain we suffer may not be our fault at all. The robbers illustrate the attitude toward life of "I'll take from others."

Ignoring Others

A second attitude toward life reflected in this parable is "I will ignore others." This is seen in the response of the priest and the Levite. Some scholars believe the priest may have been going toward the Temple to perform his religious duties. There were so many priests at that time in Israel, a priest only worked about two weeks a year in his official priestly duties in the Temple. Priests were divided into twenty-four different units to perform their functions. If the priest were traveling toward the Temple to do his two-week tour of duty there, he knew that he could be defiled if he touched this man who was lying by the road and he discovered that he was dead. Touching a corpse was one of the worst kinds of defilement a Jewish person could experience. The priest couldn't take a chance and touch him. It might keep him from doing his sacred functions.

He also knew that the Jewish law decreed that whatever had happened to this man was the will of God. You know that attitude. We sometimes sing, "*Que sera, sera.* Whatever will be will be." The fact that this man had been beaten and robbed was simply the will of God. He couldn't do anything to change that. It was decreed by God. He didn't want to be late for his official appointment in the Temple.

But I am not so sure from a careful reading of the text that he was going toward Jerusalem. The text states that he was "going down" from Jerusalem. I think he had already done his priestly duty and was going home. He was in a hurry to be with his family. He was too busy to change his plans. Oh, he would have been defiled if he had touched the man and found out he was dead. But what difference would that make at this point? He was going home. He didn't have to do official duties now, and in seven days he would be clean anyway. He was simply rushing home to be with his family and did not want to take the time to be bothered with this man.

The Levite was a holy person by heredity. He may have approached the man a little closer than the priest. He may have looked at his helpless form and heard his cries, but he went on his way as well. He and the priest passed by on the other side. They were too busy; they had too much to do. "I'll just go on my way," each said. "I don't have time for this." They closed their eyes to the problems around them. They could say, "I didn't see you!" If you don't see, your conscience is clear. They thought religion was more concerned with custom than charity, with being than doing, with seeing than assisting, with feeling than helping.

Helmut Thielicke, the prominent theologian and preacher in Hamburg, West Germany, told of an experience he had when he visited a well-to-do church councilman who invited him for tea one afternoon. In the course of the conversation, Thielicke expressed regret that part of the man's lovely house had been destroyed during the Second World War. Since then it had been beautifully restored. "Don't talk about regret," the man said. "Even in this loss I experienced the grace of God." Thielicke said a warm feeling came inside him toward this man, and he thought how devout and humble the man was. But then the man finished. "God left me with just enough room so that I did not have to take in any refugees after the war." You see, his motive had not been right at all. It had been all wrong. "It had never occurred to him," Thielicke observed, "that the housing shortage had anything to do with one's relationship to God and our neighbor."[1] Although the man was devout, he did not see the ethical side of this particular issue. But he is not alone.

The priest represents the noble citizens, the good folks in society, the church-going people, and the preachers. He probably told the man who was lying wounded in the ditch, "Friend, I am concerned about you. I want you to know that I hurt with you. I ache with you. I am sorry this has happened to you. As soon as I get home, I will organize a committee, and we will start a drive to clean up the Jericho Road." Oh, he had noble feelings and good thoughts toward this man. He may have even told him, "I will inform the Jerusalem Red Cross." "I will let the Jericho Salvation Army know of your plight." He was too busy with his own needs, concerns, family, and way of life. He was concerned, but he didn't do anything. He simply ignored the man on the road.

In Albert Camus' novel, *The Fall*, an attorney in Paris was taking a walk in a park one night by the River Seine. He passed a young woman who seemed to be in distress. A few moments later he heard a splash in the river and a repeated cry for help. He felt an urge to run quickly and see if he could help her. The pull was strong to go help her. He heard her cry several times. But he did nothing, and finally there was silence. Years have passed by, and he cannot escape the memory of what happened that night. He is constantly plagued with what he did not do. One day in a confession he exclaimed: "Oh, young woman, throw yourself into the water again so that I may a second time have the chance of saving both of us."[2]

Too often we just ignore people with their needs and hurts. We simply pass by on the other side.

Helping Others

There was also a third attitude in this story. It is expressed in the words, "I'll help others." Notice what an unlikely hero Jesus set before his listeners: a Samaritan. He was a despised person to the Jewish mind. This attitude of hatred had existed for 450 years toward the Samaritans. In 720 B.C. when Samaria fell, some of the citizens were deported to Babylon—but not all of them. The Jews who remained there had intermarried with foreigners. These people were called Samaritans. They were considered half-breeds, a defiled people. When Jesus made the Samaritan a hero, the hair probably stood up on the back of the necks of his Jewish hearers. Their teeth were likely set on edge; their flesh may have begun to crawl. The Jews despised the Samaritans so much that they would take a day's journey longer to go another way rather than go through Samaria.

Jesus said the Samaritan came that way "by chance." The word in Greek is better stated "coincidence." But the meaning contains more than our English word coincidence. The word is used in a religious sense of "coincidence" as though God was involved in that process of bringing the Samaritan near the certain man who was hurt. Seeing his need, he showed mercy. Mercy means "moving toward." He extended himself toward the wounded man in a deliberate act. He reached out to one in need. He saw a need and came to help. "Mercy is not traditional, not token, not sterile," Clarence Jordan wrote. "Mercy is the creative risk of unlimited involvement."[3]

Notice the personal involvement of the Good Samaritan in this situation. He went down into the ravine or desert area where the man was lying hurt and maybe unconscious. He touched him physically and began to bind up his wounds by pouring oil and wine on them to cleanse the cuts. This was the best medicine he had at that moment. He put himself at some personal risk by going to the side of the hurt stranger. Sometimes robbers used decoys to make a traveler think that somebody was hurt, and when someone tried to help them, they were attacked and robbed. He didn't know if the man was really hurt or was only lying there to entrap him. He also did not know whether this man had some kind of disease he might catch. He could have been a leper. He did not know the real condition of the man. He exposed himself to potential danger.

The Samaritan placed the hurt man on his animal, and then took him to an inn about halfway down the Jericho Road from Jerusalem. Today a hotel stands on the supposed location of this ancient inn. The owner of the inn obviously knew the Samaritan. He may have been a businessman who traveled that way often and frequently spent the night at this inn. "Let me give you two denarii," the Samaritan said to the innkeeper. That may not sound like much money today, especially when you are aware that it was only forty cents in our money today. But in that day it was the equivalent of two day's wages for a working man. "Take care of him," the Samaritan said, "and I will repay you any other costs he may run up on his bill." His repeated use of the personal pronoun "I" indicates the innkeeper knew him. He was saying in effect, "You know me. I will repay you." The way the story is told, the Samaritan may have stayed up all night tending the hurt man's needs.

The Samaritan also made personal sacrifices to assist the wounded man. He most likely had business he needed to attend to, appointments with other business associates, wares to sell, places to be. He sacrificed his time, changed his schedule, and may have missed the next caravan going East and even lost a few sales.

The Samaritan also took the risk of being misunderstood by his Jewish neighbor. If the wounded man were a Jew, and it certainly seems evident in the story that he was, the fact that a Samaritan rescued a Jew might not set well with the Jew who was rescued. He and his family might think the Samaritan had defiled him by touching him.

Kenneth Bailey observes that the Samaritan ran a grave risk of having the family of the wounded man think he may have been the one who robbed him in the first place. If an American Plains Indian in 1875 brought a scalped cowboy into Dodge City on his horse and checked him into the local hotel, that Indian might be accused of being the one who scalped the cowboy in the first place. He could have a hard time convincing some of the other cowboys in that community he wasn't the one who did it.[4]

The Samaritan was so despised by the Jews, some might have assumed he had attacked the wounded man. The family of the victim might seek revenge on him. His act of kindness would not make any difference. He took a real risk. But Jesus said the Samaritan saw a need and went to meet it.

Who Is Our Neighbor?

Then Jesus turned to the lawyer and asked: "Who do you think then was the neighbor?" Notice that the lawyer could not even say the word Samaritan. He didn't say the Samaritan was the neighbor. He said, "The one who showed mercy."

Who is your neighbor? Where do you see yourself in this story? Identify yourself. Are you the victim? Are you wounded and hurting, waiting for someone to come and tend your needs? Are you the robber or the priest? Or are you the one who shows kindness? As the story unfolds, we are actors in the drama, not merely observers.

The test of religion is in service. The test of religion as Micah proclaimed is "to act justly, to love loyalty, to walk wisely before your God" (Micah 6:8 NEB). Jesus said, "You will know my disciples by their fruits." "Do unto others as you would have them do even also unto you." "Faith without works is dead," writes James. We can't just talk about religion; it must be seen in our lives.

D. T. Niles, the Indian minister from Ceylonese, tells the story about a man who was rushing through an alleyway and tripped over a beggar. The beggar reached up and pleaded for help from him. The man looked at the beggar and said: "Friend, I would like to help you now, but I cannot. I have just become a Christian, and I am rushing home to tell my family."

Sometimes we stumble across people in need in our pathway, and we do not even recognize them. Christian love is to be spontaneous. Wherever there are needs we are challenged to reach out to help these persons. Just like the father in the parable of the prodigal son showed extravagant love toward his son, God expects our love to be extravagant. Wherever there is need, let us respond lovingly.

Recognizing Our Neighbor

"Who is my neighbor?" is the wrong question. It attempts to set limits. We are not to restrict who our neighbor is. Knowing who our neighbor is moves us beyond geography, countries, or space. Knowing who our neighbor is concerns not an area but a spirit. Our neighbor is not determined by proximity but need. Our neighbor is not identified by fences but in opportunities for ministry. Our neighbor cannot be defined. There is an absence of limits. When we understand what it means to be a neighbor, we realize that all fences and walls are destroyed. All barriers disappear. All limitations are removed. We are neighbors to persons of all races, creeds, skin colors, ranks, geography, or educational levels. God expects us to reach out to all humans with love and compassion. Wherever there is need, we are challenged to respond in kindness and grace.

Dr. Jack Witten grew up in Tazewell County, Virginia. After graduating from the Medical College of Virginia, he decided to return to Tazewell to practice medicine. He had a disappointment in love and never got married. One night Dr. Witten was ministering to a woman who was dying. She looked up at him a few moments before she died and asked, "Who will take care of my little boy?" Dr. Witten said, "Don't worry. I will." That began Dr. Witten's collection of boys. Over the years, 300 boys came into his home. More than 150 of them lived with him, and many of them went to college. Wherever there was a need, Dr. Witten simply brought one of the boys into his home, loved him, cared for him, and provided for him. He saw a need and met it.

The good Samaritan is symbolic of Jesus Christ and his ministry. Jesus' ministry is summarized in the compassion of the Samaritan. Jesus spent his ministry reaching out to persons in need—to the blind, the deaf, the crippled, the lepers, the outcast, and the lost. He reached out with compassion to all persons in their time of need.

The Jericho Road passes by your door every day. Its path may lead by the door at your home or at work or the street you travel each day. Down the Jericho Road that passes your door you encounter the hurting, the lonely, the wounded, and the needy who walk by every day. They reach out to you for help. Do you see them and hear them?

To Whom Am I Neighbor?

Who is your neighbor? That is not the right question. The right question is: "To whom am I neighbor?" Our neighbor is everyone who has need. "This parable of the Good Samaritan," A. T. Robertson wrote many years ago, "has built the world's hospitals and, if properly understood and practiced would remove race prejudice, national hatred, class jealousy, and war."[5]

A young man stopped one day to help a stranded motorist. As he got ready to leave after assisting the motorist, the man he helped asked: "What can I do to help you?" "As my father always told me," the young man replied, "whenever you see somebody else stranded, you stop and help them."

"Who was your neighbor?" "The one who showed mercy," he replied. And Jesus said, "Go and do likewise."

Notes

[1] Helmut Thielicke, *The Trouble with the Church*, (New York: Harper & Row, 1965), 11.

[2] Albert Camus, *The Fall and the Exile and the Kingdom* (New York: The Modern Library, 1957), 147.

[3] Clarence Jordon and Bill Lane Doulos, *Cotton Patch Parables of Liberation* (Scottdale, PA: Herald Press, 1976), 137.

[4] Kenneth E. Bailey, *Through Peasant Eyes* (Grand Rapids: William B. Eerdmans Co., 1980), 52.

[5] A. T. Robertson, *Word Pictures in the New Testament*, vol. 2 (Nashville: Broadman Press, 1930), 155.

Part 2

Seeing Inside the Listener's Head:
Preaching to Human Needs

It was pre-air-conditioned days in a hot southern town on a Sunday morning. The congregation sat behind funeral home fans kept constantly in motion as the preacher was "going at" his sermon. The congregation was not listening well, and not just because of the heat. The preacher had not prepared his sermon. The congregation knew it, and he knew it. He was glad when it was over, and so were they. The music had been poorly rehearsed and poorly presented. The congregation went through the motions of singing the hymns, and they daydreamed through the service. Everyone seemed glad when the service was over.

The preacher stood at the door to greet the people as they filed by. "Hot day, ain't it preacher?" one of them observed. "It's dry; we sure need rain," another commented. Then the preacher noticed a stranger coming through the line. This unfamiliar face for some reason made him uneasy. Finally the stranger stood in front of the preacher, and the preacher extended his hand and said, "My name is Robin." The stranger said, "I know." "And your name?" the preacher asked. "Oh, I'm just a watchman," the stranger replied. "A watchman?" the preacher asked. "Yes, a watchman," the stranger repeated. The preacher then said, "Well, come back." And the watchman asked, "Why?" The preacher never forgot that question. It changed his whole ministry. He vowed to take his worship leadership seriously after that experience.

The stranger's question, as told in this story in Wallace Hamilton's book, *Where Now Is Thy God?*, was indeed a disarming one. Why should anyone want to come hear you or me preach a sermon? That watchman's question continues to echo in the pews, chancel, balcony, and lobby of our churches. And it should sound an alarm the loudest in the pastor's study. Why should someone come back to listen to a sermon on Sunday?

Yet even while that question is being carried by the wind, sermons are being preached. Five million sermons are preached every year in the United States alone. Think what that number swells to when you add the other ministerial voices around the world. I suspect some of these sermons are inspiring, challenging, and profound. But others will be dull, boring, mediocre, and maybe even painful to endure.

The word went forth a few years ago that preaching was dead. "Its day is over," the critics of preaching declared. They spoke about the empty pulpit, the most wasted hour of the week, the comfortable pew, faith without dogma, the lukewarm pulpit, the God evaders, God's frozen people, and the last days of the church. These critics predicted the death of the institutional church and saw the sermon either as its last dying gasp or as the stake driven into the church's heart. Through the centuries, prophets have predicted the church is going to die—but it never has.

As for preaching, rather than killing the church, it has often served as an invigorating and renewing force. Over the past couple of decades, most major religious presses have published whole series of books on almost every facet of preaching. Preaching has not been discussed, researched, analyzed, and heralded with such vigor in all the history of the church as it has been for the past few years. Conferences, clinics, lectureships, and seminars abound. University and divinity school preaching chairs have been established. New preaching journals have been born, and old ones revised. Numerous sets of proclamation commentaries have been written, and dozens of new preaching "texts" have been published. And, pastor search committees still place preaching as the number-one gift they look for in their prospective minister.

Today, then, is an exciting time for those who want to preach, because much has been and is being written and said about the art and discipline of preaching. But it is still a frightening time. Because, if you and I are honest, we know that few preachers are really reading these books and attending these conferences or working to improve their preaching. Laypersons still complain about meagerly prepared and poorly delivered sermons and that the sermons seldom address their personal needs or struggles. For those of us who want to improve our preaching, where do we begin? Sometimes insights may come to us from strange and even unwelcome areas.

About thirty years ago, the editor of *TV Guide* asked William F. Fore to write an article on the electronic church. Fore published his article under the title, "Why TV Evangelists Can't Be Pastors." He received numerous letters, many of them hostile, in response to his article. Fore stated that these letters did not change his mind about the dangers of the electronic church, but they did change his views about the problems of the local church. Although he believed strongly that the electronic church might be providing inadequate and even misleading and harmful solutions to the needs of its listeners, the viewers felt this media did attempt to meet their needs while the local congregation did not even care. "If local churches in this country began to take the needs of the American people seriously as the electronic church now does, and if they began to meet those needs in fundamental long-term ways," Fore observed, "we would see a national revival unparalleled in our history."[2] He concluded his article with this challenge:

> The electronic church is a serious and formidable threat to the mainline churches today—not because it threatens to reduce income or attendance (although that threat may be true in some cases), but because it challenges the local church to develop a new understanding of the needs of the people in their community, people who are searching for a satisfying religious experience, people who otherwise are going to find what solace and direction they can from the superficial and ultimately harmful ministrations of the electronic church.[3]

Fore has given the church an urgent message that is still needed today. Many people do not listen to sermons because they genuinely feel the preaching they have heard or listened to on other occasions does not touch their lives. They feel their needs are unrecognized or ignored. In a study and survey by Pew Forum on Religion & Public Life that depicted the flux in religion in America in 2008, director Luis E. Lugo noted: "The American religious economy is like a market place—very dynamic, very competitive."[4] In an article published in *The Boston Globe*, Ellen Goodman commented on the Pew Forum's findings with this observation: "The researchers describe a 'vibrant marketplace where individuals pick and choose religions *that meet their needs*'"[5] (italics mine). William F. Fore's concern is still paramount today.

You and I cannot be effective preachers until we try to get inside our listener's head and know his real needs. This does not mean we have to take our answers from the pages of the electronic church's notebook and give simple, chatty, pious clichés as "solutions" to soul-searching issues and questions. This also does not imply that we merely offer our hearers a smorgasbord where they come "shopping" to see if the preacher has made them "feel" good without doing them any good. This also should not be an effort to see the parishioners as simply "customers" for whom the preacher is seeking to entice with "cheap" grace, the desire for personal wealth, healthy self-esteem, or a sense of self-satisfaction without concern for others or their needs and void of any awareness of the sacrificial way of the cross. This is not an approach to give church members a wish list of whatever they want to satisfy some selfish personal desire to make their children happy or to feel good. The church is not a cafeteria of personal wishes or longings where people hunt and pick what they desire most, nor is it a place to meet everyone's personal desires for "sweet" biblical interpretations, nor is it an institution to furnish "fun and games." However, if the hearers do not sense that the preacher is concerned with their basic needs, then they will not sit in the pew of that church very long.

Decades ago, Harry Emerson Fosdick challenged preachers to address personal spiritual problems that were puzzling their hearers or distracting the lives or burdening the conscious of those in congregations instead of simply expounding a biblical text. Tom Long acknowledges that Fosdick developed an approach to preaching that "marshaled the best learning of his day, pedagogically and psychologically, to reconnect with congregations. And it worked."[6] Long believes, however, that "the price for life-situation preaching has been high."[7] He believes that many preachers do address people's needs, but they go lacking in the preparation of the "good news" of the gospel itself.[8] Long may be alluding to the impact of "successful" TV preachers and some popular preachers he knows, but I personally have not encountered many preachers in church pulpits who are addressing people's genuine needs. I certainly agree with Long that any preaching that is genuine, life-situational, or any other kind has to proclaim the good news of the gospel and the challenge of the cross-like way of life.

William Brosend has challenged preachers to look at the same source materials Jesus used in his preaching: the Scriptures, tradition, culture, and the lives of his listeners. Most of Jesus' preaching, Brosend notes, was done in response to the questions, life situations, challenges, or charges directed to him. He reminds us that we have to listen to our listeners.[9] Says Brosend, "Preaching must be responsive to the situation, needs, and questions of the audience and not just those of the preacher."[10] Preachers have to do what he calls "dialogical preaching," or preaching that follows the example of Jesus and tries to be in conversation with Scripture, tradition, culture, and the lives of the listeners.[11]

Brosend affirms strongly that good preaching is an authentic response to the needs and interests of one's listeners. He relates a story by

Tom Long, who told about an elderly woman "with a face like a hatchet dipped in vinegar" who approached him after he spoke as a guest preacher, and asked: "You teach preaching at the seminary, don't you?" "Yes, I do," Long responded. "Well, I have something that I want you to tell your students. Tell them to take me seriously."[12] We have to take our listeners seriously and listen to their real concerns and deepest questions and issues.

"Too often we fret over what people want to hear, or what their 'needs' might be, or even what the needs of the inner psyche of ancient people might have been and how Jesus dealt with such needs," James Howell asserts. "Spiritually, people are tangled in confusion about desire, and 'felt needs' become a golden idol before whom not only people out there, but even the preachers, bow in humble adoration."[13] Howell reminds us legitimately that "sermons are not always about us," but foremost about God. "The heart of every sermon is about God, not you or me."[14] Every preacher has to keep this basic focus in her sermon as she proclaims the good news about God. Our "needs" always have to be understood in relationship to the way of Jesus Christ and not merely our own felt concerns or desires. Nevertheless, as we probe the mystery and wonder of God's majesty and grace or the sacrifice of Christ's death on the cross, we have to sense how our listener reacts to or is affected by this experience. If it does not touch him personally, it cannot have meaning for the listener.

Effective preaching will speak to the problems of the individual in the pew. The cry is directed to the pulpit from the pew: "Do you care about me and my struggles, preacher?" If you and I really care, our empathy has to be evident in our words and gestures. James W. Clark made this point clearly when he wrote: "All preaching is preaching to personal needs, if it is really preaching and not the delivery of an essay or a general address to nobody in particular or mere vocal muscle flexing. It is the transmission of God's truth through a person to a person."[15] This is what I think is appropriately called "pastoral preaching." This kind of preaching will enable us to incorporate what Fred Craddock calls the "qualities" to be sought in a sermon: unity, recognition, identification, anticipation, and intimacy.[16]

Pastoral preaching begins with the awareness that preaching is not a solo event but a joint enterprise between the congregation and the preacher. Individuals in the congregation feel they really matter to the preacher. Authentic preaching vibrates with concern. The hearers in the pew sense the preacher in the pulpit genuinely cares about them as persons. This kind of preaching is called by Charles Kemp "life situation preaching." It is an attempt to take the needs of the people in your congregation in one hand and the truth of the Christian gospel in the other and bring them together by means of the spoken word.[17] Wayne Oates described this kind of preaching as "therapeutic"[18] or "the psychological approach to homiletics."[19] Pastoral preaching might also be described as contextual or correlational because it is an effort to respond with the "Word of God" to the problems that have arisen out of the struggles to live as human persons.

I want to share three ingredients I believe will enable the preacher to see more clearly inside the listener's head. I call these the three R's for effective pastoral preaching: recognition, revelation, and response.

Recognition

Look with me first at recognition. The listener in the pew wants to feel that "the preacher is talking to me." She wants to be assured that the preacher recognizes her, knows she is present, and cares about what's bothering her. In large congregations, giving this personal touch becomes difficult for the pastor. Although there might be a few persons who attend a large church because they want to get lost in the crowd, even in their obscurity, these persons want some kind of recognition. They hunger for a "nod or shock of recognition" from the pastor in the sermon, as Fred Craddock terms it. Craddock challenges the preacher to deliver sermons that are "twice told."[20] A sermon that is "twice told" will have "the sense that there is a resonance, a resonance between the experience of the listener and the experience of the text."[21] The deepest longing, unspoken or maybe even unrealized of the listeners, is that the sermon touches them in a concrete way.

When does a sermon misfire? Ask a church member and she will let you know what poor preaching is. It is preaching that does not communicate anything to the hearer. Why? Because it does not address any particular needs in that listener's life. Preaching is not just delivering a subject—getting something out of the preacher's head into someone else's. Preaching is communicating concern, love, understanding, compassion, hope, and openness, if you please—a word from God. Preaching is communicating: "Hey, I'm listening to you; I feel your hurt; I hear your pain; and there is a God who likewise hears you and cares about you." The preacher can communicate a sense of recognition to those who listen in the pew by mirroring the listener's pilgrimage or addressing needs directly or indirectly.

Mirroring the Listener's Pilgrimage

The sermon should be a mirror of the listener's pilgrimage. If the preacher addresses an issue that is a great distance from where his listeners are—even if it is biblically or theologically sound—they will likely not hear it. "Only the preacher," Harry Emerson Fosdick wrote years ago, "proceeds still upon the idea that folk come to church desperately anxious to discover what happened to the Jebusites."[22] They do not, and only the naïve or uninformed preacher clings to that assumption. If the hearer is going to listen, he has to believe he is involved in what the preacher is talking about.

The hearers long to feel that the preacher is speaking a word he has discovered within their everyday world and not from some distant point outside their sphere of life. They believe that only one who has sat where they have sat, struggled with their burdens, borne their pain, known their joys and sorrows, hopes and failures can have a real word from the Lord for them. Pastoral preaching begins where people live. It affirms that the preacher has walked among them and understands their struggles, pressures, dreams, aspirations, fears, and frustrations. When the preacher touches the nerve of everyday life, she will not only capture the attention of the listener better but also will hold that attention longer. People always listen better to something they feel concerns them.

Julie Pennington-Russell introduced her sermon titled "Our Good Shepherd" by relating an experience a woman had during the near-fatal illness of her daughter and her struggle to find some kind of lifeline in her dark sea of fear and despondency. One day during this time she read Psalm 23 in the quietness of an interfaith chapel and related later how the words of that psalm performed CPR on her broken heart. Drawing on that woman's struggle, Russell then drew her congregation into the meaning of the psalm through these movements:

1. The shepherd leads us to green pastures where we are invited to rest, and many of us do indeed need rest.
2. After we have rested, the shepherd invites us to hit the road again as he scans what lies ahead for us.
3. As we walk through the "valley of the shadow," we sense the hand of the good shepherd and that is enough.
4. Following the shepherd, we are led to the table and cup as we trust the shepherd.[23]

In his book, *The Recovery of Preaching*, Henry Mitchell issues a call for ministers to learn to preach to the transconscious level of people.[24] This style of preaching will address not only the intellect of the listener, but also the deepest existential needs of that person. It will communicate with the whole person; touch both the conscious and unconscious levels, the intuitive dimension along with the rational. Much out of which we respond is buried below our rational level deep within our unconscious or subconscious mind. Preaching has to address the total person.

Once I was hiking up a mountain near where I lived in Tennessee. I started up a ravine and had walked up it a short distance when I came upon a huge spider whose web stretched from one side of the ravine to the other. The pathway was completely blocked by that web. I stopped for a moment and looked over the web to see if I could find the spider. After a few moments of searching, I saw the large spider over in one corner of the web. I picked up a stick and touched a distant corner of the web without breaking it to see what response I might get from the spider. The spider quickly moved toward that side to see who the intruder was and if lunch had arrived. Not finding anything there, the spider retreated back to the same corner of the web. I touched several spots on the web, and the spider would become alert for a moment and make a slight movement toward the vibrations. Soon my touching elicited no response. I walked around the web and hiked on up the mountain and left the spider in its world. I really didn't exist to the spider. I was outside its realm.

This experience became a parable for me about preaching. The preacher approaches people on their "web" of life through his sermon. Many of the listeners feel the preacher lives outside their world. Occasionally the preacher might touch the corner of the web where people live and shake it a little, as I did the spider's web, but most of the time his noisy actions are superfluous to their world. So much of our preaching fails, is ignored, falls short of its goal, or is not heard because it is seen as outside the world where our people live every day. We have to scratch them where they itch, understand their difficulties, and acknowledge that we, too, are fellow strugglers on the web of life.

When we speak as a fellow pilgrim, we acknowledge that we respond not only rationally but also sometimes instinctively, sometimes with our intellect and sometimes out of the deep unknown well of our subconscious experience. Out of the depths of our own experience that involves both intellect and emotions we address the "depth" within our listeners. We address that deeply buried depth within all of us that has memories, experiences, dreams, nightmares, joys, and tragedies stored there. We have to touch that depth sometime transconsciously with images and pictures that will open the storage door. A preacher's words or pictures may awaken in her listener's mind an instinctive or intuitive grasp of truth.

John Baillie, the Scottish theologian, stressed the significance of intuition. For a person's apprehension of the divine reality, Baillie believed that man and woman's religious insight into the element of intuition is almost everything. "Intuitive insight will here always precede formal proof, and where there is as yet no such insight, formal proof is likely to be powerless to convince."[25] In his Gifford Lectures, Baillie likewise placed a strong emphasis on the intuited element by drawing together the intuitive and the non-inferential: "All in all, therefore, the seat of human wisdom will always remain with our intuited rather than our inferred knowledge of our human situation."[26] Baillie calls this awareness of God "a sense of the presence of God."

Our understanding of God is not limited to rational perception. There is an awareness, an apprehension, a recognition, a non-sensuous dimension, an intuitive grasp, and a non-expressible sensitivity. This is not an argument against speaking to the intellect. The preacher certainly wants his listeners to think, and he fails when he ignores the thinking side of his hearers, but this is a reminder to preach to the subtle unconsciousness of your listeners along with the obvious rational element.

Mitchell believes there is an "unconscious" depth of stored religious culture within the worst of people. He relates an experience that a nurse in a Brooklyn hospital told him about women who were "divorced" from the church and living as prostitutes. No matter what profanity one of these women might have used previously, when the worst labor pains hit her, she would clean up her speech and call on God with the plea: "O Lord, have mercy!" This residue of religion, he thinks, is a foundation for later spiritual growth.[27] There is a root—cultural unconsciousness—within the soul of every person. We have to learn to address that dimension.

Addressing Needs Directly

Sometimes the best avenue into the listener's mind to accomplish recognition is a direct approach. If you preach a sermon on loneliness, for example, the antennae of many of the persons in your congregation will be open to receiving a word of encouragement and guidance. There are few persons who have not known some moments of loneliness. Others, like the elderly widow who lives alone, may know it as a daily companion. Sermons that address some personal need directly will usually find a ready audience.

Many persons in your congregation will have experienced some kind of crisis. They have known marital problems, difficulties at work, job insecurity, illness, pain or suffering, moving to a new city or state, a job change or retirement, grief, and a host of other challenges. To ignore these struggles in our preaching is to avoid the most apparent needs of your listeners.

Annie Lally Milhaven has edited a sermon collection, *Sermons Seldom Heard: Women Proclaim Their Lives*, that addresses some of the most difficult struggles or issues women face today such as incest, wife-battering, AIDS, alcoholism, abortion, and divorce. These women preach on themes rarely heard in a church or synagogue. "The sermons in this volume attest not only to the ordeals of suffering and dehumanization," according to Elizabeth Schussler Fiorenza in the foreword, "but also to the visions and voices, the hopes and struggles women today bring to their ministry, opening up their own experiences and those of their unnamed sisters to public theological reflection."[28]

One of the most helpful ways I have found to speak directly to these various needs is to preach a series of sermons on different aspects of the struggles. I have approached these in a variety of ways, for example through the following sermon series:

Facing Personal Struggles[29]
• "When Life Crashes In"
• "The Fear of Failure"
• "Living with Tension"
• "Down in the Dumps of Depression"
• "Overcoming Discouragement"

Meeting Personal Needs[30]
• "The Discipline of Patience"
• "What Makes You Angry?"
• "The Burden of Guilt"
• "Judging May Boomerang"
• "Controlling Your Tongue"
• "The World's Worst Curse Word"
• "Meeting Life's Detours"
• "When You Can't Pray Anymore"

Living with Dying[31]
- "The Fear of Death"
- "Learning How to Meet Grief"
- "Helping a Friend in Grief"
- "Death and the Meaning of Life"
- "The Mystery of Death"

On another occasion I preached an eight-sermon series leading up to Easter around the theme, "Questions about the Dark." The sermons in this series focused on questions about sin, suffering, suicide, burdens, aging, and death, and an answer to our questions in the lift out of the darkness that Easter provides.

    I have always experienced a genuine response from my hearers during these sermon series. Many of the sermons have opened doors for conversation with persons and encouraged some to seek counseling. Others have asked, "How did you know how I was feeling?" or "You must have been reading my mail." Comments, letters, and telephone calls from my listeners indicated to me that I had touched a responsive chord in their lives. Sometimes I would follow the sermon with a listening and dialogue session on the following Sunday or Wednesday night. I was always amazed at the interest and participation. The list of personal needs a minister can address is endless.[32]

    A word of warning is important here. No preacher can possibly know or speak about what everyone in a congregation may need or want to hear. The catalog of human needs is long, and every preacher must have the awareness of her limitations in perceiving everyone else's needs and the presumption that the preacher can help "solve" everyone's problems. Every preacher needs a strong dose of humility and the courage not to panic and flee in the face of a bewildering avalanche of human desires and conflicts. Remember that the one really unique insight you bring is found in rendering a word from the Lord, drawn from the Bible, and its relationship to the lives of your listeners as you have experienced in your own human struggles.

    In an age when many people feel they are merely a number in our society, if the preacher pushes the button of need in the inner depths of a person, she will respond. If you don't think you are seen primarily as a number to many today, try calling some large oil company or business and have them check your account without giving them your number. To our bank, oil company, social security office, retirement agency, IRS, the telephone company, and so on, we are recognized by our number. Pastoral preaching telegraphs the message to individuals that they are important to you and their struggles are not lost in a meaningless sea of minute details. The preacher must not only see individuals in the midst of a number of people in the congregation, but also make each individual feel the preacher is speaking to him personally.

From the preacher's perspective, he may feel the "seed" is being broadcast with a wide sweep; but nevertheless, it is carefully aimed to fall into a certain kind of "fertile" soil. From the listener's viewpoint, each person has to sense that the "seed" from the preacher's sowing has fallen into the awaiting soil of her own life. If the sermon is effective, an individual listener will say silently or sometimes verbally: "This sermon was for me. Thanks!" The preacher has to believe that kind of response is possible. Fosdick confessed that his silent prayer before each sermon was, "O God, some one person here needs what I am going to say. Help me to reach him!"[33]

I often use a brief story out of my experience with "hurting" individuals to capture the attention of the listeners and to help them sense that the sermon has their name on it. I carefully guard the confidentially of the person I mention. The following example is taken from a sermon I have preached a number of times in several churches in different states titled, "The Wilderness Places of Life."

> I could tell that John was low as he came into my study. He slumped down into the seat near my chair, and said: "Pastor, I have never felt so low in all of my life. As you know, I have not worked now for twelve months. I have tried desperately to find a job, but no one seems to want to hire someone who is fifty-nine years old. We've gone through our life savings. What do I do now?"
>
> This man was in what I would call one of the wilderness places of life. He was in that place where every one of us sooner or later will find ourselves. We can never avoid the wilderness totally, finally, or completely. Some of you this morning may find yourself in one of these wilderness places. You may be there right now. Some of you have been there in the past. Others of you will be there in the near future. But let me alert you to one thing: Every one of us will find ourselves at some point in life in some kind of wilderness.

Now I do not know what kind of wilderness yours might be. It can take many shapes and forms. Let me suggest a few wildernesses I have seen. Some of you may know these too well because you have been there before.

In this sermon I speak about the wilderness of failure, guilt, loneliness, grief, suffering, pain or death, and rejection. I acknowledge that these are only typical of the many wildernesses through which people pass. Others walk through wildernesses of drugs, alcoholism, depression, mental illness, divorce, and many others. They often feel trapped in a dead-end street with nowhere to turn. Their hopes have been broken like a discarded toy on a deserted beach. They are tired, fatigued, disturbed, and broken. They long for direction and hope. I then ask the question: "Is there any word that comes from God to us in the wilderness that gives us hope and help?" My response is drawn in five lessons from the story of Jesus feeding the five thousand people in the wilderness as recorded in Matthew 14:13-21.

Whenever I have preached this sermon, someone has always told me later about a wilderness place she has been in and how God guided her through it or how she is struggling in a wilderness currently. Those who hear this sermon see themselves in it and identify their needs.

Addressing Needs Indirectly

The indirect or inductive approach to focusing on human needs may be as effective at times or even more helpful on other occasions than is the direct method. Rather than addressing a need such as forgiveness directly in a sermon, the preacher might approach this subject in a more round-about way.

Fred Craddock, in his Lyman Beecher Lectures at Yale, *Overhearing the Gospel*, drew upon Søren Kierkegaard's concept of indirect communication and urged the preacher to let his listeners "overhear" the gospel. Craddock noted that one of the methods Kierkegaard's father used to educate his son was by having him sit and overhear the discussions among the adults. Later, Kierkegaard related an experience he had when he was walking through a cemetery late one afternoon and overheard the conversation between a grandfather and his grandson as they stood by the fresh grave of the man who had been son to one and father to the other. The grandfather spoke tenderly about life, death, and life eternal. Although the conversation was not directed to him at all, it was formative in determining Kierkegaard's sense of mission in life and his indirect method of communicating that message.[34]

We do not have to confront every need directly nor attempt to give answers to all the problems of our congregation. We have all learned that usually the best way to elicit a meaningful response from someone is not simply to supply the person with selected facts. We have all known people—or have been one of them—who had the correct information but either could not or would not act.

Preaching is not simply sharing information or propositions about religion. The preacher attempts to confront the listener with the gospel and leaves the listener free to draw her own message from "the message." The preacher does not attempt to draw the conclusions for the listener, but allows the listener that freedom. The preacher who uses the indirect style realizes that "knowing about" Christ is not the same as "knowing" Christ and that merely agreeing or disagreeing with some theological propositions does not mean one has been affected by that knowledge. The indirect method respects the listener's capacity to respond and make his own decisions.

There are many ways to "pull" the listener into the sermon indirectly. Listen to the way Charles Rice introduces an Advent sermon, "Walk, Therefore . . ."

> On a Monday in late November I joined step with the
>   commuters who hustle down our street to the
>   station five mornings a week,
>   and come dragging their briefcases up the hill, some of
>   them, long after children have gone to bed.
> As usual, the people on the 7:16, headed for mid-Manhattan
>   or the World Trade Center, most of them, were as
>   quiet as old friends at breakfast,
>   settled into their familiar routines:
>   reading, sleeping,
>   scribbling on top of a briefcase like a schoolchild
>   who hasn't done homework,
>   or just looking out the window, listening to the clickety-
>   clack.
> You could hardly help noticing how nicely turned out they
>   were,
>   fresh from the shower,
>   Oxford cloth, pinstripes, and tweed.

> Then I spied the first sign of the season, up front, on the ad
> space beside the door.
> The poster shows a child's sled, wooden, with red trim,
> sitting in a circle of snow against a dark
> background, and below, the question:
> REMEMBER WHEN THIS WAS THE ONLY THING
> YOU WANTED IN THE WHOLE WORLD?
> —Johnnie Walker
>
> There wasn't any sign on that sedate train that anyone else
> saw it. But as the good old Erie-Lackawanna
> rattled and rolled toward New York and another
> day's work, I wondered if some of my fellow travelers,
> deep into their trench coats and the Wall Street Journal,
> didn't find their eyes, too,
> wandering now and again to that Flexible Flyer.[35]

Dr. Rice's observation about the Flexible Flyer opens the listener's mind in an unexpected way and challenges her to react.

Edmund Steimle begins a sermon titled, "And How Does It All End?" this way:

> Early one summer morning, a New York policeman delivered a child in a dimly lighted Brooklyn tenement, and, less than three hours later, and only six blocks away, shot and killed a stick-up man who was pulling his gun on him. At the end of the day both the child and the gunman were still nameless. Anonymous birth and anonymous death—and the whole mystery of life and what it's all about caught up in a story of a policeman's tour of duty early one summer morning.[36]

These stories have a way of becoming our stories, and so on the listener is drawn into the story. That's the reason stories and illustrations are such effective tools for the preacher. They can become mirrors for the listeners to see themselves. Story or narrative preaching has been expounded by Eugene Lowry, Richard Jenson, Edmund Steimle, and others. Jesus was a master storyteller. His parables sounded at first so safe and about someone else. "A certain rich man had two sons . . ." Initially, the tale seemed to be about an anonymous person, living somewhere else, so the listener could relax and listen. But before the listener realized it, Jesus had drawn him into the story, and the listener recognized it was his own story. Isn't that the fact not only about the parables of Jesus, but also about the rest of the Bible? In the stories of Jacob, Jeremiah, Job, Andrew, Peter, Mary and Martha, and others, we recognize our own story. Sometimes we hear the message the clearest when it was first directed to someone else. We overhear what has been said, and we hear a message for us as well.

In the second sermon of a series I preached on "The Seven Last Words from the Cross," I looked at the cry of the thief on the cross who asked our dying Lord: "Jesus, remember me when you come into your Kingdom" (Luke 23:39-43). I would list this sermon type as doctrinal and not life-situational. But I still attempted to help the listener identify with the thief's agony and drew out an element of human need in the following manner:

> "Remember me." Listen to his plea: "Remember me." Those words fell like a pewter platter that had been dropped on a slate floor and have echoed down through the centuries. "Remember me." These words are your cry and mine. When we come to moments of loneliness and rejection, and no one seems to understand us or care, we cry: "Remember me, Lord." When we come to the times in our life when we have lost our job or are frustrated in our work, we cry: "Remember me." When we have experienced an illness or heard those dreaded words from our doctor, "It is cancer," we cry: "Remember me." When we feel misunderstood or rejected by friends or relatives, we cry: "Remember me." When we stand by the grave of a loved one or a friend, or know that we have come to our own time of dying, we join the words of the penitent thief and say: "Jesus, remember me."

Whatever way we attempt to do it—by story, vivid image, imagination, or the retelling of the ancient biblical story—our listeners have to recognize themselves. They have to feel that in some concrete way this sermon recognizes them as listeners, cares whether or not they are listening, and speaks to their personal needs. When that happens, the church bells will ring loudly that day for the man or woman in the pew. The preacher in the pulpit will be communicating.

Revelation

The Christian faith is based on God's revelation in Jesus Christ. Our preaching focuses on the unique disclosure of God in Jesus of Nazareth. In the Incarnation of God in Jesus Christ the "very face of the Most High" has been revealed. The Incarnation is the central doctrine of the Christian faith. As Paul declared: "God was in Christ reconciling the world to himself" (2 Cor. 5:19). Revelation literally means an unveiling or a disclosure of something that was formerly hidden. In Jesus Christ, God has disclosed to humanity not mere information about himself but has given self-revelation. It is a disclosure of subject to subject, not an inference, argument, or proposition but a presence. "Whoever has seen me," Jesus stated, "has seen the Father. How can you say, 'Show us the Father?'" (John 14:9).

As ministers, we have been given the ministry of reconciliation (2 Cor. 5:18). Those of us who have experienced the presence of God in Christ are charged with the responsibility of sharing this "good news" with others. Christ told his disciples that "you are the light of the world" (Matt. 5:14). We are called to shed light on the pathway of life that will lead persons to see the Light. As we have received God's revelation in Christ, we seek to disclose or make known the presence of God to others. The preacher is a vehicle through whom the revelation of God is communicated. He is an instrument to reveal "the revelation."

Revelation will "happen" through a preacher only when the listeners believe that the communicator is a full human being, has listened to them, and points beyond himself to the Word of God. The listener wants to—nay, must—believe that the preacher not only makes sense, but also is transparent to the revelation about whom she is preaching. You can achieve this by listening to the people, listening to your heart, listening to your delivery, and listening to the Scriptures.

Listening to the People

No congregation is going to listen very long to someone they feel does not listen to or care about them. Carlyle Marney used to say that if a preacher spent twenty hours a week listening to his people, he then had a right to speak for twenty minutes on Sunday morning. If a pastor faithfully does her pastoral responsibility of visiting the sick, seeing the homebound, listening to and counseling those in crises, assisting members in times of marital conflicts, counseling and performing weddings, ministering to persons who are dying or grieving, conducting funerals and following up the family's loss with grief counseling, and ministering to children, youth, young adults, and senior adults, she will encounter more personal needs than she will be able to preach about in her whole ministry.

During those times spent with people, listen with what Theodore Reik calls "the third ear."[37] You may have to "listen" to their eyes, body language, gestures, sighs, tone of voice, posture, pace of speech, and other non-verbal signals to hear the real message they are seeking to communicate. Learn to listen to the whole person—both the conscious and unconscious presentations. From pastoral contact with his flock a minister will learn the hopes, fears, burdens, joys, and sorrows of his congregation. When his preaching reveals to those in his congregation that he has heard them, they will listen.

Sometimes I hear a minister say he is or wants to be only the preaching minister of a church. I personally believe that is impossible. No one can be an effective and authentic preacher who is not also a pastor to the people to whom she preaches. The work of pastor and preacher is inseparable. Each aspect of the ministry enriches the other, and one prong without the other is insipid. Phillips Brooks expressed this well in his lectures on preaching at Yale in 1877:

> The work of the preacher and the pastor really belong together, and ought not to be separated. I believe that very strongly . . . When you find that you can never sit down to study and write without the faces of the people, who you know need your care, looking at you from the paper; and yet you never can go out among your people without hearing your forsaken study reproaching you, and calling you home, you may come to believe that it would be good indeed if you could be one or other of two things and not both; either a preacher or a pastor, but not the two together. But I assure you, you are wrong. The two things are not two, but one . . . The preacher needs to be a pastor, that he may preach to real men. The pastor must be preacher that he may keep the dignity of his work alive . . . Be both; for you cannot really be one unless you also are the other.[38]

The question is not whether preaching or pastoral ministry is more significant. Both are essential for effective ministry. But there is no question in my mind that without doing effective pastoral care of his congregation, a minister's preaching is diminished. It is weakened because the preacher—the shepherd—has not listened to, hurt with, and cared for his flock and because the people, who have not had a relationship with a minister who has cared for their pastoral needs, will be less likely to tune in on his verbal wave length on Sunday. H. H. Farmer reminds us:

> The act of preaching is part of a larger system of personal relationships and cannot be rightly understood in separation from it. The preacher, his sermon, and his hearers are embedded in the larger system and what the preaching effects largely depends upon it.[39]

As a pastor, caring for and feeding his sheep are daily tasks. They are not two separate tasks but one, each dependent upon and interacting with the other.

An effective way to keep the needs of your congregation before you is to keep a daily journal. At the end of each day, jot down a brief summary of your day's ministry, especially your counseling, hospital, or crisis work. A digest of conversations or phone calls with church members with concrete needs can help you focus. I often keep a prayer journal and begin the day by listing particular needs I know members of my congregation have and praying for them. I can tell them later that I am praying for them and really know the times I have. Sometimes a church member will write a letter to me where she states a particular need or how she has been helped. I file these for reference. Letters, telephone calls, and personal conversations with church members, or others informing me about needs of my members, keep me apprised of the many areas I can address in my preaching.

When I work on a sermon, I try to keep the needs I have learned that week before me. I try to envision the faces of some of the people to whom I will be preaching and focus on one or two in particular. I ask myself: "Will this way of explaining this thought mean anything to or help Jane Smith whose husband just died or Larry Rogers who just lost his job?" By trying to focus on particular persons, this keeps me from becoming abstract or too restrictive in my theological language. By asking myself, "Will Mrs. Jackson, who is seventy-five years old, get anything from this sermon?" I am forced to focus my thought, listen to her, and speak so she will understand me.

Barbara Brown Taylor in a sermon titled "Waiting in the Dark," based on John 1:6-8, observed that many persons are waiting for something—recognition, retirement, money to pay bills, certainty, healing, peace, love, justice, or the dawning of a new age, etc. She draws her listeners into the sermon this way:

> Whatever it is that our hearts yearn for, chances are that it has something to do with our vision of what it would mean for us to be made whole, to be transformed into people who are not afraid anymore, whose basic needs are met and whose wounds are healed and who are more nearly the people God created us to be. It is the same vision John the Baptist had of a great light that was coming into the world to outshine the darkness once and for all.[40]

It is helpful for every minister to write in the upper left-hand corner of her sermon manuscript or notes: "The pastoral concern of this sermon is _____." And then fill in that blank with your intent, for example: ". . . to help someone find strength to face his or her grief." Every sermon needs to be focused with a clearly defined purpose in the mind of the preacher. By imagining I see the faces of certain persons before me as I prepare my sermon, I can direct my attention to the needs of individuals and "listen" to them even when I am alone in my study. When we have listened to our people on Main Street and in their ordinary and critical times of life, they will listen to us when we speak on Sunday.

Listening to Your Heart

The preacher proclaims a gospel about the Word that became flesh—incarnate. God chose human flesh to reveal his presence to us. Incarnational preaching may be the most effective method of proclamation. "The incarnation, therefore, is the truest theological model for preaching," Clyde Fant states, "because it was God's ultimate act of communication. Jesus, who was the Christ, most perfectly said God to us because the eternal Word took on human flesh in a contemporary situation. Preaching cannot do otherwise."[41]

We have to become transparent for the gospel we proclaim to be through us. We are indeed vehicles, instruments, mediums, means, clay pots through whom the Word is revealed. We communicate the gospel through our own personality. "The decision that a message is worth listening to," Craddock observes, "is a decision that the teller is worth listening to.

If the speaker is not in his (or her) speaking . . . The hearers feel deceived and deprived . . . When we respond, we respond to *Someone*."[42]

By speaking out of his own human needs, the preacher clearly identifies with his congregation in their daily struggles. Our people know we really can't walk on water, so why pretend we do not have weaknesses and difficulties in life just like everyone else?

All authentic preaching is autobiographical. We share our story to point persons to the story. Wasn't that the Apostle Paul's method before Felix and Agrippa? I do not believe the "humanness" or personableness of our preaching is a weakness but rather a strength. I have often heard preachers say, "Please excuse my personal reference." What does this mean? How can I preach without the gospel filtering through my life? We do not stand at some distance from what we proclaim as ticket sellers who merely hand a ticket to the person who purchases it. The gospel is not something the preacher passes on objectively as information from the past. He is subjectively involved within the story. His life has been made different by the gospel he preaches. It is not just the gospel, but like Paul he speaks about *my* gospel (2 Tim. 2:8).

Leslie Tizard relates an experience he had as a student at Oxford with the Old Testament scholar H. Wheeler Robinson. As they were walking one day by the river at Oxford, the two began to talk about preaching and Robinson, who was the supervisor of Tizard's studies, asked him how he was doing in his preaching. Tizard told him he felt he was preaching too much about his own needs and the things that interested him. "But what else should you preach about?" Robinson asked him. "What else could you preach about with conviction?"[43]

The preacher is, to use Henri Nouwen's image, "the wounded healer." He has the courage to share the gospel with others out of his own struggles, doubts, fears, longings, hopes, darkness, and confusion in his spiritual journey. He does not pretend to stand ten feet above known sin and remain aloof from the normal demands of living. What we preach arises from within our own soul as we have passed through the crucible of encountering our own pain and suffering, joys and laughter, victories and defeats.

John Claypool was probably one of the finest representatives of what has been called confessional preaching. "We will make our greatest impact in preaching," Claypool declared, "when we dare to make available to the woundedness of others what we have learned through an honest grappling with our own woundedness."[44] Rather than pretending he had all the answers and was devoid of doubts and fears, Claypool freely preached out of his "woundedness."

When Claypool's eight-year-old daughter was diagnosed as having acute leukemia, he bore with his congregation through his sermons his "encounter with darkness" and his struggle with the drama, suffering, and eventual death of his daughter. He later recounted his personal struggle with grief in a book titled, *Tracks of a Fellow Struggler*. The introduction in the first sermon in the book illustrates his confessional approach:

> It has never been easy for me to stand in this place and try to preach a sermon, but I must confess to you this morning that it is doubly difficult. As many of you know, the last two weeks have been full of trauma for me and my family. During these days my eight-year-old daughter was diagnosed as having leukemia, and we have been called upon to shift very swiftly from the shock and numbness that first comes with such a disclosure to the task of learning to care for her and now to live with a degree of normalcy in the shadow of such an enormity.[45]

Confessional preaching enables the listeners to see through the "window pane" of the preacher's personal struggles into the house of their own mind and heart. His story helps the woman in the pew identify her own story as she looks for light from "the" story to guide her in life's journey. The listener knows she is not alone in her struggles, and the preacher understands her because he too has known struggles, whether or not it is her particular struggle. This touches the transconscious level deep within a person. Often the most private and personal feelings a preacher shares will resonate most vividly with the deepest—sometimes unexpressed—feelings of his listeners. Paul Scott Wilson speaks of "confession" or "testimony" as one of the "genres" of the proclamation of the gospel. Wilson draws upon David Lose and Anna Carter Florence in particular to describe the meaning of testimony or confession as a witness to one's deepest convictions through preaching.[46]

One of the most powerful sermons the noted Scottish preacher Arthur John Gossip ever delivered was "But When Life Tumbles In, What Then?" In that sermon, the first one he preached after his wife's sudden and unexpected death, he spoke about those who experienced loss and bereavement and in the midst of their sorrow flung away from the faith. Asserting his sense of Christ's presence, he said: "You people in the sunshine may believe the faith, but we in the shadows must believe it."[47] His congregation heard him more readily because he had walked the "valley of the shadow of death" with them.

David Buttrick and some other teachers of homiletics have been critical of the use of personal references in preaching. Buttrick states his view forcefully: "To be blunt, there are virtually no good reasons to talk about ourselves from the pulpit."[48] William Brosend in an article titled "Enough about Me" in *The Christian Century* and in his book, *The Preaching of Jesus: Gospel Proclamation, Then and Now*, argues boldly that there is no "I" in preach and the preacher should avoid at all costs inserting himself or herself into the sermon. He continues:

> The preacher who prefaces every story with a bit of autobiography dulls the ears of the listener. When the time does come to share something important that can be shared only autobiographically—self-disclosure rather than self-reference—the preacher may have already trained the listeners to tune out; the listeners know that the important material won't come until after the mention of self.[49]

John M. Buchanan in his editorial for *The Christian Century* titled "I Statements," observes that when he came through seminary there was nearly a phobia against making any "I" statements in the sermon. But one day in a seminar led by James Forbes from Riverside Church, Forbes observed that preaching among other things is testimony and if it is not testimony, it isn't going to work. He said that Forbes' words struck home to him when he declared: "If you don't believe this stuff and tell them you do, why would you expect them to believe it?" That sentence hit him, Buchanan stated, like "a fax from heaven." He indicated that he still was cautious in his use of "I" in his preaching. "But I learned from Forbes that preaching is one of those vocations where personal testimony is called for."[50]

There are clearly dangers in using any kind of personal references. If a preacher uses any personal reference in a narcissist way to call attention to himself, his strengths or accomplishments, then obviously this kind of reference will be self-defeating. Any attempt to speak personally is not to focus on the preacher but on his humanity and his dependence on God like all the rest of the congregation. A continuous or unending reference to one's self in preaching the Word obviously directs the focus in the wrong place and, I agree with Brosend, this self-reference can soon cause the congregation to tune the preacher out.

But I believe the revelation of the preacher's humanity through personal references or confessional preaching far outweighs the risks. The listeners need to see the preacher in the pulpit as a whole human being, searching to know and serve God as he is. In a sermon titled, "Lord, I Keep Getting a Busy Signal," I spoke about my own difficulty in praying. I exposed myself to my congregation in this way:

> To be very frank this morning, I have to tell you that it has never been easy for me to understand people for whom praying comes easily. It has always been a struggle for me. It has been a struggle to find the time, to keep the time, to make it meaningful, to avoid interruption, and to sense the reality of the presence of God always in my prayer time.

Preachers who carefully preach out of their own spiritual pilgrimage, who identify with their people in their quest for spiritual knowledge, and who do not try to come across as religious experts will be heard more readily by their people. Remember the Lyconian confession of the Apostle Paul: "We are men like yourselves . . ." (Acts 14:15). We confess our own humanity and sinfulness and point to our own redemption and only then how others can experience God's salvation. If people are going to listen to a preacher, they have to be interested in what she is saying. Etymologically, interest is rendered "*inter est*"—that which the speaker and hearer have in common between them. Our humanity is what we have most in common with our people. Listen to your own humanity and speak out of what you discover.

Listening to Your Delivery

The way we deliver the gospel is as important as what we have to say. You may have a great sermon on paper about love, but if you preach it as though you are angry and hate your listeners, you will communicate the opposite message from what you intended. Marshall McLuhan has reminded us that "the medium is the message." We have to listen to how we deliver our sermons because the moments of sermon delivery are inseparably bound to the reception of the sermon we want to communicate to our people.

Listen to your sermons on audio-cassette or watch a video tape or a DVD of a sermon. Some seminaries offer refresher courses for pastors where the preacher is given an opportunity to preach a sermon in a studio and have a video tape made. He and a professor of homiletics discuss the presentation later. A wise preacher will ask her spouse or a friend in the congregation to listen to and evaluate both the sermon's content and the delivery style.

Learn to tell stories and paint pictures effectively for your listeners. People need pictorial buckets to carry their thoughts in when they leave. Abstract, theological jargon will not nail down the ideas in their mind. I think Henry Mitchell is correct when he says: "If you have an idea that can't be translated into a story or a picture, don't use it."[51] Why? Because your listeners will neither understand what your point is nor find it relevant to their lives. Vivid illustrations, graphic images, parabolic stories, descriptive language, and personal experiences make the sermon come alive. Mitchell states this truth forcefully: "Theology and ethics and anything else worth preaching may and perhaps must be stated in careful argument. But it won't reach the whole person until it is translated into moving and graphic art and symbol-word pictures and narrations."[52]

The preacher needs to prepare his sermon notes or manuscript carefully. I will sometimes write eight or ten legal size pages of handwritten notes. Some sections may be written out in full. But when I preach I do not take anything with me into the pulpit other than a few quotations I want to have exactly as they were given. A free delivery or extemporaneous style, as it is often called, allows for a greater sense of communication. The oral, conversational style will permit the preacher to have better eye contact and to engage and interact more readily with the body and eye language of the congregation. There is a naturalness and freshness about extemporaneous preaching. The people in the congregation feel the preacher is talking more personally to them as individuals. Fant offers some helpful suggestions in his book, *Preaching for Today*, on how to prepare an "oral manuscript." I encourage you to read that book in its revised and expanded edition.[53]

A preacher may be able to communicate effectively with skillful use of sermon notes, but where is the preacher who can read a sermon and keep the attention or interest of a congregation? A read sermon usually communicates more interest in what one has written than in the congregation to whom the preacher is speaking. The pastoral preaching approach, Wayne Oates believed, "implies a conversational, eye-contact, extemporaneous delivery rather than a more impersonal, formal, and oratorical delivery. It rules out histrionics and other appeals to the more superficial emotions. Yet, being united to the sense of touch, to sound, and to rhythm makes the message more concrete."[54] People respond better to an oral style than a written one. Spoken sermons are meant to be heard and not read.

Listening to the Scriptures

People are not interested primarily in hearing what the preacher's opinion is on a subject. They want to know if there is any word from the Lord. If a preacher who prepares pastoral sermons is not careful, she may end up with nice essays on psychological problems about loneliness, stress, guilt, grief, anger, and so on. Preaching needs to be grounded in the Bible. The best pastoral preaching will arise not only out of listening to your people, but also by careful, daily Bible study. The Bible contains a broad slice of human experience. It contains countless stories about men and women in almost every circumstance of life. We overhear their struggles and victories, sins and repentance, joys and sorrows, doubts and faith, curses and blessings, strengths and weaknesses, births and deaths. Their stories are in many ways your story and mine. God made himself known to these persons in various stages and times in human history. And we are confident it continues to work in our lives in the same way today.

Elizabeth Achtemeier has reminded us that "the one basis of our authority is the Holy Scriptures, and if we do not preach out of them, we should not be preaching at all."[55] The Bible has to be our common starting point and the ultimate source by which we measure our word. "The Bible became the authority for the church," Achtemeier continues, "because the church learned, over decades of worship and practice, that the biblical story was the one story that created and sustained its life."[56]

Preaching a sermon without a biblical base is like offering our people bricks made with straw or giving a lecture on food to people dying of hunger without offering them bread to eat. Preaching without a biblical base is akin to building a house on a sandy beach where the waves from the ocean will soon wash it away. Preaching without a biblical base reduces the communication to "a noisy gong or a clanging cymbal" (1 Cor. 13:1). Preaching without a biblical base cuts the preacher off from his source of power, his map through the wilderness of life, his light through the dark valleys, his guide up the mountains of difficulties, his ship across the stormy seas of doubt and confusion, his comforter in moments of grief and pain and the words that lead us to the Word.

The Bible provides us with an inexhaustible well from which to draw. No matter how often we draw from its depths, we always discover there is still more water there. We fill the empty cups of our lives from it as generations before us have and future generations after us will continue to do.

The text we use for our sermon should be more than a self-starter. It is not something we simply quote and then depart quickly from it. The biblical text we use should influence the outline, direction, and content of the sermon. We need to explore the text and determine why that passage was a part of the Scripture in the first place. What were the events, experiences, issues, or needs the original writer or narrator of the story was trying to address? From this study we try to determine two factors: (1) what the text meant then—the ancient story—and (2) what the text means today—the analogous story for us today. The New Testament scholar, Leander Keck in his book, *The Bible in the Pulpit*, argues this case forcefully and then observes:

> To preach biblically is to take full account of the concrete issues to which the text was addressed in the first place; it is to reckon with the fact that what the biblical writers found necessary to say was determined not by truth in general but by needs in particular. The situation of the community, as perceived by the writer, set the agenda, and the traditions provided some of the resources for addressing it; the text is a selected and focused truth in the form of a literary response.[57]

After we sense what we believe was the original intent of the biblical writer for including this passage as a part of the Scriptures, we then try to hear the text addressing us today in a similar way the ancient writer wanted it to speak to his readers or hearers of the story. If we can discover the need or issue this passage was addressing originally, then we can draw a parallel for our modern-day listeners. Our listeners do not need a simple exposition of the text but rather an explanation of how they are confronted by the text today. Whether the preacher starts with the Bible or with people, the goal is to meet a need in the life of the listener and not simply explain a passage of Scripture. The passage was written originally out of a historical concern for a person or persons—in the Old Testament for example, Moses, Jacob, David, or the nation Israel—or in the New Testament for example, Jesus, Peter, Paul, or the church.

The preacher has both hands full. One hand holds the Bible, and the other hand holds the needs of her people. The Bible calls out to us with its claim for our attention, and our people call out to us with their needs. The tension need not be unhealthy or divisive. In reality it is two faces pointing us back to one truth: God's concern for people. As Wayne Oates reminded us, "The Bible is the pastor's 'royal road' to the deeper levels of the personalities of his people."[58]

In a sermon I preached on Jeremiah 15:10-21, titled "When Life Crashes In," the outline and movement followed the text but also addressed the analogous needs of people today. Here is an example from that sermon on how I tried to link the concern of past and present needs.

> Jeremiah recorded his personal confessions, and out of his agony cried, "I sat alone." This is the aloneness of a leper, who is isolated from all the rest of society. In his aloneness Jeremiah longed to sense the presence of God.
>
> Too often we think the ancient prophets always walked in unparalleled fellowship with God. We assume they always felt the strength of God's strong arm by their side at every moment. But Jeremiah in his honesty tells us this was not always true for him. There were times when he was caught in the floods and storms of life that swept him away from his foundation. He reached for the bottom but could not find it. He groped and searched for a word from God. He reached the point that he questioned his calling, purpose, his message, and even God. "Where are you, God?" he cried. "I sat alone."
>
> Jeremiah, however, is not the only one who has had that kind of experience, is he? You and I have known those kinds of feelings, haven't we? If we are honest, we have to admit it. Have there not been times in your life when you have felt alone and wondered where God was in your pain, rejection, ridicule, loneliness, despair, and depression? Have there not been moments in your life, like Jeremiah, when you have cried out to God and said, "I sit alone"?

I attempted to follow a similar approach in a series of sermons I preached on Old Testament heroes of the faith. In fact, no matter what kind of sermon I preach—doctrinal, textural, expository, or life situation—I seek to show the correlation of the ancient story with our human story today. Paul Tillich called this "the principal of correlation." This principle states that the questions to which the gospel is directed have to be genuine, human (existential) issues and the response of the church has to be true to the gospel and expressed in language that can be understood by those to whom it is addressed.[59] When we read the Bible in a reflective way, we will hear both the question and the response that have arisen out of the hearts of men and women through the ages to know God.

Response

When we preach, we should anticipate some kind of response. A sermon is delivered, hopefully, not merely for the preacher's personal satisfaction or a solo performance to be seen, heard, and applauded. A sermon should have with its delivery a summons to action. Our listeners will say to themselves: "I ought to think and act differently because of what I have heard the preacher say today." A preacher who is not concerned with motivating his listeners to some kind of response is only going through the motions of preaching. From Pentecost on, Christian preachers have called their listeners to react to the message of the gospel. If we want a response to our pastoral preaching, the following factors should be present to motivate our listeners to respond: conviction, respect, and dialogue.

Conviction

If the preacher is going to awaken a response from her listeners, then they have to be convinced the proclaimer believes what she is heralding. If the listeners think the preacher is not genuine or is disguising her real thoughts or feelings, then her words will sound hollow and empty. The listeners may sometimes wonder: "Does the preacher really believe that? How can she? Is she really being honest?" When we have been willing to let our humanity be seen, then our listeners are more likely to believe that we are authentic. A faithful pastor will have demonstrated his character to the people in other settings, so they will trust him in the pulpit. His credibility will be low in the pulpit, however, if he has ignored their needs in times of crises.

A preacher honestly must believe what she preaches. This does not imply that she has all the answers or never has doubts. If that were the case, most of us would have to stop preaching. Out of our humanness we may struggle with tough questions at various times in our life. Although all of our intellectual questions may not be satisfactorily answered, or all of our emotional states put at ease, we do have an abiding sense of the presence of God that sustains us. With John we declare: "That which we have seen and heard we proclaim also to you, so that you may have fellowship with us" (1 John 1:3). Or, "I had heard of you with the hearing of the ear, but now my eyes have seen you" (Mark 8:18).

The gospel we preach is not secondhand information we merely pass on to others. The preacher's life must be transformed by the Lord about whom he speaks. We share out of our personal experience with a living Lord. Like the Apostle Paul, we acknowledge that we are captives to Christ. This kind of knowledge is brought about by a personal relationship and not by hearsay. Only fire will kindle fire. A preacher's genuine depth of sincerity and conviction will be detected by a sensitive congregation.

A young man, who was a student under James Stewart when he was a professor at the divinity college at Edinburgh, told his father one day, "Dad, that man doesn't just turn on a light in you when you sit under his teaching; he lights a blazing torch in your life."

People will respond to a preacher who believes what he says he believes, who proclaims it with sincerity, and who lives out his faith in his private devotional life and in his pastoral care of church members.

Respect

Listeners will respond to a preacher whom they feel respects them as individuals and as listeners. If the preacher talks down to them or over their heads, she is not taking them seriously as persons. When the preacher attacks her listeners or belittles them, communication is averted. Whether the listeners agree with the preacher or not, they want to feel they have the right for the preacher to take their perspective seriously. A preacher needs to convey through words and body language that he thinks his listeners are persons of worth who can think for themselves and are capable of interpreting what he is saying and can make a responsible decision in the light of his sermon. An authoritarian stance by the preacher, a patronizing tone or manner, an attempted manipulation of the hearers, putting a guilt trip on them, or attempts to think for them are all stances of disrespect.

A preacher who respects her listeners will acknowledge that she is a fellow pilgrim with them in her quest to follow Christ. She will acknowledge her vulnerability and remain open to further insight from others and to a continual spiritual growth. She will admit that she has not arrived and is genuinely open to fellow Christians to share with her their insights into the Christian faith. A preacher who respects her listeners will remain humble and teachable, lovable and approachable, a fellow searcher and struggler—and not pretend to be a person with all the answers.

David Switzer has described the authoritarian preacher as the sort of person about whom a colleague of his once observed: "He may be in error, but he is never in doubt."[60] Switzer believes that a preacher who respects his listener will use what he calls "tentative language:" "After serious study, my conclusion is . . ." "It seems to me as if this is a valid way of viewing this issue." "I wonder if a way of going at this is not to . . ."[61] Our congregations will respect us more as speakers if they feel we have shown them respect and seek to walk with them as a part of the community of faith in our quest together for truth.

Dialogue

Surely every preacher hopes his sermon will provoke some kind of dialogue in his congregation. He hopes the listener will engage in a dialogue in her own mind about what she has heard. He hopes she might enter into dialogue with another member of the congregation about the sermon or with someone outside the church. He would be delighted to think it might open up a dialogue between the preacher and the listener. He also longs to believe it will encourage the listener to engage more readily in dialogue with God.

In some African-American traditions and Deep South churches, there is verbal reaction from the congregation. In most African-American congregations this verbal dialogue will continue throughout the course of the entire sermon. The response the preacher may most desire is not, however, an outward verbal dialogue but a dialogue taking place within the mind of the listener. If the preacher does not want some kind of response from those listening to him, why should they bother to listen?

Reuel Howe has reminded the laity they are partners in preaching with the clergy. He believes the laity have a responsibility for the delivery of the preacher's sermon. He encourages the listener "to practice active listening." Both clergy and laity need each other. He continues:

> In a sense it is true that laity have a responsibility to pull the preaching out of the minister by the urgency of their questions, by their sense of excitement resulting from their

experience of the meeting of meaning in their lives, by their devotion to their work in the world, and by their regular participation in the worship preaching dialogue. What is not always realized is that the quality of the hearing has a great deal to do with the quality of the speaking, and that this is a ministry of the laity.

In one local church, where dialogical preaching has become the norm, a layman said to his preacher after the service, "We didn't do so well today." "What do you mean?" asked the preacher. "I mean," replied the parishioner, "your sermon was not as helpful as it might have been because I wasn't working along with you. In fact, I think I was pushing down in me the meaning of something that happened to me this past week."[62]

The layman was right, of course. Preaching is a two-way street. It is a joint venture of both the preacher and the laity. Sermons would be greatly improved if the quality of listening was enhanced.

If the congregation feels the minister's sermon is a monologue, then he cannot expect much response from them. The hearer has to sense that the preacher wants the sermon to be a cooperative enterprise between himself and the congregation. The preacher's style and content need to send out a clear signal: "Hey, I have heard you. I have felt your pain and brokenness. Let's see now if we can converse together so we can hear what God is trying to teach us through his Word today." Expressions such as the following can help us communicate this attitude:

- "I know that some of you can't see how this could possibly be true, but let's inquire if it could be true."
- "You may think that your burden of guilt is so heavy that nothing can ever lift its crushing load from your back, but take hope in Jesus' forgiveness of Simon Peter."
- "The Apostle Peter might have experienced forgiveness, but Jesus was standing there beside him on the shore of the Sea of Galilee. Almost two thousand years separate me from those events."
- "I don't know how to pray anymore. God seems remote and uncaring."
- "Let's consider a few questions that might arise."

These kinds of comments or questions help open doors into the minds of your listeners or beckon them to pause and notice that you are taking them and their needs seriously. Pastoral preaching may open the way for personal counseling with some members of your congregation. Your sermon on Jeremiah's loneliness or Job's suffering or Paul's thorn in the flesh may provide the catalyst for someone to make an appointment to talk with you about personal problems. If you do not want to counsel with persons, then don't preach about human needs. Pastoral preaching will open doors to persons in your congregation who are longing to talk with someone. When I was pastor in a university community and spoke on human needs, there were weeks when I hardly had time to see the students who wanted to talk with a minister.

Sometimes the minister might engage in a planned dialogue with the congregation. I have on occasions preached a series of sermons and then had a "talk-back" session with the congregation on Sunday night or Wednesday night following the sermon. I always found this an exciting and stimulating exchange. If the preacher and laity will trust each other to be honest and not be intimidated or threatened every time someone doesn't agree with one another, this can be a healthy experience in the life of a congregation. It reveals and requires openness on the part of both clergy and laity.

Pastoral Preaching That Invites Change

Fosdick observed that preaching to human needs was "counseling on a group level."[63] Arthur L. Teikmanis declared that "dynamic preaching is basically pastoral care in the context of worship."[64] William Willimon wrote a book some years ago with the title *Worship as Pastoral Care*.[65] Granted that all of these claims may sweep with a broom that is too wide; they do, however, all stress the preventive factor in effective preaching and the importance of the worshipping community in the health and wholeness of Christian persons.

Clement C. Welsh, in his book *Preaching in a New Key*, notes a striking difference between preaching as providing information and preaching as helping people make sense of their lives.[66] Pastoral preaching addresses many of the needs in the congregation and provides some avenues for recognizing them, confronting them, overcoming or bearing them, and knowing they do not carry them alone, but they have the support of their pastor, the Christian community, other professional resources, and ultimately the presence of God.

Pastoral preaching may be, in an odd way, a more evangelistic sermon than a direct "repent and believe" appeal. Why? Because the listener might feel the preacher has spoken not to a general sense of sinfulness, but to his deep sense of guilt or his heavy burden of feeling rejected. He may "overhear" the good news that confronts his loneliness, fear, grief, suffering, or death. By localizing the need of particular persons, individuals may be more open to the "persuasion" of the gospel. The minister's own "confessional" approach may touch a need within a listener's life. The preacher's openness may persuade him to be open to hearing the good news, and ultimately to be open to receive acceptance from God.

Christians on all levels of the spiritual journey and with a wide variety of ages, both male and female, gather on Sunday to hear a word from the Lord. When the words from the preacher bring that word to meet the deepest needs of their hearts, people will respond. They will recognize the aliveness of the preaching event, because it avoids generalities and focuses where they live.

I heard a student say one day that his former pastor's sermons were like the old TV show *Journey to the Bottom of the Sea*. The TV show had the same set each week; only the costumes and monsters changed. His preacher changed the text, but it was always the same old sermon. Preaching to human needs makes us focus, and often our listeners will exclaim: "The sermon is focusing on me."

The dialogue created by the cooperative venture of preaching will, hopefully, make the listener want to take some positive steps to seek help, to find resources to change what can be corrected, or to experience more fully the grace and power of God. The listener needs to know she is not thrown back upon her strength and resources alone. She has the presence and power of God to sustain her. Hopefully, the sermon will also call forth a deeper commitment to God. Knowing she does not have to face her struggles alone, the listener vows to recommit herself to the common journey of faith with fellow believers in her Christian community. Together they will seek to grow in their knowledge and service for the Lord. Hearing the preacher's challenge that arises out of the Word of God as it addresses her particular need, she cannot remain neutral. She is invited to change. Following Jesus is changing.

I am convinced the most effective preaching is that which is clearly directed to meet human needs. Pastoral preaching continues the ministry of our Lord who reached out to heal the lame, blind, deaf, ill, diseased, grieving, rejected, outcast, poor, needy, old, young, male, and female. Preaching to human needs is good news to many who have only experienced bad news. We let them know that God has heard their cries, seen their pain, felt their hopelessness, and knows their sorrow. When the preacher really sees inside the head of his listeners, he will sense their deepest needs and respond out of the depths of his own being where he too has been already addressed by God. But you and I have to confess that we have to return again and again, as our laypeople do, to sense the presence of God.

In a London church the caretaker was getting ready to close the building and he asked a visitor, who was still there, if he would leave. The man begged that he might have another moment. The caretaker noticed the visitor was standing by a sign that read: "Here God laid his hands on William Booth." The caretaker overhead the man praying: "O God, do it again." Suddenly the caretaker recognized that the man who was praying was William Booth himself.

Our prayer as a preacher of the gospel each Sunday is the same: "Lay your hands on me again, O God." May we be transparent so those in need can see God through us and the words we proclaim.

Notes

[1] Wallace Hamilton, *Where Now Is Thy God?* (Old Tappen, NJ: Fleming H. Revell Co., 1969), 91-92.

[2] William F. Fore, "Beyond the Electronic Church," *The Christian Century* (January 7-14, 1981), 29.

[3] Ibid., 30.

[4] Luis E. Lugo, "Faith is in flux in America, survey finds," *Richmond Times Dispatch*, February 28, 2008, 1 and A4. See also www.pewforum.org.

[5] Ellen Goodman, "Shopping for Religion," *The Boston Globe*, February 29, 2008. See a similar article, "American Religion as a Spiritual Shopping Center," by Eric Gorck, *The New York Times*, February 29, 2008.

[6] Thomas G. Long, "No News Is Bad News," in *What's the Matter with Preaching Today?* ed. Mike Graves (Louisville: Westminster John Knox Press, 2004), 147.

[7] Ibid., 148.

[8] Ibid., 149.

[9] William Brosend, *The Preaching of Jesus: Gospel Proclamation, Then and Now* (Louisville: Westminster John Press, 2010), 35.

[10] Ibid., 35-36.

[11] Ibid., 47.

[12] Ibid., 60. Quoting Thomas G. Long, "Taking the Listener Seriously in Biblical Interpretation," in *The Folly of Preaching*, ed. Michael P. Knowles (Grand Rapids: Wm. B. Eerdmans Publishing Co., 2007), 73.

[13] James C. Howell, *The Beauty of the Word: The Challenge and Wonder of Preaching* (Louisville: Westminster John Knox Press, 2011), 38.

[14] Ibid., 40.

[15]James Clark, *Dynamic Preaching* (Westwood, NJ: Fleming H. Revell Co., 1960), 68. See also David H. C. Read, *Preaching about the Needs of Real People* (Philadelphia: Westminster Press, 1988).

[16]Fred B. Craddock, *Preaching* (Nashville: Abingdon Press, 1983), 153ff.

[17]Charles F. Kemp, *Life Situation Preaching* (St. Louis: Bethany Press, 1956), 16.

[18]Wayne Oates, *The Christian Pastor* (Philadelphia: Westminster Press, 1951), 67.

[19]Wayne Oates, *The Christian Pastor*, 3rd ed. (Philadelphia: Westminster Press, 1982), 149.

[20]Fred B. Craddock, *Craddock on the Craft of Preaching*, ed. Lee and Kathryn Sparks (St. Louis: Chalice Press, 2011), 117-136.

[21]Ibid., 91.

[22]Harry Emersion Fosdick, *The Living of These Days* (New York: Harper and Row, 1956), 92.

[23]Julie Pennington-Russell, "Our Good Shepherd," in *This Is What a Preacher Looks Like: Sermons by Baptist Women in Ministry*, ed. Pamela R. Durso (Macon, GA: Smyth & Helwys, 2010), 87-91.

[24]Henry Mitchell, *The Recovery of Preaching* (San Francisco: Harper and Row, 1977), 30ff.

[25]John Baillie, *The Roots of Religion in the Human Soul* (London: James Clarke and Co., 1937), 112.

[26]John Baillie, *The Sense of the Presence of God* (New York: Charles Scribner's Sons, 1962), 61.

[27]Mitchell, *The Recovery of Preaching*, 28.

[28]Annie Lally Milhaven, ed., *Sermons Seldom Heard: Women Proclaim Their Lives* (New York: Crossroad, 1991), vii.

[29]See my book, *Facing Life's Ups and Downs: The Struggle To Be Whole* (Macon, GA: Smyth & Helwys, 2010), for some examples of these types of sermons.

[30]Ibid.

[31]This series was published under the title, *Facing Grief and Death* (Nashville: Broadman Press, 1975).

[32]Edgar N. Jackson in his book, *How to Preach to People's Needs*, lists seventeen different areas with brief sermon résumés from various preachers as examples. In three of the books he has edited, *The Preaching Pastor, Pastoral Preaching*, and *Life Situation Preaching*, Charles Kemp has selected some examples of sermons written and delivered to meet the haunting needs of people. Other recent books that offer resources for preaching to human needs are the following: Joe Cauthen, *The Pulpit Is Waiting: A Guide for Pastoral Preaching*; Donald Capps, *Pastoral Counseling and Preaching*; Charles B. Bugg, *Witness a Fragile Servant: A Personal Look at Pastoral Preaching*; Gary D. Stratman, *Pastoral Preaching: Timeless Truth for Changing Needs*; Edward P. Wimberly, *Moving from Shame to Self-Worth: Preaching and Pastoral Care*; David J. Schlafer and Roger Alling, ed., *Preaching as Caring (Sermons that Work)*; Annie Lally Milhaven, ed., *Sermons Seldom Heard: Women Proclaim Their Lives*; LeRoy H. Adams and Robert Hughes, *Preaching God's Compassion*; and Barbara Brown Taylor, *God in Pain: Teaching Sermons on Suffering*.

[33]Fosdick, *The Living of These Days*, 100.

[34]Fred Craddock, *Overhearing the Gospel* (Nashville: Abingdon Press, 1978), 105-106.

[35]Charles Rice, "Watch Therefore . . ." in *Twentieth Century Pulpit*, vol. 2, ed. James W. Cox (Nashville: Abingdon Press, 1981), 157-158.

[36]Edmund Steimle, *From Death to Birth* (Philadelphia: Fortress Press, 1973), 3.

[37]Theodore Reike, *Listening with the Third Ear* (New York: Farrar, Straus, 1948), 146.

[38]Phillips Brooks, *Lectures on Preaching* (New York: Dutton & Co., 1877), 75-77.

[39]H. H. Farmer, *The Servant of the Word* (Philadelphia: Fortress Press, 1964), 66.

⁴⁰Barbara Brown Taylor, *Gospel Medicine* (Cambridge: Cowley Publications, 1995), 68-69.
⁴¹Clyde Fant, *Preaching for Today* (New York: Harper & Row, 1975), 29.
⁴²Craddock, *Overhearing the Gospel*, 43.
⁴³Leslie J. Tizard, *Preaching, the Art of Communication* (New York: Oxford University Press, 1959), 16.
⁴⁴John Claypool, *The Preaching Event* (Waco: Word Books, 1980), 86-87.
⁴⁵John Claypool, *Tracks of a Fellow Struggler* (Waco: Word Books, 1974), 25.
⁴⁶Paul Scott Wilson, *Setting Words on Fire: Putting God at the Center of the Sermon* (Nashville: Abingdon Press, 2008), 151-152.
⁴⁷Arthur John Gossip, *The Hero in Thy Soul* (Edinburgh: T & T Clark, 1928), 111.
⁴⁸David Buttrick, *Homiletics* (Philadelphia: Fortress Press, 1987), 142. For another study on this issue, see Richard L. Thalin, *The "I" of the Sermon* (Minneapolis: Fortress Press, 1987).
⁴⁹William Brosend, "Enough about Me," *The Christian Century* (February 23, 2010), 37-38. See also for more details *The Preaching of Jesus: Gospel Proclamation, Then and Now* (Louisville: Westminster John Knox Press, 2010), 98-123.
⁵⁰John M. Buchanan, "I Statements," *The Christian Century* (February 9, 2010), 3.
⁵¹Mitchell, *The Recovery of Preaching*, 45.
⁵²Ibid., 47
⁵³Clyde Fant, *Preaching for Today* (New York: Harper & Row, 1987), 165-173.
⁵⁴Oates, *The Christian Pastor*, 3rd ed., 149.
⁵⁵Elizabeth Achtemeier, *Creative Preaching* (Nashville: Abingdon Press, 1980), 18.
⁵⁶Ibid., 19.
⁵⁷Leander Keck, *The Bible in the Pulpit* (Nashville: Abingdon Press, 1978), 115.
⁵⁸Wayne Oates, *The Bible and Pastoral Care* (Philadelphia: Westminster Press, 1953), 21.
⁵⁹Paul Tillich, *Systematic Theology*, vol. 1 (Chicago: University of Chicago Press, 1951), 59ff.
⁶⁰David H. Switzer, *Pastor, Preacher, Person* (Nashville: Abingdon Press, 1979), 80.
⁶¹Ibid., 81.
⁶²Reuel L. Howe, *Partners in Preaching: Clergy & Laity in Dialogue* (New York: Seabury Press, 1967, 91.
⁶³Fosdick, *The Living of These Days*, 94.
⁶⁴Arthur L. Teikmanis, *Preaching and Pastoral Care* (Philadelphia: Fortress Press, 1964), 19.
⁶⁵William H. Willimon, *Worship as Pastoral Care* (Nashville: Abingdon Press, 1979).
⁶⁶Clement Welsh, *Preaching in a New Key* (Philadelphia: United Church Press,1974), 33.

Sermon

The Wilderness Places of Life
Exodus 16:9-15; Matthew 14:13-21

I could tell that he was low as he came into my study. He slumped down into the seat near my chair, and said: "Pastor, I have never felt so low in all my life. As you know, I have not worked now for twelve months. I have tried desperately to find a job, but no one seems to want to hire someone who is 59 years old. We've gone through our life savings. What do I do now?"

This man was in what I would call one of the wilderness places of life. He was in that place where every one of us sooner or later will find ourselves. We can never avoid these wilderness places totally, finally, or completely. Some of you this morning may find yourself in one of these places. You may be there right now. Some of you have been there in the past. Others of you will be there in the near future. But let me assure you of one thing: All of us will find ourselves at some point in life in some kind of wilderness.

Now I do not know what kind yours might be. It can take many shapes and forms. Let me suggest a few wildernesses I have seen. Some of you may know these too well. For some, you may sense your own wilderness in those I suggest. There are many others.

The Wilderness of Failure

One of the wilderness places where some people find themselves is what we might call the wilderness of failure. Life often teaches us rather early an unfortunate lesson: We are never supposed to fail at anything we ever try. That is a bad lesson to be taught, because it is simply not true. Every one of us, if we are honest, will have to confess there are things in life we have wanted to do that we have not quite pulled off like we wanted to. There are things we have tried desperately to do, and we really have failed at our attempts to succeed.

There is a young teenager who desperately wants to make the football team, so he begins doing everything possible to accomplish his goal. He works hard at all the exercises. He practices throwing, kicking, running, and everything that goes with the game. He eats, trains, and sleeps well. But then when the players are selected for the team, he is cut. He does not make it.

There is a young lady who wants to make straight A's in high school so she can go to the college of her first choice. She studies hard, long into the night, and carefully does every assignment. But when she gets her report card, it still has B's and C's. She tried, but could not achieve the grades she desired.

There is a man who climbs up the ladder in business. He wants to be number one in business, and so he works hard to reach the top, but when he gets to a certain spot, he suddenly discovers there is a host of other folks also climbing up the same ladder. And he finds that after awhile he has reached a certain point and cannot go further. Similarly, a young woman has attempted to make her way in the business world only to find one door after another close in her face.

All of us carry around with us a "bag of dreams" we hope someday we can realize. But we all have dreams that have never been fulfilled; aspirations, hopes, and desires that have never been realized totally and finally. That is true for all of us. Some of us are like that man who said, "Here I am, 54 years old, and I still don't know what I want to be when I grow up." There are too many of us like that, because we have tried one thing and we have not quite succeeded or made it. We tried another thing over here, and did not quite realize what we wanted. Life finds us sometimes in a wilderness surrounded by different kinds of failures.

The Wilderness of Guilt

For some of us, the wilderness may take a different turn, and it may be a wilderness of guilt. Who among us has not said or done things that quickly and immediately we wish we could retract? We say something to another person, and the word is in the stream of life. It has penetrated into that person, and we wish for anything that we could grab it and pull it back. But it has gone into that person's life. It has been said, and we cannot stop it. It has hurt, cut, stabbed, and wounded like a knife. We feel the black-and-blue marks left by the stinging words of criticism, rebuke, insult, and gossip. Then, we live with a sense of guilt for having said it. It hurt someone, and we know it hurt, but we cannot retract it. There are things in the past we have said or done. There are sins and acts for which we have never really been able to forgive ourselves. They may be things we have said to our husband, our wife, our children, or our friends. They could be deeds we have done in the wilderness, or in the quietness, or in the brightness of day, or in the loudness of the crowd, or in a moment, or carefully planned, or in desperation, or in anxiety, or in frustration. From them we have deep within us a lingering sense of guilt for which we have never heard the words come to us, "You are forgiven!" The late theologian Paul Tillich said that each of us must learn "to accept his acceptance by God."[1] We must learn to accept God's acceptance and forgiveness of us.

Many of us live with a heavy load of guilt in our lives. We could symbolize it in the following image. Our guilt is like a huge chain stretched far behind us, and on it would be linked all of the junk in our lives: old trash cans, an old sink, old tires, garbage cans, refuse, and pieces of every kind of trash. We have never heard the words deep down inside of us that say: "You are acceptable and you are forgiven." Some of us continue to live with an agonizing sense of guilt. That is our wilderness.

The Wilderness of Loneliness

For others, their wilderness is loneliness. The woman looked up at me as I left the nursing home and said, "Pastor, come back soon." I was the only person other than her doctor and nurses who ever came into her room. She had no family, no friends. She lived in a world of constant loneliness. "Come back, Pastor, soon."

There are many people who go day after day to the mailbox, looking for a letter from a child, or a friend, or a parent. There is a young man overseas, a young girl off at college, or someone in another state living constantly in a sense of loneliness while eagerly waiting to hear a word from home, or to receive a letter or a telephone call or an email, or to hear someone saying in some way or another: "You count as a person, and I remember you and care about you."

There are those who sit across the table from an empty chair. There is a loved one who has been in their lives for so many years who is no longer there. Now they live with the loneliness of not having this companion. Oh, this is not just the problem of older folks, either.

I was pastor of a college church where a university was just two blocks away. When I preached on loneliness once in that church, I was invited to come to the college campus the next week to speak because of the loneliness many college students were constantly wrestling with. It is also a problem for teenagers.

Some of us, who have gotten older, forget that it was hard to be a teenager. It seems there is no one who really seems to understand you. Your parents do not understand you, your friends do not understand you, and you do not understand yourself sometimes. And so it is tough growing up, and sometimes it is lonely to be a teenager.

A teenager came home almost in tears from her first day in a new school in a large city. She had just moved from a small city, where she had lived for many years. She looked up at her mother and exclaimed: "This has been the loneliest day of my life." But it is also lonely and tough to be the parents of teenagers.

John Killinger has written a striking book about *The Loneliness of Children*.[2] We have all known loneliness, and we reach out for some kind of security blanket to put around ourselves to feel warmth and comfort.

The Wilderness of Grief, Suffering, and Death

For others of us, the experience of the wilderness is grief, suffering, pain, or death. None of us escapes this wilderness. Every one of us, sooner or later, walks through that dark valley. It is there. I was a pastor too long. I walked in too many hospital corridors. I have embraced too many people in their moment of grief. I have sat by too many bedsides and have seen young and old slip from this life. I have seen the experience of grief, denial, frustration, anger, hostility, acceptance, and other emotions as people have wrestled with the valley of the shadow of death. Grief has brought to us that choking feeling, the desire to run, to scream, to cry, and to faint. An empty feeling has pulled at us within our stomach. We have had a sinking feeling and felt we were out of control.

I remember his face well. He was one of our bright-eyed teenagers. He was a young man who, when you thought you had answered all of the questions in the youth group, would then raise his hand and say: "Pastor, I've got one more question." He would always ask the penetrating questions for which no one had the simple answers. He seemed to be so bright-eyed, full of hope, alive with possibility for making rich contributions to society and his church. But then at a football game in Baton Rouge, Louisiana, he stepped from behind a bus into the pathway of an oncoming car and was killed instantly.

I remember standing in the pulpit on one occasion, looking into my congregation, and seeing seated before me a middle-aged couple with their nine-year-old, blond-haired daughter. She was the only child they had ever been able to have. They could have no other children. And now she was dying of leukemia.

Grief and suffering break into our lives in so many ways. Just a few weeks ago my wife and I were in a hospital visiting a young couple whose three-month-old child had an incision across his body because he had cancer. We do not think the child will live. The parents are heartsick. It is not easy to walk through this kind of wilderness.

Some of you have lost a mother or father or a grandparent. Others have known the sadness of the death of a wife or husband or a child. The shadow of death has crossed all our paths at some time or will in the future. I remember persons whom I met in a hospital corridor and had to say to them, "Sit down. I have some bad news for you. Your husband just had a heart attack." The reality of the wilderness of grief, suffering, and death is there for every one of us to walk through at some point or another.

The Wilderness of Rejection

For some of us, the wilderness is rejection. I suppose one of the hardest things for a young person is to wait for sides to be chosen on the playground, and always to be chosen last. What a sense of rejection! Some of us feel rejection in so many places in life. We learn early that there are some places where folks do not want us. We are not welcome. There are "keep-out" signs that say: "Don't come in here." It is hard when we feel that we do not measure up to someone else's image. We are not tall enough for their occasion. It is difficult to live when we feel rejected here or there in life.

Do you know what the two most stolen books in the New York City Public Library are? Number one is *Emily Post*. This book tries to tell us how to get along with other people. The other one is the Holy Bible. In desperation, some people reach out to find a way to relate more effectively with others and with God. Why? Because of the awful fear of rejection.

I do not know what kind of wilderness you may be walking through in your life today. Maybe the wildernesses I mentioned are not your particular ones, or maybe they are. Many people feel trapped in a dead-end street with nowhere to turn. Their yearnings are unfulfilled. Their hopes are broken like a discarded toy on a sandy beach. Their dreams have vanished. Their bodies are fatigued and their minds disturbed. They long for direction. Many walk through wildernesses of drugs, alcoholism, depression, mental illness, divorce, and so on. Sooner or later, all of us walk through a wilderness of some kind. Now then, is there any word that comes from God to use in the wilderness that gives us hope and help? I think there is, and insight for this direction comes from the passage we read this morning. I want to share with you very briefly some points that give us direction from those verses.

The Setting of the Biblical Texts

Capture the setting of these Scripture passages for a moment. The children of Israel knew about wildernesses. They had wandered through one for forty years. They had known hard, lean days. Their cries went against Moses and they longed for food to eat, even if it was given by Pharaoh's men and they had to return to slavery:

> Would that we had died by the hand of the Lord in the land of Egypt, when we sat by the flesh pots and ate bread to the full; for you have brought us out into this wilderness to kill this whole assembly with hunger. (Exod. 16:3).

God told Moses to lead the people to the Sinai Peninsula and he would provide for them there. He provided meat for them in the quails that came that way as a part of their regular migratory pattern. The bread God provided was found in the manna that was geographically limited to the Sinai Peninsula. Manna was a sweet secretion of a local plant still found today in that region. When the Israelites first saw it they cried: "Man-ha" ("manna")—"what is it?" This fine, flake-like substance was the bread the Lord had provided for Israel. It came to them in their wilderness experience as a sign of the providence of God.

Turn now to the New Testament story. Jesus has just received word that John the Baptist has been beheaded. Luke tells his readers that Herod wanted to kill Jesus as well as John, because Jesus had been openly criticizing Herod. Jesus departed to escape Herod. On this particular day, Jesus had been teaching a long time. He was frustrated and frightened by what had happened to John. Jesus instructed his disciples to go across the Sea of Galilee to a "desert place" on the other side so he might find some rest. But the Sea of Galilee is a small sea, as seas go. It is only thirteen miles long and eight miles across. When the people saw that Jesus was going to the other side, some of them quickly got in their boats and started toward the other side. Some of them probably hiked around the lake. When he got to the other side, Jesus saw the great host of people waiting for him there in that wilderness place. He had compassion on them, taught them, and healed the sick.

Late into the day, his disciples said, "Master, you had better send this crowd away, because there is nothing to eat." And Jesus said: "Feed them yourself." And they said, "We do not have anything, Lord. The only thing in this whole crowd we have found to eat is the sack lunch of a young boy." Jesus said, "Bring it to me. It is enough." He blessed it. He broke it. And he fed the multitude.

Lessons from the Wilderness Places

From the experiences of Moses and his people and those of Jesus, there are some lessons we can learn about how to live in the wilderness. I want to mention a few of these.

No One Escapes the Wilderness

The first lesson is this: Learn to expect to spend some time in the wilderness. The children of Israel knew that the journey to freedom would be difficult. They had to go through a wilderness to get to the promised land, and so may you and I. Jesus withdrew to a lonely place. This lonely place has been translated "desert" or "wilderness." Jesus knew that other wildernesses lay before him. His hour of conflict was coming. The agony of his rejection, suffering, and death were drawing nearer. Jesus was not surprised when he found himself in a wilderness. In this wilderness place on the other side of the lake, even when he attempted to escape to be apart, he was met by people and their needs. Even in the wilderness he attempted to help others in their time of need.

Most of us act surprised when we end up in the wilderness. Why should we be amazed at that? When sometimes I stay up late working on sermons or articles I am writing or I stay up late talking to someone and miss several good nights of sleep, I should not be surprised when my body is tired and my eyes are bloodshot and have huge bags under them. I should expect that, because that is the kind of abuse that comes from misusing my body. When we overeat, over-drink, under-exercise, and overindulge, why should we be surprised when we become ill and too tense? Why should we blame God all the time, as though it is something God has done to us? We ask: "Why did God do this to me?" We know full well it is something we should expect from what we have done to our bodies. It is strange, isn't it, that we expect to go through life with only comfort, convenience, joy, and happiness. We act surprised if any difficult spot ever comes.

One of my favorite theologians is Charles Schultz. If you do not know the theologian Charles Schultz, let me introduce him. He is the one who writes the "Peanuts" comic strips. In one of them, Charlie Brown and Lucy are engaged in conversation. Charlie Brown is telling Lucy his philosophy of life, and he says: "You know, life sometimes has its ups and its downs. Sometimes we're up and sometimes we're down." And Lucy, putting her hand on her hips, says: "Well, why should it be like that? Why should life sometimes be up and sometimes down? Why can't we go from one up to another up? And why can't I go from that up to an even higher up? And from that up, just up, up, up?" And Charlie Brown walks off, saying: "Good grief. I can't stand it."

There are too many of us in life who want to live like Lucy. We expect life always to be lived on the mountaintops, and never to have to walk in the valleys. We expect to go through life always with balmy, beautiful weather. We do not anticipate any storm or excessive heat. The weather of life will always be cool and nice. But life has its storms and difficulties. They are a part of life, and we need to learn to expect them. It rains on the just and the unjust.

After Jesus was baptized, and his Father said: "This is my beloved Son in whom I am well pleased," Jesus was immediately taken into the wilderness and experienced temptation. Even our Lord experienced times in the wilderness. He also warned his disciples that they would experience many kinds of wilderness experiences (Mark 13:9ff). So, we need to learn to expect these wildernesses as a part of life and not to be surprised when they confront us.

Use the Resources Around You

Second, we need to learn to use the resources we have around us. God instructed Moses and his people to eat of the migratory quail and to partake of the manna found on the Sinai Peninsula. They used the resources at hand. God's special blessing is often linked with our use of natural surroundings.

Notice that Jesus asked his disciples: "What have we got to eat in this crowd?" They said: "Only one lunch." Jesus said: "Bring it to me. This is enough." Then he took the small loaves and the few fish, blessed them, and distributed them to the disciples and the disciples to the people. And the multitude was fed.

No matter how meager our resources, God will bless their use. I think God expects us, when we get in our wildernesses in life, first to see what resources we have. It is amazing what resources you and I do have. So often we simply give up and say: "Oh, woe is me" or "Ain't it awful?" We do not try to find what resources we already have at hand. God is expecting you to use your mind, your heart, your strength, and whatever other means you have. For those who have lost their hearing, they may have learned to use their eyes and their hands better. For those who have lost their sight, they may have learned to use more effectively their ears and their hands. For those who have lost both, they may have learned to use other senses.

Let me give you an example of a beautiful woman in one of my former congregations. She was crippled with arthritis. She had to remain in a wheelchair and could almost never come to church. She seldom was able to go anywhere. I tried to visit her as often as I could, in order to give her some word of encouragement. When I would knock on her door, she would greet me, fling open the door, and, with a smile say: "Pastor, come in and let me tell you what I've been doing." Then she would proceed to tell me what she had been busy doing since I last saw her. She told me about the telephone calls she had made to cheer people who were sick and lonely; the letters she had written to college students; the cards she had mailed to shut-ins; and the bulletin articles, pastor's paragraphs, sermon excerpts, quotations from books, and readings she had shared with other people. She was crippled with arthritis; she could not walk; she could not leave home very often. But she was able to use the resources she had: the telephone, the pen, the letter, the gift of kindness, an understanding heart, and a joyful spirit. She was a radiant personality who had learned to use whatever limited resources she had.

Whatever kind of wilderness we are in, God expects us to learn to use the resources around us and within us.

God Is Concerned About Our Needs

Third, notice that both of these biblical accounts tell us about a God who is concerned with the bodily needs of persons. God was moved by the hunger of the Israelites, and Jesus had compassion on the crowd and fed them. God is aware of your hunger, pain, hurt, and other human needs. God is not interested in just your soul but with your total person—body, soul, and mind.

Your physical needs are important to God as they are real and significant to you. Jesus reminded us of God's care when he taught us to pray: "Give us this day our daily bread." Although Jesus refused to perform miracles of turning stones into bread to meet his own personal need, he did perform a miracle to feed the multitude. He has also reminded us that we have an obligation, no matter how small our resources are, to feed those who are without. "Inasmuch as we do it unto one of the least of these," we have done it unto him. God cares about our needs, and he challenges us to care for the needs of others.

You May Learn Something About Yourself

Fourth, when you find yourself in the wilderness, the amazing thing is that you might learn something about yourself that you did not know before. Jesus instructed the disciples to feed the people. They found they were unable to do so. They discovered their own inadequacies. In some of the translations of this New Testament passage from the Greek, it has been rendered that Jesus called his disciples to come apart to the wilderness "by yourselves." But the Greek word is "for yourselves." In this wilderness experience and this lonely place he reminds them and us: you may find out something about yourself that teaches you a lesson you have never known before. While wandering in the wilderness for forty years, the nation Israel learned about God's faithfulness, judgment, and covenant love. It was while the people of Israel were in the wilderness that they were bound firmly into a nation.

Do you know that sometimes God can only teach us lessons in the wilderness? That, unfortunately is the only place some of us ever learn them. In the brightness of the sunshine and in the joy of life, we almost seem to be unteachable. God cannot penetrate our thick skins and hard hearts. He has a difficult time communicating with us. I have learned in the churches where I have been a pastor to send a person who has had a grief experience and effectively come through it to talk to someone else who has a similar grief experience. Someone who has found the healing power of Christ can go to another and say, "I understand"—and really mean it. Those who have been in the wilderness of grief can help others find their way through it. Those who have experienced loneliness can understand the loneliness of others. Those who have known difficulties, frustration, sinfulness, guilt, forgiveness, and restoration can talk to others who have not yet found the path Christ gives through this kind of wilderness. Those who have found the presence of God in the wilderness can communicate that message to others.

I read about a dream a woman had several years ago. In her dream she saw a huge Christmas tree that stretched high into the heavens. She noticed that the tree was loaded down with all kinds of gifts and presents. She turned to a figure standing by her, who represented God, and asked: "Who are all these presents for?" "They are the gifts I wanted to give you in life," God responded, "but you were always too busy and preoccupied to receive them." Too often we are busy and God cannot touch our lives. Sometimes it is only in the wilderness where God can get our attention.

There is an old Eastern tradition that has turned one of our American sayings upside-down, and it goes like this: "Stop doing something; just stand there!" Some of us are never still long enough to hear God who wants to come into our lives. We never seek him until we are in some kind of wilderness. He wants to speak to us in our joy and in the light, and he is certainly present there. But some of us cannot hear him in the light. It is only when we come into the darkness, when our resources are so few, that some of us hear him.

You May Meet God in the Wilderness

Finally, the most important message taught in these Scripture passages is this: In the wilderness, we may meet God. The Bible has many images of our God. One of the great images is that of host: "Thou preparest a table before me in the presence of mine enemies." It is the God who fed the children of Israel as they wandered in their wilderness for forty years. God was the host who provided for their needs. Manna has become a metaphor for God's grace and providence. In Matthew's miracle story, which all the other Gospel writers record, we are told Jesus Christ meets us as the host in the wilderness experiences of life. God had fed Israel in the wilderness. The covenant God made with Israel had been sealed by a meal. The feeding of the multitude in the wilderness by Jesus was a sign of the messianic banquet for which all of Israel longed.

The meal also had eucharistic images of the Last Supper because Jesus took the bread, blessed it, broke it, and gave it to the disciples and they to the people. John's Gospel makes the symbolic message plainer: Jesus is himself "the bread of life." He is the one who feeds us and meets our basic needs. The "how" of the multiplication of the bread and fish cannot be explained scientifically. But the miracle or "sign" is accepted as a part of the tradition of the early church. The story points us to the one who is God's Messiah. "He who comes to me," Jesus said, "shall never hunger and he who believes in me shall never thirst" (John 6:35). In the wilderness, you and I may meet God. God comes to us, and we can feast upon his presence and find the power to go on.

The Scriptures do not tell us that God will keep us from getting into all kinds of wildernesses. We are not told that we may never be lonely, frustrated, or depressed, or experience grief or have other difficulties. But

God tells us this: There is absolutely nothing that can separate us from him when we are in Christ Jesus. There in the wilderness God comes to sustain us. When we walk through the dark valley, we are not alone, but we walk through it with the power and the presence of the God of the universe. In the wilderness places of life, you and I can meet God. He is seeking to come to us, to sustain us, to comfort us, to strengthen us.

A number of years ago on the southern coast of Wales, a man had reached the low point of his life and was at the point of committing suicide. He sat alone on the shore watching the waves as they broke on the sand and rocks. Finally he decided there was only one option open to him. He had lost his marriage, his money, his ministry, and his faith. At one time he had been a noted journalist and a minister, but now everything he had ever loved and held dear had collapsed. He sat in the sand, feeling he was a dismal failure. He threw himself into the water and began to swim out into the darkness of the night to let the waves swallow him. This was his way to commit suicide. Suddenly after he had been swimming a great distance, he cried: "Good God! What am I doing?" He turned around in the water and struggled back to the shore and collapsed on the sand in a convulsion of weeping. His mind flashed back to the times when he was a small boy and his mother tried to teach him about God. She would open the small catechism book and ask him: "Who is Jesus Christ?" And he found himself responding out loud: "Jesus Christ is my Savior." Suddenly, he said, a deep peace settled over him. There, where D. R. Davies had least expected to find God, in his own agony, he met him. "In the final anguish, hovering between life and death, I found myself, as I was, and in my utter nakedness and worthlessness I found God."[3]

Many of us, in the midst of the wilderness places of life, may find that God comes into our lives as never before. Now again I remind you that God is always trying to come to us in the bright, beautiful days, so we might sense his presence. But be assured of this: Whatever wilderness you are in now, or may be in the future, the great God of the universe, who has revealed himself in Jesus Christ, is there with you and he is seeking to strengthen you and sustain you. He never leaves you alone in your wilderness. He is there with you! May God give you and me the strength and the insight to sense his presence.

Notes

[1] Paul Tillich, *The Shaking of the Foundations* (New York: Charles Scribner's Sons, 1948), 162
[2] John Killinger, *The Loneliness of Children* (New York: Vanguard Press, 1980).
[3] D. R. Davies, *In Search of Myself* (London: Geoffrey Bles, 1961) 189-190.

Part 3
Pulpit and Pew Rediscovering Theology:
Preaching as a Ministry of the Word

Søren Kierkegaard, the Danish philosopher, told a striking parable about a preaching goose. This wild goose saw a flock of geese nibbling on some grain in a fenced lot on a farm. He flew down to where the other geese were and landed on the fence. From that vantage spot he got their attention and began to preach to them. He told them they were free creatures like he was and did not have to remain confined to a barnyard. They had mighty wings that would lift them above the fences, and they could fly high into the skies and visit distant lands. The geese listened attentively to the preaching goose and even applauded his oratory. But they did not follow him and fly out of the barnyard. They continued to remain inside the fence, feeding off the bits of grain they found and living in safety and security.

Our Lord has commissioned his disciples to go and preach the gospel in all the world. The gospel we have is a powerful message about God's grace, but too often we as preachers of this gospel have confined ourselves to a small fenced section, nibbling off scraps of the Word we discover from secondhand sources, and we never attempt to soar to the majestic heights of the gospel's splendor. Much that goes for biblical preaching is often a shallow glance at the obvious in the text or a tiptoe through an essay on easy living and how to feel better sooner or later. These sermonic dishes are often piled high with how to feel good about one's self and are often garnished with religious clichés, pious slogans, backslapping cheers, and trips down nostalgic lanes instead of confronting the hard—sometimes painful—questions about life. Some wit has observed that we know the gospel is true, because it has withstood so much bad preaching.

Instead of feeding off the kernels or particles of the Word, the preacher is challenged to serve the meat of the Word. The Scriptures are not shallow puddles but deep wells from which we can draw an endless supply of water to offer those who thirst after righteousness. Rather than confining ourselves to some corner of biblical familiarity, we can scale the highest summits of theological thoughts in the Scriptures. Brood over the great texts of the Bible and affirm with the Apostle Paul, "I did not shrink from declaring to you the whole counsel of God" (Acts 20:27). Our calling is not to be recognized as great preachers, but to preach a mighty gospel. With Paul, let the preacher declare forcefully: "I am not ashamed of the gospel of Christ" (Rom. 1:16).

The preacher must also believe in the power of preaching to communicate this great gospel. No one is going to become an effective preacher who does not really believe in preaching. God has chosen "the foolishness of preaching" (1 Cor. 2:4) as the medium to proclaim his mighty acts. Preaching is still the minister's primary duty, and all of his other labors enrich or inform that task. Our first calling is to preach the Word. We dare not fail to remember that Jesus "came preaching the good news of the kingdom of God" (Mark 1:14). And our Lord has commissioned his disciples to preach the gospel (Luke 9:2). Through the activity of the spoken word, the listener encounters the eternal Word.

The pulpit is the prow of the ship of Zion. Herman Melville in *Moby Dick* draws this image for us:

> The pulpit is ever this earth's foremost part; all the rest
> comes in the rear; the pulpit leads the world. From thence
> it is the storm of God's quick wrath is first described, and
> the bow must bear the earliest brunt. From thence it is
> the God of breezes fair or foul is first invoked for favor-
> able winds. Yes, the world is a ship on its passage out, and
> not a voyage complete; and the pulpit is its prow.[1]

One of the central ways to focus on the "high calling" of the preacher is to preach the cardinal doctrines of the faith. Burton Cooper and John McClure wrote their book, *Claiming Theology in the Pulpit*, to help "bring a preacher's theological knowledge and perspective . . . to bear upon biblical texts, and questions or issues arising from the world."[2] They raise serious concerns about the lack of "theology" in many preachers' sermons. Richard Lischer has noted that "although preaching is central to the life of the church, it has had to struggle continually against its exclusion from the church's self-reflection, its theology."[3] In *The Pastor as Theologian*, the contributors challenge the preacher to remember that effective pastoral ministry and theological reflection must depend on each other as a condition of authenticity.[4]

I don't see how a preacher can avoid preaching on doctrines. If he listens to the people in the pews, their questions are often doctrinal in nature and demand a theological response. As the pulpit listens to the questions that come from the congregation, there will be a rediscovery of a deep-seated theological need. Members of a congregation often ask their pastor:

- "Why do good people suffer?"
- "What have I done to deserve this pain?"
- "Can I be forgiven for what I have done?"
- "Why did God give my son cancer?"
- "How can I know the will of God?"
- "Does God hear my prayers?"
- "How do I know there is a God?"
- "Why did Jesus die?"
- "What do we mean by atonement?"
- "How was Jesus raised from the dead?"
- "Will I live after death?"
- "How do I become a Christian?"

These are theological questions that often arise out of the hurt, pain, sin, brokenness, and longings of the human heart. They are not abstract or theoretical questions, but come from the sobs of the human heart; out of the longing for truth or the desire to love and follow God. They demand a response from the preacher, one who takes the questions seriously and touches the need of her listener.

In a book in which several writers revisit Harry Emerson Fosdick's question, "What's the matter with preaching?" Mike Graves declares boldly that "theology is the matter (the problem) with our preaching because theology is no longer the matter (the substance) of our sermons, at least not in responsible ways!"[5] Tom Long also expresses concern that our proclamation today has lost the deep sense of the "good news" of the gospel. He notes that he means this "in the theological sense" about what God has done, is doing, or will do that makes a life-changing difference.[6]

The pulpit has to rediscover and utilize "the queen of the sciences" in communicating the gospel. Much of our modern preaching is heresy, because it has removed the central grain of the gospel and offers instead the "husks" of a mild form of Christianity, devoid of the mighty act of God revealed supremely in the life and death of Jesus Christ. Heinrich Ott, Karl Barth's successor in Basel, has reminded us that "theology is there for the sake of preaching" and that "theology is the conscience of preaching."[7] Theology and preaching are interwoven. Each needs and assists the other. A sermon without doctrinal content is not Christian preaching. William H. Willimon reminds the preacher:

> Preaching is a theological act, an attempt to do business with a God who speaks. It is also a theological act in that a sermon is God's attempt to do business with us through words . . . It is based upon the conviction that preaching is not about us—not about you the listener or about me the preacher. Preaching is about God and by God, or it is silly.[8]

Although David Buttrick has challenged some of Barth's high claim for preaching, he still affirms Barth's strong tie of theology and preaching. In fact, when Barth's lecture notes on preaching were translated and published in the United States, Buttrick wrote a foreword for the volume. Barth had affirmed that theology should be "nothing other than sermon preparation." In concluding his observations in the foreword, Buttrick observes: "Barth's thoughtful wrestling with homiletic definitions and issues is still worthy of attention because, to reverse Barth's own claim, sermon preparation after all is nothing other than theology."[9]

The preacher often excuses herself for not preaching directly on Christian doctrine by saying, "Well, I'm not a theologian." You may not be a professional or academic theologian of the caliber of Karl Barth, Paul Tillich, Hans Küng, Douglas John Hall, Rosemary Radford Ruether, or Wolfhart Pannenberg, but you are indeed a theologian. You are either an informed or uninformed one, a good theologian or a bad one.

In their book, *The Pastor as Theologian*, Shelp and Sunderland remind every preacher that he is indeed a theologian. Our congregations are taught—well or poorly—most of their theology through the minister's sermons. Much of our listener's theology is learned in a worship context through the sermon, hymns, anthems, prayers, and responses. Although he has not considered preaching adequately in his 583-page book, *Doxology: The Praise of God in Worship, Doctrine and Life,* Geoffrey Wainwright has written the first systematic theology based on the church's worship practices.[10] Our theology, good or bad, is acquired for the most part in our experience of worship.

The preacher who, with pretended modesty, attempts to ignore the theological dimension of her preaching does so only at the peril of the congregation. This disclaimer says in essence: "Don't ask me any questions about the faith or about your struggles in life. I can't answer them; I'm only a pastor." But just as people go to their doctor for medicine when they are physically ill, they seek out their pastor when they have spiritual questions or problems. What is the minister's business if it is not to respond helpfully to his congregation's needs?

The Apostle Paul's letters arose out of his relationship to the struggles and questions of young churches in Asia Minor. The Gospels were composed originally by their authors in response to the early church's need to know more about the life and teachings of Jesus. The writings of Clement, Ignatius, Polycarp, Justin, Augustine, Gregory, Luther, Calvin, Schleiermacher, and Jonathan Edwards and the formative thought of Walter Rauschenbusch, Karl Barth, and Reinhold Niebuhr all come out of the responses of these pastors to the questions and needs they experienced with their congregations. We, of course, may not express our theologies as they did, but we have to accept the reality that every pastor is the principal theologian for his congregation.

No matter what our training or experience, we all feel inadequate for this task. We often feel like one of the students in Elton Trueblood's classes in philosophy at Earlham College some years ago. At the end of the semester the young man had not turned in fourteen papers. When the professor told him he was failing and asked for a reason why he failed to turn in his papers, the student gave this classic reply: "My standard of excellence is so high that I cannot bear to hand in the poor things of which I am capable."

Let's confess it early in our ministry: No one is an expert on God. No preacher or theologian or anyone else can legitimately claim that he sees from God's perspective. No one is sufficient to claim that he alone has the only correct interpretation about the vast riches of the Christian gospel or about the nature of God or the final insight into the totality of the Christian faith and doctrines. We always look at truth and life with eyes clouded with ignorance, fear, superstition, and prejudice. But speak we must. We seek to offer to God and our congregations the best we can—after careful thought, study, prayer, and listening to our people. This awareness of our own limitations and weaknesses demands from us excellence and professionalism. King David said before he offered a burnt offering to God, "I will not offer to the Lord burnt offerings which cost me nothing" (2 Sam. 24:24).

Robert Lifton has reminded us that the root idea of the word "profession" originally meant "a personal form of out-front public acknowledgement." This original meaning focused on personal commitment, advocacy, renewal, and enhanced sensitivity. Until the sixteenth century, that which was acknowledged had to do with religion. This word became secularized and came to mean that a person was professional when she was an expert or proficient in an enterprise of any kind.[11] Of all persons, the minister needs to recover the true sense of "profession" and demonstrate sensibility to her calling and people. Up front we confess our limitations, but we also offer to God and our congregation the best gifts we are capable of rendering.

The preacher also acknowledges that the gospel she proclaims is filtered through her personality. There is a gospel according to Matthew, Mark, Luke, and John. Each one of these writers communicated the gospel through his grasp of it. Likewise, there is a gospel according to you. Each preacher communicates her sense of that message. I believe this was what Paul was saying when he wrote "according to *my* gospel" (Rom. 2:16, 2 Tim. 2:8). There is *the* gospel, but it was essential for Paul and is essential for us that we speak of "my gospel." As Keats said, "Nothing ever becomes real till it is experienced. Even a proverb is no proverb to you till it is experienced." "The" gospel has to possess the preacher until it becomes "my" gospel. Only then can we share it with another. Every congregation deserves a pastor who knows God other than by hearsay. Knowing God's love personally, the preacher communicates that experience of love with others. We cannot preach what we have not experienced.

Robert W. Dale, minister of Carr's Lane Congregational Church in Birmingham, England, was working on his Easter sermon one day, according to the reminiscences of his assistant, George Barber, when the reality of the resurrection of Jesus broke in upon Dale's thought in a vivid manner. It transformed his preaching and outlook. The gospel was now his gospel. He expressed this transformation like this:

> Christ is alive! I said to myself; alive! and then I paused—alive! And then I paused again; alive! Can that really be true? living as really as I myself am? I got up and walked about repeating "Christ is living!" "Christ is living!" At first it seemed strange and hardly true, but at last it came upon me as a burst of sudden glory; yes, Christ is living. It was to me a new discovery. I thought that all along I had believed

it; but not till that moment did I feel sure about it. I then said, "My people shall know it; I shall preach about it again and again until they believe it, as I do now." For months afterwards and in every sermon, the Living Christ was his one great theme; and then began the custom at Carr's Lane on every Sunday morning of singing an Easter hymn.[12]

Before the preacher can convince others, he has to be empowered by the gospel, believe in its power, and be gripped by the authority of Christ. A preacher will have no "authority" unless he preaches not only the gospel, but also a gospel of his own. Having experienced the incarnate presence of God in Christ, we imperfectly try to model through our lives and words the incarnation we have known. With John we declare: "What we have seen and heard we proclaim to you also" (1 John 1:3).

Reasons for Preaching Christian Doctrine

It seems in some ways strange to raise the question, "Why should a minister preach Christian doctrine?" But a sampling of sermons from congregations across our country will show only a minimal impact of theology on the sermons preached in these churches.[13] The call to preach doctrinal sermons is not an attempt to focus on every passing theological fad such as the secular city, the death of God, hope, play, liberation, story, narrative, or the new quest for the historical Jesus. Instead it is an imperative for proclaiming the foundation of our faith. Theology first arose out of preaching and is continually taught through preaching. The preacher has been sent to proclaim not his opinion but the gospel message. I'm sure there are more, but I would summarize the reasons for doctrinal preaching under three headings: to preserve the faith, to communicate the church's faith, and to clarify the faith.

Preserve the Faith

Faith is used here in the sense of what constitutes the biblical heritage and basic Christian doctrines. Church members cannot share with others what they do not know or understand themselves about the faith. The congregation must first be taught the great doctrines of the faith. It is almost embarrassing to hear some church members talk about what they believe. Many of their theological concepts are so vague or ambiguous, they struggle to verbalize any kind of clear statements about what they believe.

From the beginning of the Christian church, preaching and teaching were vitally linked. Preaching by necessity carries with its nature a teaching dimension. Converts have to be taught the Christian gospel and what constitutes the Christian way of life. A new Christian must become as Paul says in 2 Corinthians a "new creation," but that "new creature" is not instantly mature in the faith. Just as doctrinal teaching was essential in leading a person to an awareness of Christ and his redemption, so doctrinal teaching is necessary to guide that individual further into a knowledge of the Christlike way. Preaching should always have a strong doctrinal element.

The New Testament scholar, Frank Stagg, argued forcefully against making a distinction between the New Testament concept of *didache* (preaching) and *kerugma* (teaching):

> No sharp distinction between preaching and teaching is to be found in the New Testament. From the earliest days *kerugma* (what was preached) and *didache* (what was taught) together made up *euangelion* (the gospel). Although no sharp distinction is to be made between *kerugma* and *didache*, preaching and teaching, some difference in emphasis is to be observed.[14]

Stagg noted that the early Christians were continuing to teach and evangelize daily (Acts 5:42). Paul, Barnabas, and others were preaching and teaching in Antioch (Acts 15:35). The teaching ministry Paul refers to in Ephesians 4:11 is linked with the work of the pastor. Jesus' followers were called disciples, which means learners. "Doctrinal preaching takes the category of tradition seriously," C. Colt Anderson argues in his book, *Christian Eloquences: Contemporary Doctrinal Preaching*, "both in terms of how we receive and how we pass on God's revelation given in the person of Jesus Christ."[15] Anyone who follows Jesus seeks to be taught how to walk more fully in his way. We follow our Lord who "came preaching" and challenged his disciples to "go and preach."

All authentic preaching bears a teaching component. The pastor is normally the chief teacher in a congregation. He is not the only teacher, but by training and usually by experience normally assumes that role. More than a hundred years ago John Broadus, the distinguished teacher of preaching, observed:

> Doctrine, i.e., teaching, is the preacher's chief business. Truth is the life-blood of piety, without which we cannot maintain its vitality or support its activity. And to teach men truth, or to quicken what they already know into freshness and power, is the preacher's great means of doing good.[16]

Let me offer a word of caution to the preacher: Do not minimize or trivialize the great beliefs of our faith in seeking to communicate the gospel. Some preachers seem more intent on entertaining their listeners than teaching the rich meaning of the Christian faith. Barbara Brown Taylor shares an experience that illustrates this point vividly:

> I listened to an Easter sermon once in which the preacher stood up in front of a church full of people hungry for good news and told us Easter bunny jokes, one after another. He never met our eyes. He looked up at the light fixtures as he delivered his punch lines, never noticing how we laughed less each time. Finally he said something about how Easter was God's joke on death and we should all laugh more. Then he said Amen and sat down. I have never in my life wished so badly for pulpit police. I wanted someone with a badge to go up and arrest that guy, slap some handcuffs on him, and lead him away.[17]

Through doctrinal preaching a congregation deepens its biblical and spiritual knowledge and fortifies its knowledge of and dependence upon God. A part of the great commission of Jesus was the command "to teach" his disciples (Matt. 28:20). As someone has observed, "The Christian faith is always one generation away from extinction." Unless the current Christian community teaches the Christian doctrines to its family and contemporaries, the message will not be carried forward. Our Christian heritage is preserved through the lives changed by the preaching of the Word of Life.

Communicate the Church's Faith

If the gospel message is going to reach a person, it has to be communicated through some channel. Throughout the centuries Christian preachers have drawn on the symbols, images, and vocabulary of the church's theological traditions to share the gospel with others. There is no way this can be done effectively, even if the language and style of the communicator is conducive to the contemporary setting, without some reference to or use of theological language. Though they may be translated differently or only alluded to, the theological words themselves or images that convey their meaning through graphic story or pictures cannot be avoided without distorting the gospel. Through words or pictorial images the great doctrinal "symbols" such as faith, grace, sin, salvation, creation, conversion, atonement, church, and eternal life are essential to witness to the Christian faith.

Any attempt to strip away or substitute a new vocabulary that denies or ignores the historic language of the Christian traditions is doomed to failure. This is like discarding the diamonds in a mine for the common stones that encase them. P. T. Forsyth in his monumental work, *Positive Preaching and the Modern Mind*, captures that truth this way:

> I cannot conceive a Christianity to hold the future without words like grace, sin, judgment, repentance, incarnation, atonement, redemption, justification, sacrifice, faith, and eternal life. No words of less volume than these can do justice to the meaning of God, however easy their access to the minds of modern men.[18]

The great doctrinal words of the faith are essential to bear witness to the faith. The preacher's purpose in preaching is not only to make people feel better about themselves or to have a greater sense of self-esteem, but also to bear witness to God's unique expression of self-love disclosed through Jesus Christ. The preacher is not merely giving a theological lecture about God, but is seeking to convict and convert his listeners. This is the evangelistic imperative: "Go therefore and make disciples of all the nations" (Matt. 28:19).

Jesus said he had come to seek and to save the lost (Luke 19:10). The Gospel of John reminds us that Christ revealed how much God loved the world and that he came not to condemn the world but that the world might be saved (John 3:17). Through our preaching we declare the redemptive activity of God's grace. Broadly speaking, David Buttrick has stated his conviction that "the purpose of preaching is the purpose of God in Christ, namely the reconciliation of the world."[19] We have been commissioned to carry forward the redeeming message and ministry of Christ into the world. We labor to bring reconciliation within the lives of persons with themselves, with other people, and with God. As Paul reminds us, we have been given "the ministry of reconciliation" (2 Cor. 5:18).

Preaching communicates the gospel so that a decision will be made in the life of the listener. A sermon, H. H. Farmer wrote, has failed "unless it carries to the serious hearer something of a claim upon, or summons to, his will, to his whole being . . . A sermon . . . should have something of the quality of a knock on the door."[20] We preach in anticipation of a response from the one hearing the gospel. This is evident in our summons to repentance, faith, and a commitment to follow Christ. This does not imply that there will always be a positive response to our preaching. Often the listener may refuse to "hear" the message of redemption and reject or ignore it. But this refusal does not remove our basic responsibility to proclaim the good news of God's redemption in hope of a positive response.

The New Testament makes an astounding claim for the gospel: It is the power of God unto salvation (Rom. 1:16). The preacher has seen evidence in the changed lives of people by the persuasive power of preaching. Doctrinal content is as essential to evangelistic preaching as steel girders are to the stability of a tall building. Persons are not persuaded to respond in a vacuum. They must know Christ by first hearing about him through the proclamation of the gospel. This has to entail theological content.

The parables of Jesus, although told as stories, are filled with doctrinal content. How can a person hear the parable of the prodigal son and the loving father and not hear the theological messages about sin and grace? His parables illustrate a graphic way to communicate theological truth about God without being confined to abstract language.

Now do not misunderstand my insistence on doctrinal preaching as a summons to accept a list of theological propositions about God and Christ. We have failed to communicate if we lead the hearer merely to assent to a set number of theological propositions. Our doctrines are means, instruments, or vehicles to persuade persons to meet the living God in a personal encounter. Doctrines are not a means in themselves but an avenue to confront the God who was revealed in Christ. The purpose of preaching doctrinal sermons is to communicate the possibility of the listener's personal encounter with God. We are concerned with the *sitz im Leben*. The end goal is knowledge *of* God that is personal, not knowledge *about* God that is secondhand.

Robert Dale has reminded us that the city of God has twelve gates and everyone of them is a gate of pearl. We are not to presume there is only one gate through which a person can enter into the presence of God. He encourages persons to enter by the gate nearest to them.[21] Our preaching strives to open that gate so the listener can confront the God who has already reached out to meet her. We announce, awaken, and point persons to God. It is God they need to meet—and not settle for our descriptions of or directions to him.

Clarify the Faith

This is the apologetic dimension of preaching. The preacher takes seriously the instruction of Peter, "Always be ready to give a defense to everyone who asks you a reason for the hope that is in you" (1 Pet. 3:15). Paul Scott Wilson reminds the preacher that "good teaching is a necessary and profound asset for any pulpit."[22] The preacher engages in an unending dialogue with those to whom she preaches. Their questions, doubts, fears, hopes, and longings are a catalyst that drives her back for a word from the Lord. The preacher also listens carefully to the questions that arise outside the church from the secular world. We cannot respond to questions we have not heard or refuse to take seriously.

The discoveries of modern science and medicine; the insights of psychologists; the advancements and inventions of a secular society; the problems of evil, suffering, grief, and death; the questions about the meaning of life; and countless other voices challenge the pulpit today. The modern apologist will need much wisdom and skill to try to answer the questions arising out of contemporary society. But to ignore these questions is to flee into useless chatter about issues seldom on the minds of your congregation. What a tragedy it would be for ministers to hide behind their stained-glass windows and close their ears to the world shouting to be heard outside the church walls.

John Killinger tells about the consternation of a young priest who spent four years at Vatican II and went to Paris to attend a meeting of bishops and theologians. The meeting took place in one of the comfortable hotels of the city. The purpose of this meeting was to discuss the geometrical design of the Pall, which is the little piece of cloth (sometimes it is cardboard covered with cloth) used to cover the chalice in the Mass. In the midst of the discussion the noise in the street became so loud that the churchmen had difficulty concentrating. One of the bishops rose and closed the wooden shutters on the window to insulate them from the noise outside so they could continue their discussion. "Do you know what the noise was?" asked the priest. "Do you know what the clatter was coming from? It was the student revolution of May 1968!"[23]

It should not be surprising, Killinger observes, that this priest is highly critical of the structures of his church.

We shut the noise of the world out of our church offices and sanctuaries at a great price. When we fail to hear the noise—outcries and inner pleas—of men and women in the real world, we are likely turning ourselves away from the God "who so loved the world that he sent his only begotten Son."

The preacher's challenge is to announce and clarify the good news about God. What the world needs from us is not a judgmental voice denouncing its sinfulness, but an ear that hears painful cries and aching sobs and responds with a word of hope and love. The young and old struggle daily with perplexing questions about life and religion. They should be able to look to the pulpit as a place that will take seriously their perplexity and offer a word of understanding, guidance, encouragement, and hope. As an apologist for the Christian gospel, you will not have all the answers, but you do need to take seriously the questions and needs communicated to you. Feel the heartbeat of humanity and respond. Don't offer your hearers abstract doctrines; instead, offer Christ who is available today. "It is good," declared Phillips Brooks, "to be a Herschel who describes the sun, but it is better to be a Prometheus who brings the sun's fire to earth."

As you prepare doctrinal sermons, hear the voice of a teenager in your congregation who queries, "Tell me what God is like." Hear the plea of the ashen-faced man who holds his dead child in his arms and sobs, "Why did God take my baby?" Hear the words of the college student who wonders, "How can I know God's will for my life?" Hear the young woman who asks, "Why did God permit a graduate student to kill twelve people and wound fifty-eight others in a movie theater in Aurora, Colorado?" Hear the many questions: "How is Jesus the Son of God?" "What does the Trinity mean?" "Can there be life after death?" "Why didn't God prevent 9/11 from happening?" "Why does God allow devastating hurricanes like Katrina to kill so many people and do so much damage?"

Do you remember the story about the company of gypsies who followed Borrow crying, "Give us God." Fumbling in his pocket, he offered them some coins. But the gypsies threw them away. "We don't want money," they cried. "Give us God." When you sit down to offer an apology for the faith, hear the hurts of the people and feel their sobering plea: "Give us God."

Approaches to Preaching Doctrinal Sermons

We can preach doctrine in a variety of ways. The following list does not pretend to be all-inclusive, but is presented only as suggestions for a lifetime pilgrimage of learning new and more effective ways of proclaiming the good news. As preachers of the Word, we affirm with Paul: "We do not preach ourselves, but Christ Jesus the Lord, and ourselves your servants for Jesus' sake" (2 Cor. 4:5).

Indirect

You will preach doctrines indirectly in all your sermons. Frankly, it would be difficult not to address some theological theme in almost any sermon. Whether it is an Easter, Christmas, expository, ethical, or life-situation sermon, some Christian doctrine will be stated or implied. A baptismal or communion sermon has doctrinal roots that can arise out of the biblical text or interpretation of the ordinance. For example, the following is an indirect doctrinal statement about Christ I made in a Communion sermon titled, "The Abiding Presence":

> John 1:17 reads, "Grace and truth came through Jesus Christ." The word for truth is translated by James Moffatt as "reality." "Grace and *reality* came through Jesus Christ." Jesus Christ has come as the reality of God among us. For us, he represented the real, authentic presence of God in our world, and he is still real with us today. We do not focus just on a memory. We have not come to this table merely to reflect, to think, and be thankful. We gather to celebrate that Jesus Christ is a living Lord with us. We commune not with a memory but with the real presence of Christ who is here with us. My point is not that he is present in the elements. The elements are symbolic of the real Christ who is here with us in our lives.

This is a theological statement about the eternal presence of Christ. It is a way of preaching doctrine indirectly, and we all will do this in some fashion in our preaching. The only way to avoid preaching on doctrines is to give a long series of bumper-sticker clichés. And even these statements may be a type of theology—as poor or shallow as they might be. But surely every preacher wants to attempt to express her thoughts with theological accuracy.

When John Claypool, in a confessional sermon, "Casting Out Fear," confronted the mysterious "knockings in the night," he had assurance, which is theologically sound, that "even if the presence at the door turns out to be a foe, there is only so much he can do to me. He cannot destroy what is most important about me—my rootage in God, the source of all life and joy."[24] Claypool underscored the providence of God's grace. Every preacher will want to work to improve his doctrinal awareness so that he will not be hazy in his thought even when his theological observation is only touched on incidentally. Here the presentation arises out of the biblical text at hand.

Systematic

Effective doctrinal preaching requires long-range study. Though a preacher will perhaps preach doctrines indirectly in most sermons, a more systematic and carefully planned approach will make your preaching more informed and meaningful to your congregation. Select a doctrinal theme you want to study more carefully, and then choose some books to read in that area of thought.

Suppose you decide to study, for example, the meaning of Christian revelation. You might consult copies of books such as H. Richard Niebuhr's *The Meaning of Revelation*, Emil Brunner's *Revelation and Reason,* or Eric Rust's *Religion, Revelation and Reason.* As you read these books, note in a journal the major themes or ideas that stand out to you. Mark significant quotes, insights, or helpful images that would make that doctrine come alive. If a series of sermons is suggested by your study, separate the emphases and make notes under each heading.

As you read about revelation, you will struggle with how God makes the divine presence known to us, how we experience God, the role of reason and feelings, whether or not humans can prove the existence of God, revelation through nature, the special revelation of God in Jesus Christ, the role of the Bible in revealing God, progressive revelation, revelation in history—especially Israel's history—revelation and other world religions, the role of God's Spirit in revelation, and many other themes. The vastness of the subject will impress upon your mind a broad variety of possibilities for preaching on this subject. Scripture texts will be discovered that will make a solid base for your sermon. This will demand discipline, planning, and thoughtful study.

I would encourage you to dig into one or more of the writings of a major theologian rather than drawing on secondhand versions of their thought. Draw water from the deep wells of John and D. M. Baillie, Barth, Brunner, Bultmann, Tillich, H. R. and Reinhold Niebuhr, Rauschenbusch, Schleiermacher, Kierkegaard, Forsyth, Otto, Temple, Bonhoeffer, Küng, Pannenberg, Moltmann, C. S. Lewis, Thielicke, Don Browning, Douglas John Hall, Rosemary Ruether, and others. This will demand a lifetime of reading, and for many preachers will be taken only in small doses. But when carefully taken, the preacher will deepen her own spiritual knowledge and will enrich her preaching profoundly. Granted, some of this reading will not and should not be passed on to your congregation without a careful translation into the vernacular.

I try to purchase as many of the books I can that I want to study. This enables me to read them at my pace, mark them, and reflect on them. When I preach, I try not to quote too many heavy passages from these writings. If I find a clear, short, and helpful quote, I will use it, however. As John Oman observed: "Preach with authority, not with authorities."[25] Absorb your mind in the writings of these theologians and digest their thoughts until they become translated into your own. Then, what you share will be informed but still your own.

Result of Bible Study

Many of your theological insights will arise naturally out of careful Bible study. My theological studies make my biblical exegesis come alive, and my exegetical work enlightens my study of theology. In this way, all sermons become doctrinal preaching. I could not possibly divorce theological thought from sermon preparation of any kind. A sermon is not a theological treatise, but it is not a valid sermon if it is not theologically sound. Likewise, no sermon can be theologically sound and be unbiblical. Our theological insight should arise out of the text for the sermon. This will demand thorough Bible study.

Suppose you decide to focus on Paul's epistle to the Ephesians for your Bible study. I would suggest that you begin your study several months in advance of the time you plan to preach. Read through the epistle in several translations. Make notes in a notebook. Jot down thoughts or ideas for preaching that come to you. You may begin to notice that your thoughts have fallen into several divisions such as doctrinal, ethical, or topical. Then consult several commentaries. I usually begin by reading through one or two commentaries in their entirety and then consulting others on a section-by-section basis. I make marginal notes, underline key phrases, and put notations in my notebook. I list again any sermon thoughts or ideas that have come out of my study. I have found it helpful to spread my study over several months to give myself time to reflect and let the thought simmer on the back burner of my mind.

In Ephesians many themes seem apparent. But the preacher needs to focus on selected key words or themes. Having discovered what you believe is the biblical theme (or themes) you want to direct your attention upon, set the boundaries of the portion of Scripture you want to be your basic text for that sermon or sermons. There seem to be seven central themes in Ephesians that could be the source for a series of seven sermons:

1. The Eternal Purpose (1:1-10)
2. Unity in Christ (3:8-10)
3. The Church (3:14-21)
4. The Gospel of Grace (2:1-10)
5. Imperatives of Christian Living (4:17-5:21)
6. The Christian Family (5:21-6:9)
7. The Christian Conflict (6:10-20)

These suggested themes can in no way exhaust the richness of this epistle. Doctrinal sermons could be preached under various categories. For example, an expository sermon on "The Whole Armor of God" (6:10-15) could be the focus. Each piece of the spiritual equipment forms the base for a division of the sermon:

- "The Girdle of Truth"
- "The Breastplate of Righteousness"
- "The Sandals of Peace"
- "The Shield of Faith"
- "The Helmet of Salvation"
- "The Sword of the Spirit"

There are two essential focuses for preaching on any biblical text. One is to determine the original meaning of the text and the meaning that is possible in our contemporary setting. The preacher has to be concerned with what the original writer was trying to say then—in the past event—and in what analogous way the text addresses us today. The then and now are both essential for effective biblical preaching. We try to proclaim what is already implicit in the Word of God. As persons were addressed by God centuries ago by the original thrust of the preaching of this passage, so today we are confronted by the power of its message.

Listen again to P. T. Forsyth. "But the great reason why the preacher must return continually to the Bible is that the Bible is the greatest sermon in the world," he writes. "Above every other function of it the Bible is a sermon, a *Knpugga*, a preachment. It is the preacher's book because it is the preaching book."[26] The Bible is the Word of God that points men and women to Christ, the living Word of God. And study it we must.

Address Human Needs

Doctrinal sermons should be preached to address the human needs of our listeners. As Andrew Blackwood, the noted teacher of preaching for many years at Princeton Theological Seminary, observed: "In the pulpit the stress ought to fall, not on explaining a doctrine, but on meeting a need, and that by preaching a truth about God."[27]

Our preaching is bifocal. It is concerned with the Word of God that is communicated and secondly the people who are addressed by that Word. It is not enough to get a subject off your mind through a spoken word. Our congregation needs to be helped personally by that word. The listeners have a right to know what that particular doctrine has to do with their everyday lives. It does not matter whether or not it is biblical if they cannot grasp what it has to do with them and their world. "The sermon that correlates the hunger of the congregation with the rich sustenance of systematic theology presented creatively," Ronald Allen observes, "can nourish the understanding of the congregation, strengthen the heart of the community, and swell the glory the people give to God."[28]

The experience of the three disciples with Jesus on the Mount of Transfiguration might be helpful here. Peter wanted to remain on the mountaintop, to build three tents and savor that exalted experience. But Jesus told him and the other disciples they could not remain on the mountaintop, but they had to leave and go down into the valley below where a person in need was waiting to be helped. Some preachers are tempted to remain on the mountaintop of profound religious thought, rich in symbols and mystery, and refuse to come down into the ordinary streets and paths in the valley where regular folks live. We are called not to remain on mountaintops and hide the gospel inside sacred, verbal tents of theological abstraction. Instead, we are charged with the responsibility of folding our theological tents and coming down the mountainside to the valley below and communicating clearly to help heal the brokenness of hurting men and women. We cannot do this if our listeners do not understand our message about God because it is covered over with pious, nonsensical verbiage.

Some years ago I preached my first sermon on the Ascension of Jesus. I have preached many sermons on the crucifixion and resurrection of Jesus, but for some reason I had avoided speaking on the Ascension. As I studied Acts 1:9-11 and Galatians 2:20 and theological works on the Ascension, I slowly warmed to the study. My excitement grew as I began to see the relationship of this doctrine to life. In my introduction to this sermon titled "What About Christ Today?" I stated:

> The Ascension of Jesus focuses on the reality of the presence of Jesus Christ in the world today. It is the New Testament's audacious way of proclaiming that Christ is the Eternal Contemporary. Rather than the cloud of departure obscuring the picture of Jesus for the disciples, it made clear to them the way he was to be present to them in the future.

My sermon unfolded with three basic movements of thought as I examined the following question:

> What then did the Ascension mean to the early church? To begin with, the Ascension was a strong statement about the glorification of Jesus Christ. As God's Incarnate Son, Jesus lived in our world as a human being. But, following his crucifixion and resurrection, it was obvious that the body of Jesus was already different. It had become a spiritual body.
>
> But the Ascension portrays more than that. The Ascension also represents the continuous presence of Christ in the world. "It was expedient," Jesus said, "that he should go away" (John 16:7). It was "expedient," because as long as Christ remained in his earthly body, in one particular place, he could not be the Universal Spirit and be present everywhere in the world and available to all persons (John 14:16, 15:26).

The Ascension of Christ represents even more. In the ringing words of Galatians 2:20, Paul declares that God is continuing the work of the crucified and risen Christ. What God accomplished in Jesus Christ is still available to men and women today.

I concluded the sermon with these words of challenge and assurance:

> Christ is not a figure trapped in the past; he is not contained in an ancient book or in a remote land. He is the eternal contemporary who confronts you and me in our need and leads us to God. Luther's refrain is still correct. "I care not whether he be the Christ, but whether he is the Christ to you." Who is Jesus Christ to you? You must decide and respond. His spirit will continuously beckon you to give him your allegiance.

I know you cannot tell a great deal about the flow and development of thought in this sermon from this brief outline. But the one factor I am trying to call to your attention at this point was my effort to make the sermon relevant to the lives of my listeners.

No matter what the doctrine is, we should seek to communicate its truth in a way that touches our listeners. We are heralding a message about an event that changed the world and continues to change lives today. May our doctrinal sermons pulsate with the power of the gospel to change the lives of men and women today. Preach so they can be forgiven of their sins, have their burdens of guilt lifted, their brokenness made whole, their sorrows borne by another, and their faith strengthened. This type of doctrinal preaching will be listened to and will transform those who hear the message proclaimed.

Follow the Church Year

One clear way to preach some doctrinal sermons is to follow the church year. The set observances and special seasons of the Christian calendar continue on a regular pattern year after year. These occasions offer the minister and the congregation times of joy and satisfaction as they focus together on major observances throughout the year. One of the great advantages in following the Christian calendar in your preaching is that it gives you an opportunity to present the gospel message with a sense of wholeness. Rather than picking a doctrine out and stressing its importance in isolation from others, by following the church year you look at the total story and show how each doctrine you preach is tied in with the whole Christian story. As you move through the church year, beginning with Advent and Christmas, Epiphany, the Lenten season and Easter, Pentecost, Ascension, Whitsuntide and Trinity, and back to Advent again, you have preached on the major themes of the Christian faith.

Many preachers who observe faithfully the church year in their preaching follow the lectionary.[29] The lectionary not only provides the theme emphasis for the particular Sunday on the Christian calendar, but also gives several Scripture lessons for each Sunday. This layout furnishes the preacher with both the doctrinal emphasis and the biblical base for study. You also join a large element of the Christian community who follow the Christian calendar faithfully in their preaching.

I have never personally followed the church year in a rigid way. Instead I have focused on selective emphases throughout the church calendar year. This method has fit more comfortably into my approach to preaching and has served more effectively the congregations where I have been pastor. I have always tried to follow Advent and Christmas and Lent and Easter emphases with a special series of sermons for each occasion. Although the sermons may appear to be topical, the underlying theme is doctrinal. How can a minister preach about Christmas—the occasion of the Incarnation—and the sermons not be doctrinal? Here are the sermon titles from a series I did one time for the Advent season:

"The Advent of Hope"	(Ps. 131, Rom. 15:4-13)
"The Gospel According to Mary"	(1 Sam. 2:1-10, Luke 1:39-56)
"Christmas and the Beast"	(Isa. 40:9-11, Matt. 2:18-20)
"In the Mood for Christmas?"	(Judg. 13:8-11, Matt. 2:1-3)
"The Wrong Side of Christmas"	(Ps. 72:1-8, Acts 8:26-40)

A church I served always observed a Hanging of the Greens Service, a Christmas Eve Communion service, and several special Christmas programs with children, youth, and adult choirs presenting sacred music. Through the spoken word, symbols, and music we proclaimed the mystery and wonder of Christmas.

The Sundays leading up to Easter also provide a grand occasion to focus on one of the central doctrinal themes of the Christian faith: the cross and the resurrection. Some time ago I preached a series of sermons on the Seven Words from the Cross. Here are their titles:

"A Prayer of Forgiveness"	(Luke 23:26-34)
"The Promise That Life Goes On"	(Luke 23:39-42)
"Words of Human Devotion"	(John 19:26-27)
"The Cry of Dereliction"	(Matt. 27:46-48)
"The Haunting Voice of Human Need"	(John 19:28-29)
"The Triumphant Shout"	(John 19:30)
"The Prayer of Trust"	(Luke 23:44-46
"Easter: The Final Word"	(John 20:26-31)

Again these sermons may appear to be topical or textual, but they are no doubt doctrinal sermons. Occasions such as these offer the preacher a wonderful opportunity to draw the minds of those in your congregation to a theme they are already in a sense anticipating because of the approach of Easter.

Sometimes I follow more carefully a section of the lectionary to guide my preaching. Whether or not you use the lectionary, I want to encourage you to follow as much as possible some part, if not all, of the church calendar. This discipline will guide your preaching along more doctrinal lines as you plan your preaching.

Concentrate on Theological Themes

Another helpful approach to preaching doctrinal sermons is to focus directly on selected theological themes. As I mentioned above, you can always do this at Advent/Christmas and at Lent/Easter. After listening to my people and determining some of the needs of individual members of my congregation or the congregation as a whole, I have focused in on certain theological issues. I try to work at this emphasis in advance to give myself an opportunity to purchase theology books and read widely in this area. I don't think good preaching can be rushed. We all need time to read and reflect.[30]

There are many examples of doctrinal areas where a preacher could focus that are not addressed by the church calendar, such as the doctrines of man, sin, forgiveness, creation, the Fall, providence, prayer, and the meaning of human existence. Let me suggest a few among many you might select for preaching purposes.

The Doctrine of God. At some point every preacher must state in some way his belief about God. You surely can't preach if you don't believe in God. J. S. Whale said that a young minister called one day on William Stubbs, bishop of Oxford, and asked his advice about preaching. The bishop was silent for a moment and then replied: "Preach about God; and preach about twenty minutes."[31]

Undergirding all of our theology is our belief about God. Every other belief we hold is colored by our perception of the reality of God. This is also true for the laypersons in our congregations. But to many of them, God is an oblong blur. God's reality and nature need to be drawn more clearly into focus by the preacher. This, of course, is no easy task.[32]

In a sermon series I preached on the question of "What is God like?" I introduced the first sermon, "Making God in Our Human Image," this way:

> The way some people talk about God, it would seem that he is "a vague, oblong blur." The image appears so unclear in their minds that God is devoid of any real meaning or significance. Most people say they believe in God, but when asked to tell what they think God's nature and activity are like, they are at a loss for words. Can it be true that many believe in "something" that is not clear or adequate for a sound faith?

The other sermons in the series included the following titles:

- "On Studying God"
- "The Idea of Holiness"
- "If We Are Faithless, God Remains Faithful"
- "A Love That Will Not Let Us Go"
- "Jesus Called God 'Father'"
- "The God of Persons"

I built another series around the theme, "The Creator and the New Creation," with these sermon topics:

- "Beginning at the Beginning"
- "Maker of Heaven and Earth"
- "From Everlasting to Everlasting"

- "Beginnings and Endings"
- "Freedom Within Order"
- "Creation and the Meaning of Life"

I have also preached on the doctrine of God in a series of sermons from the parables or on the Lord's Prayer. When our new sanctuary at St. Matthews Baptist Church in Louisville, Kentucky was dedicated, I preached a series of sermons based on our three large stained glass windows that depict God as Creator, Redeemer, and Spirit, and the carved images on the pulpit and Communion table. Although the emphasis was on the dedication of our sanctuary to God, the themes were theological:

- "Maker of Heaven and Earth
- "The Lamb of God"
- "The Spirit at Work in the World"
- "Your God Is Too Small"
- "Sharing the Lord's Cup and Eating His Bread"

Questions about the will of God, suffering and evil following natural disasters, grief and death, and countless others provide occasions for a series or single sermons on the doctrine of God.

The Doctrine of the Incarnation. Our understanding of Christ is central to our faith. Yet, many people in our congregations hold only a fuzzy image of Christ and his ministry. They do not know where to begin in a discussion about the meaning of the Word that became flesh; how Jesus revealed God, was, and is the Son of God; the meaning of the Trinity; or Jesus' death, resurrection, and ascension.[33] On this theological theme I once preached a series addressing the question, "Who Is This Jesus Christ?"[34] The titles and texts included the following:

"Who Is This Jesus Christ?"	(Matt. 16:13-21)
"The Incarnate Christ"	(John 1:1-14)
"The Healing Christ"	(Ps. 111:1-4, Luke 4:16-21)
"The Teaching Christ"	(Jer. 38:14-17; Matt. 4:23, 7:28-29; John 3:1-2)
"The Rejected Christ"	(Jer. 2:20-21, Luke 20:1-20)

"The Crucified Christ"	(Isa. 53:1-6, Matt. 27:27-31, 1 Cor. 1:23-24)
"The Risen Christ" (Easter Sunday)	(Hosea 6:1-2, 1 Cor. 15:1-22)
"What About Christ Today?"	(Ps. 90:1-4, Acts 1:9-11, Gal. 2:20)

I raised the question about the nature of Christ in the first of these sermons in these words:

> "Who do you say I am?" That question has continued to be asked through the centuries. This is not an answer but a question. We sometimes say that Jesus is the answer. But here Jesus is the question, and he is the questioner. "Who do men and women say that I am?" Most of the heresies of the Christian church have arisen in response to that question. "Who do men say that I am?" The Apostle's Creed came into existence in response to that question. The Councils of Nicaea and Chalcedon were called to respond to that question . . .
>
> Christians through the ages have attempted to give a reply. His footprints have been seen across the pages of history. The answers continue to come to that question, "Who do men say that I am?" Listen to some of the replies . . .
>
> Who is Jesus Christ? The answers seem to be "written in the wind." First this, and then another. "Who do you say that I am?" Is he simply a mannequin we dress in whatever manner we like? Is he a lump of clay we can mold any way we want? Is he an empty canvas on which we can paint any picture we desire? The variety of responses to him through the centuries makes one wonder if this is not the case. Who has seen his real face? Can he be whatever men and women want him to be?
>
> "Who do you say that I am?"[35]

Much of our preaching will be directed to understanding Jesus, his life, death, resurrection, and ministry. His parables and other teachings will form the bases for many sermons—doctrinal—in some way or another. Don't buy into the attitude that doctrinal preaching has to be boring or dull. Of course, we know that some preachers seem to be invested with the ability to put guardian angels to sleep with their preaching. You may have heard that Fosdick was once asked if he ever went to sleep while he was preaching. "No," he replied. "But I have preached in a lot of other people's sleep." We all know that problem. You may have heard about the preacher who dreamed he was preaching to his congregation. He woke up and sure enough he was!

But let's not let the thrill of the gospel elude us. We have good news to proclaim. The New Testament's concept that the Word was made flesh is a startling and revolutionary event in human history. "If this is dull," Dorothy Sayers exclaims, "then what in Heaven's name is worthy to be called exciting?" Lift the trumpet to your lips each week and exclaim, "We have good news for you today!"

The Doctrine of the Cross. The cross stands at the heart of our preaching about Christ. Yet many preachers only preach on it once a year or a week or so before Easter.

Some years ago I was talking with a minister friend of mine as we were both preparing for the Lenten/Easter season. He observed how difficult it was for him to think about preaching on the cross. I understand something of his reluctance and timidity in speaking about such a theme. But I have been daring enough to try and focus the attention of my congregation upon the cross of Jesus for a seven-part sermon series. There was no way I could possibly speak on all that was involved in the great message of the cross in several sermons. Thousands of books have been written about the cross; thousands of sermons have been preached on it. Yet all of them have only touched the edge of the truth contained in its message.

The Gospel writers struggled to understand why Jesus was crucified, and the Apostle Paul, without hesitation, put the cross at the center of his preaching. If the church is to be the authentic church, the cross will always be at the center of our preaching and way of life. The church cannot really exist as "the church" without the memory and the impact of the cross being a vital part of our message and ministry.

When one studies the Scriptures, there is no question that the cross was at the center of the preaching about Jesus Christ in the early church. A cross-shaped cavity was found in the wall of an upper room in Pompeii, a city destroyed by Vesuvius in A.D. 79. About twenty inscriptions of the cross were found in the catacombs at Rome that scholars date in the second and third centuries. In most of our churches the cross is still the central symbol of the Christian faith. The cross is the symbol placed on the altar, in stained glass windows, and on the steeple of the church.

In some church traditions a cross is woven into the stoles or other vestments worn by the minister. In some worship settings the choir processes in, and one of the ministers or someone else may carry a processional cross. Some church buildings are constructed in the shape of a cross. Crosses are sometimes imprinted on Bibles, hymnbooks, and other religious books. We sing about the cross in our hymns. The cross is depicted in poetry, art, sculpture, and in many other ways. Without question, the cross is the church's central symbol. Yet many people are uncomfortable with what the cross symbol really means. It has become an offense once again to many.

Vincent Taylor in his book, *The Cross of Christ*, has challenged the church to think again about the cross. "Perhaps our greatest need today, if we would rise above the poverty of much of our worship, is to experience once more the wonder of reliance upon Christ's ceaseless saving ministry, which is the true center of Christian devotion and the abiding source of Christian living."[36] The cross needs to be at the center of our life. If our Lord gave his life, are we not challenged to give our lives in devotion and ministry for him?

Eric Rust told about visiting Laacher, which was the burial place of many kings. In the royal chapel there was a strange fitting in the reading desk of the pulpit. Hidden inside the cross on the pulpit was a microphone. What a parable about life.[37]

The cross, when really understood, becomes a microphone through which the voice of Christ and the voices of his disciples spread the good news of God's grace everywhere. The cross of Jesus Christ declares that God has reconciled humankind to himself. The cross reveals to us the costly nature of sin, the love of God, the sacrifice, self-denial, and surrender of Christ, and the limitless grace of the Father. Having been reconciled to God by Christ, we are challenged to share this message of love with others and to live the Christlike, cross-like way of life. It is not the easy life, but I am convinced it is the Christian way. We bow before the mystery of the cross and follow in its light.

Following is a list of sermons I preached in the series, "The Church Under the Cross":[38]

"The Cross and the Gospel Paradox"   (Isa. 53:4-6, 1 Cor. 1:18-24)
"The Cross and the Face of God"   (Ps. 40:1-3, 16-17; Phil. 2:5-11)
"The Cross and the Silence of God"   (Job 23:1-7; Mark 15:21-27, 33-36)

"The Cross and Our Atonement"	(Ps. 110:1-4, Rom. 8:1-3, (Heb. 7:23-28)
"Easter: Living Beyond the Cross"	(Job 14:12-17, Luke 24:13-35)
"Bearing Your Own Cross"	(Gen. 13:1-13, Luke 9:23-25)
"The Church Under the Cross"	(Exod. 20:1-3, 2 Cor. 5:17-21)

I encourage you to put the cross at the center of your preaching. Consult the many books and articles available for study on the cross.[39]

The Doctrine of the Church. Like the doctrine of the cross, numerous books have been written about the church. In my library I have two shelves of books on the church.[40]

The church has changed in many ways over the years. Down through the centuries many voices have said that the institutional church is not very close to what the authentic church should be. The philosopher Santayana once said that "the shell of Christendom is broken." "In every age," Gustau Weigel declared, "the institutions (of religion) are dying." But he added, "They never do." Swinburne, the poet, stated that he had great admiration for Christ but despised his "leprous bride"—the church. Bertrand Russell, the agnostic, once wrote: "I say quite deliberately that the Christian religion as organized in the churches has been and still is the principal enemy of moral progress in the world."

When it looks like the church has been destroyed or is dead, God continues to give it new life. There have always been times when the church seemed ineffective and impotent. Dorothy Sayers once observed that "the average church member is about as equipped to do battle on fundamentals with a Marxist atheist as a boy with a peashooter facing a fanfare of machine guns." Today, as times in the past, the church appears weak and inefficient against the forces of evil. Yet Christ continues to work within his church to strengthen and empower it to meet the powers of darkness. Disciples who have been disciplined and trained will be able to serve Christ more courageously in our modern world.

The Greek word for church (*ecclesia*) in Matthew 16:18 means "the called out ones." Jesus envisioned the church not so much as an organization but as an organism—a living group of people—a covenant of believers—a fellowship of disciples. The church grew out of the group of disciples gathered together in deep commitment to him. But the church cannot exist merely as an ideal without some kind of institutional form for its habitation.

Persons such as Leonard Sweet, Brian McLaren, Robert Weber, and others have written about the "emerging church" that is constantly changing and taking new shapes and images in the postmodern twenty-first century. While we do not need to do away with all the established churches, churches need to be reborn in the image Christ intended them to be initially. This may not be a rejection of the institutional church but a "reshaping" or new "fleshing" of the form or structure it takes in the modern world. Harvey Cox believes the church is undergoing a revolution or reformation that may be even greater than the one under Martin Luther. "Faith is resurgent," he declares, "while dogma is dying."[41] "All the signs suggest," he believes, "we are poised to enter a new Age of the Spirit and that the future will be a future of faith."[42]

In an attempt to examine the intention of Jesus for his church, I preached a series of sermons on the church.[43] Below is the list of the sermon topics in that series:

"The Foundation of the Church"	(Luke 24:13-35)
"The Church Nobody Knows"	(Eph. 4:11-16)
"Why Go to Church?"	(Isa. 6:1-7, Heb. 12:22-25)
"To What Church Do You Belong?"	(Ps. 42:1-8, 1 Tim. 3:14-16)
"Being Irreligious in Church"	(Luke 18:9-14)
"Evangelism in the Church: Journey Inward, Journey Outward"	(Exod. 6:2-9, Luke 4:16-21)
"The Ministry of the Church"	(Eph. 4:9-16)
"The Rebirth of the Church"	(Matt. 16:13-19, 24-27; 1 Pet. 4:8-11)

The Doctrine of the Last Things. Another significant theme that most mainline church ministers rarely preach on is eschatology, or the theology of the last things. Few preachers have the boldness to address the issues of death, the last judgment, the second coming of Christ, hell, and heaven. Yet, many of our parishioners long to hear some helpful word about these topics.

Thomas Long in his Lyman Beecher Lectures, *From Memory to Hope*, challenged the preacher to have the courage to meet a real need and desire on the part of laypersons to have this issue addressed.[44] Too often the church allows persons such as Tim LaHaye and Jerry Jenkins to establish the theology that many think is the authentic teaching of the faith. I personally think their theology is harmful and that they substitute the concept of rapture for the biblical teaching of resurrection. In my book, *The Left Behind Fantasy: The Theology Behind the Left Behind Tales,* I offer a critique of their theology and suggestions for approaching an interpretation of the end times and the Book of Revelation.[45]

A proper understanding of the genres of the biblical time in which the writers of Revelation and other apocalyptic books were written will help us to reflect on the end times but, as Paul Scott Wilson suggests, "ought to assist preachers in preaching boldly about social injustice in the present."[46] A medical doctor in one of my congregations challenged me to preach on these themes. I found it one of the most challenging and satisfying preaching adventures I have pursued. And I received probably the most enthusiastic response I have ever gotten from a series of sermons.[47]

Following are examples from a sermon series I preached on the Doctrine of Last Things:[48]

"The Mystery of Death: Behind the Veil"	(1 Cor. 15:12-20, 26, 42-44, 50-57)
"The Last Judgment: How God Sizes Us Up"	(Matt. 25:31-46; John 3:16-21, 12:44-50)
"The Second Coming of Christ: Christ Came and Comes"	(Matt. 16:28, 24:3-36)
"Hell: Vindictive or Remedial?"	(Matt. 13:36-43, Gal. 6:7-8, Rev. 14:9-12)
"Heaven: The Undiscovered Country"	(John 14:1-4; Phil. 3:20; 1 Cor. 2:9; Rev. 21:1-4, 10-14, 22:1-5)

There are, of course, many other possibilities for doctrinal sermons. If you are Baptist, you might preach a series on "What Baptists Believe" and stress personal religious experiences, the priesthood of believers, the acceptance of the Bible as the only guide for faith and practice, religious liberty, and liberty of conscience. I once preached a series on Sunday nights on "Selected Baptist Theologians as Models for Ministry" in which I focused on the life and theology of Baptist theologians such as John Broadus, Walter Rauschenbusch, E. Y. Mullins, W. O. Carver, Harry Emerson Fosdick, Frank Stagg, Martin Luther King, Jr., and Wayne Oates who taught Baptist theology through the life models of ministers rather than through the study of their doctrines.

Whatever your denominational affiliation, you can preach a series of sermons on your group's distinctiveness. You might also do a series on the Apostle's Creed. Use your imagination. The possibilities and study helps are endless.[49]

Focus on Ethical Issues

Another important part of theological preaching is focusing on ethical issues. To preach the whole gospel, the preacher cannot ignore the needs of the total person, and this means she often has to address social issues that confront the hearers.

In his inaugural message at his hometown synagogue at Nazareth, Jesus began his ministry linking his message of salvation with his concern for the poor, enslaved, blind, and oppressed (Luke 4:18-19). On another occasion Jesus indicated that the question God would ask us at the judgment would focus on our concern for those in need (Matt. 25:35-36). When Jesus was asked what the greatest commandment was, he listed two: we are to love God with all our being and secondly, we are to love our neighbor. The two were joined as one. Jesus' concern for the poor, feeding the hungry, the blind, deaf, lame, sick, and other human needs model for us genuine ethical concern. He also taught us to petition God for our "daily bread." His teachings, miracles, and compassion for human needs and social concerns have inseparably tied ethical concerns with kingdom concerns.

Our models for preaching on social issues also reach back to the great Old Testament prophets of Israel such as Amos, Micah, Hosea, Isaiah, and Jeremiah who called the people to the awareness that religious ritual, animal sacrifice, or objective ceremonial rites and private morality were not sufficient as real worship. Amos was fierce in his denunciation of the shallowness of much of Israel's worship: "I hate, I despise your feasts, and I take no delight in your solemn assemblies . . . But let justice roll down like waters, and righteousness like an ever-flowing stream" (Amos 5:21, 24). Worship and our daily living are intertwined. The Christian way of life is personal, but it is never depicted as private.

Jesus was crucified because he dared to challenge those who wanted to separate religion from one's daily life and confine it to an observance of rules and rigid ecclesial traditions. If we are to follow the model and teachings of our Lord, we cannot ignore as none of our business the problems of war, racism, prejudice, poverty, famine, drugs, alcohol, gambling, pollution, the ecological crises, corrupt politics, sexism, and many other issues facing us today. To love or hunger for righteousness is to long for it in these areas as well as within our own personal lives. To ignore the giant social issues of our day is to be unlike our Master and leave the woman at the well, the beggar at the gate, the lame in his bed, the blind in his darkness, and the poor in his poverty. Our sense of righteousness can never be satisfied until it has both a social and a personal dimension.

There are several reasons why we should preach on ethical issues, for example:

- By preaching on ethical themes, the preacher joins the great Old Testament prophetic tradition of Amos, Hosea, Isaiah, Jeremiah, and others, as well as linking his voice with our Lord in concern for the poor, oppressed, and needy and for justice and righteousness.

- We preach on ethical themes to show that our proclamation that Jesus is Lord is directed to us as individuals in the church, and that Jesus is Lord not only of a person's religious life but of all life.

- We preach on ethical themes to confront the secular and pseudomorality of our day and to challenge our listeners to follow the example our Lord gave in his teachings and sacrificial life and death.

- We preach on ethical themes to offer guidance for our listeners as they seek spiritual discernment to respond to the controversial social and ethical issues of our day.

- Ethical preaching can help people to see that the awesome power of evil reaches beyond personal sinfulness and has a corporate dimension, as Walter Rauschenbusch, Reinhold Niebuhr, and others have reminded us. This will entail preaching that confronts the social factors in our society that lead to prejudice, racism, war, alcoholism, business and government corruption, gambling, AIDS, and so on.

- Ethical preaching can affirm the church as the social factor in redemption, as Walter Rauschenbusch said, to confront the many and varied forces of evil in our society.

- Ethical preaching can offer spiritual direction for our listeners about Christian values and principles that lift us beyond selfishness to authentic living as we seek to follow the way of Christ.

Having established the rationale for preaching on ethical issues, here are some suggested guidelines the preacher can follow:

- Avoid projecting the image that you alone have the only correct insight into all the profound issues of life. Offer your insight and understanding, but do not try to act like you have a direct line to God for your view. Humility will likely get you a better hearing than haughtiness.

- Avoid preaching partisan politics. There is no place for political party positions in the pulpit as though one or the other was or is the mind of God on certain issues. The preacher is free to remind the people to vote, but is not free to instruct them in how or for whom to vote. Remember that church and state are separate. Do not make the image fuzzy or blurred by preaching politics instead of religion.

- Avoid fragmenting your church by taking a political stand instead of an ethical position. We can preach an ethical sermon that notes the needs of the poor, for example, and we can offer concrete ways to assist or how we can get involved or to what church agency we can give financial support without making it a political matter or saying which political party in our opinion may be doing a better job on this particular issue.

- Avoid preaching in broad generalities about ethical issues. A sermon on sin will need to focus on a particular ethical issue if it is likely to communicate your concern. A sermon may need to focus on the call for ecological awareness or the low moral values of young and old in our society or the real problem with heavy drinking on our college campuses or the lack of integrity in many of our business practices or the challenge and call to assist the hungry of the world or those across town. There is a time to be as specific as we can be without putting a name or face on the challenge before the church that will cause hurt or ridicule.

- Avoid proclaiming that politics is dirty and everyone should stay clear of it as a profession. We need all the Christians we can get in politics without those persons trying to impose their views on others.

- Avoid preaching an absolute ethic. No one person or preacher has the mind of Christ on all the great social issues of humankind with only one simple possible answer to them all. The Pat Robertsons or Jerry Falwells of the world with their pat, absolute answers are usually ignored by most of the thinking people of society. We are all seeking to know the mind of Christ on the profound issues of the world. We listen in humility and awareness that we are searchers after truth, not those who always know the mind of Christ ahead of time.

Through the years I have tried to focus on ethical issues in sermons such as the following:

- "Waging Peace"
- "What Color Is Love?"
- "A Pollution Revolution"
- "A Theology for Ecology"
- "Family Values"
- "The AIDS Crisis"
- "Whose Situational Ethics?"
- "The Playboy Philosophy of Life"
- "Do You Really Want to Live by the New Morality?"
- "The Separation of Church and State"
- "The Gospel for City Folks"

I have also preached series of sermons on the Ten Commandments, the Beatitudes of Jesus, and the Old Testament Prophets and Their Teachings and participated in pulpit exchanges with ministers of black churches on Race Relations Sunday. In addition, I have presented special studies or sermons on books or issues dealing with such themes as situational ethics, the new morality, ecology, war and peace, AIDS, ecology, the secular city, marriage, sexuality, euthanasia, liberation ethics, bioethics, women's liberation, drug addiction, and Black Power. I have drawn on a variety of excellent resources that inform my preaching on ethical issues.[50]

Provide Theological Translation

If the Word is to be proclaimed through our words, then theological translation is a necessity for the preacher. Too often we hide behind biblical or theological jargon, thinking it gives us the appearance of being scholarly or mature. Sometimes we are simply unconscious of our use of such language, because it is second nature to us, and we forget this is not true for people in the pews. This is one of the chief criticisms of laypersons about preaching.

They say preachers assume that laypersons have a greater knowledge and understanding of biblical and theological terms and language than they actually do. "Do not talk to me," they say, "as though I were from Athens, Jerusalem, or Laodicea." When asked some of the words preachers use that are meaningless to them, they have mentioned "salvation," "redemption," "myth," "gospel," and "Synoptic Gospels," for example. These are words right at the heart of the Christian faith but are unknown to many.

The preacher has the responsibility of putting the great biblical and theological truths into the language of the common people. As James Russell Lowell once wrote, "We need the tongue of the people in the mouth of the scholar." We do not help people to know the gospel and the Bible better if we present them in ways listeners cannot grasp. The Gospels were originally written in *Koine* Greek, the language of the common persons. Part of our preaching task is to continue that process and translate the Gospels into the language of our people today.

Some seminary wag drew a cartoon several years ago that pictured Jesus talking to Simon Peter at Caesarea Philippi. He has responded to the first question, "Who do men say that the Son of Man is?" And now Peter is replying to the question, "But who do you say that I am?" Peter answers: "Thou art the paradoxical *Kerygma,* the epistological manifestation of the existential ground of ontological ultimacy." Jesus responds simply: "Huh?"

Many of our listeners look at us with blank stares because we have left them when we preach in the jargon of our theological discipline. Our words should not conceal the Word but reveal it. Most vocations or disciplines have their own jargon, and anyone unfamiliar with it could not follow the conversation. For example, a sign in the Pentagon, a place not noted for clear talk, reads: "This thorough way is not conducive to traffic for an indefinite period." The meaning? "Keep Out!"

We all know what it is like to have a medical doctor talk to us in her jargon. "Tell me so I can understand it, Doctor. What's wrong with me?" We want it clear and plain, and so do our listeners. There is a real art and task involved in learning to speak without being simplistic or clear without being trite. We need to know that difference and practice it if we are to communicate the faith today.

This is not a plea for avoiding the learning of biblical and theological language and its meaning. You and I ought to read and master the best theological, philosophical, and biblical books we can. Good preaching and good thinking go together. Learn then to translate the conventional religious language into words that address people today. This will be hard work.

Let me raise a warning flag here. Do not try to discard all of the great words of the Christian vocabulary. We need to interpret, paraphrase, and translate them but not reject them completely. Whatever our new theological words are, they must know and build on the old categories. I agree with Barbara Brown Taylor when she asserts that she is "not ready to let go of these words. The realities they point to are still very much with us," she affirms, "and we need to know their names."[51] But we need to avoid abstraction and vagueness. Focus your thought so the meaning of the doctrine under discussion is clear to your hearers. Separate your primary emphasis from secondary matters so your target is apparent. Say what you mean. Try to be simple without being trite or simplistic.

Helmut Thielicke gave an imaginary story as an illustration about the necessity for translating some theological phrases if communication is going to take place in the mind of the hearer. In his imagination he saw a demonstration by the German Faith Movement in the Berlin Sportpalast with the appropriate anti-Christian agitation. As the hate tirades reached their climax, a Christian in the audience could stand it no longer. He stood up and shouted loudly, "Christ is the Messiah." A few people near him turned around in their seats with surprise at the interrupter but looked again back to the platform. But another person stood up and shouted: "Christ is the only Lord and Leader and without him, Hitler and all the apostles of this false faith will go to hell." This man was mobbed and killed.[52]

Why? He spoke so those around him could understand him. The term Messiah was interpreted by him, so it hit home. We need that same kind of directness and translation in our proclamation of the gospel. Base your preaching on sound biblical and theological foundations, but avoid abstract theological jargon. It is essential that our listeners understand the meaning of the truth we expound and not get lost in nonsensical vocabulary. The language of Zion and the vocabulary of the theologians do not belong on the tongue of the contemporary proclaimer of good news.

Preach with Conviction

Preach with conviction tempered with humility. R. E. C. Browne says it is not the preacher's business "to make us believe *what* he believes, but to make us believe *that* he believes. He must convince us that he is convinced."[53] Conviction in a preacher is not so much his trying to make us believe certain ideas, but rather communicating that what the preacher is proclaiming is vitally real to him. Through the person of the preacher, an inner meaning of assurance is conveyed.

State your case strongly, but with the awareness that none of us can put on God's glasses. Our knowledge is always imperfect and partial. Avoid dogmatism. Even the preacher is a pilgrim in search of truth. The prize of the upward calling is always before us, never in our grasp. We are disciples—learners—trying to learn as we are at the same time being taught by our Lord and fellow Christians. None of us have arrived in our faith. We always preach in awe at the wonder and mystery about which we proclaim.

Edward Farley reminds us of this truth in these words: "Insofar as the *what* of preaching is the world of the gospel, preaching is not supplied with a clear doctrinal, ethical, or exegetical given. Rather, its given is the very mystery of God's (present) activity in the situations of the world."[54]

We, too, are still learning, growing, and seeking to "eat the meat" of the Word. Do we all not feel the sense of inadequacy that Reverend John Ames noted in his letter to his young son? "So often I have known," Ames wrote, "right there in the pulpit, even as I read the words, how far they fell short of any hopes I had for them. And they were the major work of my life, from a certain point of view. I have to wonder how I have lived with that."[55]

"The minister of the Word does his clearest thinking on the edge of error," Browne observes. "He is more orthodox when on the point of coming to heretical conclusions."[56] We follow our Lord, who is the Way, the Truth, and the Life, and seek to understand him and his way. Therefore, I will explore any theological system and not be boxed in by some predetermined system of belief to which I have to ascribe.

Arthur John Gossip, the noted Scottish preacher, said that George Whyte walked part of the way home with him after he preached at St. George Church one night as a young minister. Among other things, Whyte said this to him: "You chose a great subject. That was right. You cannot always do it. But do it as often as you can."[57]

That is solid advice. Choose a great doctrine and preach on it. Climb into the pulpit with a renewed thrill of preaching the great doctrines of the faith. With Paul, cry out: "I am not ashamed of the gospel, because it is the power of God unto salvation" (Rom. 1:16). Let your Christian flag wave proudly in the breeze. Speak with a new song in your heart, fire in your mouth, and Christ's mantle about your shoulders. "Be ready at any time," as Peter advised, "to give a quiet and reverent answer to any man who wants a reason for the hope that you have within you" (1 Pet. 3:15, Phillips).

Notes

[1] Herman Melville, *Moby Dick* (New York: Dodd, Mead and Co., 1942), 66.

[2] Burton Z. Cooper and John S. McClure, *Claiming Theology in the Pulpit* (Louisville: Westminster John Knox Press, 2003), 1.

[3] Richard Lischer, *A Theology of Preaching* (Nashville: Abingdon Press, 1981), 13.

[4] Earl E. Shelp and Ronald H. Sunderland, eds., *The Pastor as Theologian* (New York: Pilgrim Press, 1988).

[5] Mike Graves, "God of Grace and Glory," in *What's the Matter with Preaching Today?*, ed. Mike Graves (Louisville: Westminster John Knox Press, 2004), 111.

[6] Thomas Long, "No News Is Bad News," in *What's the Matter with Preaching Today?*, 149.

[7] Heinrich Ott, *Theology and Preaching*, trans. Harold Knight (Louisville: Westminster Press, 1961), 23.

[8] William H. Willimon, *Proclamation and Theology* (Nashville: Abingdon, 2005), 7.

[9] David Buttrick, foreword to *Homiletics* by Karl Barth, trans. Geoffrey Bromiley and David E. Daniels (Louisville: Westminster John Knox Press, 1991), 10.

[10] Geoffrey Wainwright, *Doxology: The Praise of God in Worship, Doctrine and Life* (New York: Oxford University Press, 1980).

[11] Robert Jay Lifton, *The Life of the Self* (New York: Simon and Schuster, 1976), 165-171.

[12] A. W. W. Dale, *The Life of R. W. Dale of Birmingham* (London: Hodder and Stoughton, 1898), 642-643.

[13] Cooper and McClure, *Claiming Theology in the Pulpit*, 1-6.

[14] Frank Stagg, *New Testament Theology* (Nashville: Broadman Press, 1962), 272.

[15] C. Colt Anderson, *Christian Eloquence: Contemporary Doctrinal Preaching* (Chicago: Hillenbrand Books, 2005), 4-5.

[16] John Broadus, *On the Preparation and Delivery of Sermons*, ed. Jesse E. Weatherspoon (New York: Harper & Row, 1944), 60.

[17] Barbara Brown Taylor, *When God Is Silent* (Cambridge: Cowley Publications, 1998), 22.

[18] P. T. Forsyth, *Positive Preaching and the Modern Mind* (London: Independent Press, 1907), 197.

[19] David Buttrick, *Homiletic: Moves and Structures* (Philadelphia: Fortress Press, 1987), 452.

[20] H. H. Farmer, *The Servant of the Word* (Philadelphia: Fortress Press, 1942), 44.

[21] R. W. Dale, *Nine Lectures on Preaching* (London: Hodden and Stoughton, 1878), 217.

[22] Paul Scott Wilson, *Setting Words on Fire: Putting God in the Center of the Sermon* (Nashville: Abingdon Press, 2008), 17.

[23] John Killinger, *The Second Coming of the Church* (Nashville: Abingdon Press, 1983), 1974.

[24] John Claypool, *The Light Within You* (Waco: Word Books, 1983), 110.

[25] John Oman, *Concerning the Ministry* (New York: Harper & Brothers, 1937), 56.

[26] Forsyth, *Positive Preaching and the Modern Mind*, 6

[27] Andrew W. Blackwood, *Doctrinal Preaching for Today* (Nashville: Abingdon Press, 1956), 28.

[28] Ronald J. Allen, *Preaching Is Believing: The Sermon as Theological Reflection* (Louisville: Westminster John Knox Press, 2002), 36.

[29] Several denominational presses publish their own lectionary resources. The following are some older resources I have used through the years: *Handbook of the Christian Year*, ed.

Hoyt L. Hickman et. al. (Abingdon Press); H. Boone Porter, *Keeping the Church Year* (Seabury Press); *Preaching Through the Year*, David Steel (John Knox); Perry H. Biddle, Jr., *Preaching the Lectionary* (Westminster Press) and *Lectionary Preaching Workbook* (C.S.S). *The Minister's Manual*, edited formerly by James W. Cox and now by Lee McGlone, and published annually, contains a helpful lectionary section. Ronald J. Allen and Clark M Williamson have produced several lectionary commentaries for Westminster John Knox Press, for example, *Preaching the Gospels without Blaming the Jews* and *Preaching the Letters without Dismissing the Law*. Abingdon, Fortress, Westminster, and other religious presses produce aids for interpreting the lessons of the church year that can be used with the Common, Episcopal, Lutheran, and Roman Catholic lectionaries. There are also many resources on the internet for lectionary worship and preaching planning. Baptists will find helpful resources at www.helwys.com/worship.

[30] In addition to individual books you select for your study of any doctrine, I would suggest you also check what is written on that particular doctrine in *The Interpreter's Dictionary of the Bible* and Kittel's *Theological Dictionary of the New Testament* and the companion volumes on the Old Testament. Bible dictionaries published by Harper, Eerdmans, and Westminster will be helpful. The biblical or New Testament Theology works by Alan Richardson, A. M. Hunter, Miller Burrows, Frank Stagg, Rudolf Bultmann, and others will be useful. Examine also the Old Testament theologies of writers such as Gerhard von Rad, Walter Eichrodt, Ludwig Kieller and A. B. Davison. *A Handbook of Christian Theology*, ed. Marvin Halverson; *A Theological Word Book of the Bible*, ed. Alan Richardson; and *A New Handbook of Christian Theology*, ed. Donald W. Musser and Joseph L. Price will offer a summary of most doctrines. You will also want to look at the way various theologians present a given doctrine in single-volume treatments or systematic theologies. These are available from every theological perspective.

[31] J. S. Whale, *Christian Doctrine* (London: Fontana Books, 1958), 11.

[32] In preparing to preach on the doctrine of God I have examined books such as Jack Miles' *God: A Biography*, Douglas John Hall's *Professing the Faith*, Emil Brunner's *The Christian Doctrine of God* and *The Christian Doctrine of Creation and Redemption*, Paul Tillich's *Systematic Theology* (vol. 1), Karl Barth's *Church's Dogmatics: The Doctrine of God* (II/2), Wolfhart Pannenberg's *Jesus God and Man*, and E. Frank Tupper's *A Scandalous Providence*. I underline as I read, make notes, gather sermon themes and questions, and jot down ideas for sermon outlines, illustrations, or helpful quotes.

[33] For this study you will want to read the classic work *God Was in Christ* by D. M. Baillie. I also suggest reading A. M. Hunter's *The Work and Words of Jesus*, Rudolf Bultmann's *Jesus and the Word*, Wolfhart Pannenburg's *Jesus, God and Man*, Piet Schoenenberg's *The Christ*, Eduard Schweizer's *Jesus*, John A. T. Robinson's *The Human Face of God*, Luke Timothy Johnson's *The Real Jesus*, John P. Meier's *A Marginal Jew*, Marcus J. Borg's *Jesus: Discovering the Life*, John Killinger's *The Changing Shape of Our Salvation: Teachings and Relevance of a Religious Revolutionary*, and Douglas John Hall's *Professing the Faith*.

[34] In a slightly different format, this series was later published under the title *The Compelling Faces of Jesus* (Macon, GA: Mercer University Press, 2008).

[35] Ibid., 8-10.

[36] Vincent Taylor, *The Cross of Christ* (London: Macmillan & Co. Ltd, 1956), 104.

[37] Eric C. Rust, *The Word and the Words* (Macon, GA: Mercer University Press, 1982), 127.

[38] This series was published under the title *The Church under the Cross* (Gonzalez, FL: Energion Publications, 2012).

[39] Books by the following writers can provide many suggestions for approaching the doctrine of the cross; Jürgen Moltmann, *The Crucified God* and *The Way of Jesus Christ*; James

E. Tull, *The Atoning Gospel*; Emil Brunner, *The Mediator*; William J. Wolf, *No Cross, No Crown*; Vincent Taylor, *The Cross of Christ*; Douglas John Hall, *The Cross in Our Context*; John Stott, *The Cross of Christ*; David Buttrick, *The Mystery of the Passion*; Fisher Humphreys, *The Death of Christ*; and the popular treatment by Leslie Weatherhead, *A Plain Man Looks at the Cross*.

[40] Among the many books available, I would encourage you to examine the following: Harvey Cox, *The Future of Faith, Fire from Heaven*, and *The Secular City*; Wolfhart Pannenberg, *The Church*; Douglas John Hall, *Has the Church a Future?*; George Hunter, *Church for the Unchurched*; Jürgen Moltmann, *The Church in the Power of the Spirit*; J. Robert Nelson, *The Realm of Redemption*; R. Newton Flew, *Jesus and His Church*; Hans Kung, *The Church*; Robert Raines, *New Life in the Church*; William H. Willimon, *What's Right with the Church*; John Killinger, *Preaching to a Church in Crisis*; Brian McLaren, *Church on the Other Side*; Leonard Sweet, *The Church of the Perfect Storm*; Jeff C. Woods, *Congregational Megatrends*.

[41] Harvey Cox, *The Future of Faith* (New York: Harper Collins, 2009), 213.

[42] Ibid., 224.

[43] One of my series of sermons on the church was published under the title, *The Church in Today's World* (Cleveland, TN: Parson's Porch Books, 2011).

[44] Thomas Long, *From Memory to Hope* (Louisville: Westminster, 2009), 111ff.

[45] William Powell Tuck, *The Left Behind Fantasy: The Theology Behind the Left Behind Tales* (Eugene, OR: Wipf and Stock, 2010).

[46] Wilson, *Setting Words on Fire*, 68.

[47] I found many helpful resources. Here are a few: Jürgen Moltmann, *The Coming of God*; John A. T. Robinson, *Jesus and His Coming*; Emil Brunner, *I Believe in the Living God*; John Baillie, *And the Life Everlasting*; S. Lewis, *Till We Have Faces*; John Killinger, *You Are What You Believe*; Leslie Weatherhead, *Life Begins at Death*; N. T. Wright, *Surprised by Hope*; Rob Bell, *Love Wins*.

[48] This series was later published in a revised form under the title *The Journey to the Undiscovered Country: What's Beyond Death?* (Gonzalez, FL: Energion Publications, 2012).

[49] The following books might provide some suggestions on how to preach on doctrinal themes: *A Faith to Proclaim* by James Stewart, *Living Doctrines in a Vital Pulpit* by Merrill R. Abbey, *Preaching for Today* by Andrew W. Blackwood, *Preaching as Local Theology and Folk Art* by Leonora Tubbs Tisdale, *Preaching as a Theological Task* edited by Thomas Long and Edward Farley, *Theology Is for Proclamation* by Gerhard O. Forde, *Preaching Is Believing: The Sermon as Theological Reflection* by Ronald J. Allen, *Claiming Theology in the Pulpit* by Burton Z. Cooper and John S. McClure, *Christian Eloquence: Contemporary Doctrinal Preaching* by Charles Colt, *Great Doctrinal Themes* by Charles R. Wood, *Sermons as God's Word: Theology for Preaching* by Robert Duke, *Theology for Preaching* by Mack B. Stokes, *Preaching Doctrine* by Robert Hughes and Robert Kysor, *Proclamation and Theology* by William H. Willimon and Mark Ellingsen, *Doctrine and Word: Theology in the Pulpit* by Mark Ellingsen, *Prophetic Preaching: A Pastoral Approach* by Leonora Tubbs Tisdale, *The Preaching of Jesus: Gospel Proclamation Then and Now* by William Brosend, *Setting Words on Fire: Putting God at the Center of the Sermon* by Paul Scott Wilson, *Speaking of Sin: The Lost Language of Salvation* by Barbara Brown Taylor, *The Collected Sermons of William H. Willimon*, *The Collected Sermons of Fred B. Craddock*.

[50] Leonora Tubbs Tisdale, *Prophetic Preaching: A Pastoral Approach* (Louisville: Westminster John Knox Press, 2010). William Sloane Coffin, *The Collected Sermons of William Sloane Coffin* (vols. 1, 2) (Louisville: Westminster John Press, 2008). Paul Simmons' book, *Faith and Health: Religion, Science, and Public Policy*, (Macon, GA: Mercer University Press, 2008), offers the preacher a solid resource for the issues of suffering, aging, health care, suicide, stem cell research, abortion, euthanasia, and other controversial themes. Through the

years I have drawn on books from the following ethicists for resources to inform my preaching in this area: Walter Rauschenbusch, Reinhold Niebuhr, Paul Simmons, Henlee Barnette, James Gustafson, Roger Shinn, John Yoder, Stanley Hauerwas, and many others. Leonora Tubbs Tisdale has written a very helpful resource, *Prophetic Preaching: A Pastoral Approach*, in which she offers a variety of forms that prophetic or ethical preaching can take with examples from preachers such as Ernest Campbell, Barbara Lundblad, and Martin Luther King, Jr. Sermons by William Sloane Coffin, the late minister at Riverside Church in New York City, also offer some sterling examples of ethical preaching.

[51] Barbara Brown Taylor, *Speaking of Sin: The Lost Language of Salvation* (Cambridge: Cowley Publications, 2000), 7.

[52] Helmut Thielicke, *The Trouble with the Church* (New York: Harper & Row, 1965), 37.

[53] R. E. C. Browne, *The Ministry of the Word* (Philadelphia: Fortress Press, 1976), 77.

[54] Edward Farley, "Toward a New Paradigm of Preaching," Thomas G. Long and Edward Farley, eds., *Preaching as a Theological Task: World, Gospel, Scripture* (Louisville: Westminster John Knox Press, 1996), 169.

[55] Marilynne Robinson, *Gilead* (New York: Farrar, 2004), 69.

[56] Browne, *The Ministry of the Word*, 46.

[57] Arthur John Gossip, *In Christ's Stead* (Grand Rapids: Baker Book House, 1968), 166-167.

Sermon
A Word on Behalf of Sin
Matthew 1:21; Romans 5:6-11

There is an old conversation about sermons that goes something like this: "Did you hear the preacher today?" "Yes." "What did he preach about? " "He preached about sin." "What did he say?" "He was against it."

This morning I am going to do something a little different. I am going to speak a word in favor of sin, a word on behalf of sin. Before you seek to have my ordination certificate revoked, though, let me explain what I am trying to do. I am not seeking to promote sinning. But I do want us to understand that sin is a valid category in human experience. Sin is a proper way of talking about the way people live at times. I am saying this because it is not popular today to talk about sin. You don't find many books written about sin in the theological world. Sin has become almost a taboo subject. You and I will see and read more about sin on the marquees of the theater, on TV, or in the paperback book selection of the bookstores. There you see people talking about sin—the movies and the theater and the paperback world. But the pulpit and the church today have become almost silent about sin, except in the ultra-fundamentalist quarters.

In our text today, the Apostle Paul does not hesitate to speak about the reality of sin. In the fifth chapter of Romans, he states, "God commands his love toward us—that while we were sinners, Christ died for us" (v. 8). Here, Paul contrasts human love with God's love. He draws a distinction between the amazing love of God and the unworthiness of the sinner. Let us begin first with Paul's comments about the fact that we are sinners.

Our Sinful Nature

In Romans 5:6-11, Paul uses four expressions to describe the sinfulness of men and women. These words translated are: without strength or powerless (v. 6), ungodly or wicked (v. 6), missing the mark (v. 8), and enemies (v. 10). We do not have the strength to live as we want to. We do not have a real sense of the sacredness of God. We do not have the ability to stay on course, and our sinfulness has caused us to be enemies with God.

Missing the Mark

Jesus was confronted by some religious leaders in his day who attempted to make rules and regulations about life exact and formalized. All one had to do was to abide by the rulebook. If he did, his relationship with God would be alright. That approach got difficult very early, because those who drew up the rule book began to add footnotes to their regulations and then footnotes to the footnotes.

Some of the rabbinical schools in the day of Jesus began to split hairs over whether or not a woman was bearing a burden if she stuck a needle in her dress when she was sewing. If a person traveled more than a prescribed distance from his home on the Sabbath, he was committing a sin. They even debated whether or not one could eat an egg laid on the Sabbath. We still have those persons today who want to legitimize morality for us. They want to prescribe morality for us and tell us what to do. We have to follow their morality code. The legalists are still with us today.

Then, there are those who want to be on the other end of the moral scale and say: "Well, just let me make my own decisions. I will decide. My conscience will determine what is right and wrong for me. I do not need any church, any God, or any person telling me how I should live or how I should act."

I guess my problem with that approach is that I am troubled with the untroubled conscience of some people. It will let them do anything, any place, any time. There was a time when the conscience of some said, "It's okay to make human sacrifices"—and they did. Neither Hitler nor the German soldiers involved in Nazism let their conscience stop them from annihilating six million Jews. Saddam Hussein had a conscience that put a low value on human life. I am very troubled by those who want to say, "I will let my conscience be my guide," because the history of the world is filled with pages stained by blood based on individual decisions about right and wrong.

Weakness

Paul uses "weakness" or "powerless" (v. 6) as another image for sin. Some people reveal the weakness of their own character when they cry out, "I am not responsible for the sins of society. I am not responsible for my own sin. I am really free from blame."

You may occasionally read the cartoon in the daily newspaper called the "Family Circus." That cartoon often depicts an "invisible" figure. This figure usually appears in the background. The mother or father will ask the children if they have done something. They might be asked, for example, if they have left their father's paintbrush on top of the open can to dry, or if they have left his tools in the woods, or if they have put their fingerprints on the wall. Each time, when they are reprimanded for various things, they reply, "Not me." This "invisible" figure is seen in each of these pieces as symbolizing another person called "Not me."

In our society today some of us almost always want to say "Not me." We point to someone else for the blame. We know how to place responsibility: We blame heredity, we blame the environment, we blame illness, we blame circumstances or emotions or a person. It is always someone else's fault. We do this individually and as a nation. You see it all the time in politics. "It was the previous administration that caused this problem." Some parents even place the blame for their actions on their children. It is always someone else—"not me." This attitude manifests itself at various times in the life of everyone after childhood.

Lucy walks up to Charlie Brown one day and says to him, "I want to talk to you, Charlie Brown. As your sister's consulting psychiatrist, I must put the blame for her fears on you." "On me?" Charlie Brown responds. "Each generation," Lucy continues, "must be able to blame the previous generation for its problems. It doesn't solve anything. But it makes us all feel better!"

Each of us wants to place blame on another. This does not mean that heredity, the environment, and/or circumstances have nothing to do with who and what we are. They are a significant part. But these factors do not remove our personal responsibility for whom we have become.

Karl Menninger, who is not a practicing theologian but a psychiatrist, has written a book titled, *Whatever Became of Sin?*, in which he focuses on the reality of sin in the behavior of people. Although he is well aware of the factors that constitute and influence a person's background, he calls for an awareness of personal responsibility in moral values. We can't always blame circumstances and others for our present state. Our sense of guilt, anxious mind, loss of direction, and confusion of thought are rooted in our need for the recognition of sin. The fault with our present state, Menninger reminds us, is a result of the sin within us.

Harvey Cox, a theologian at Harvard University, has written a book titled, *On Not Leaving It to the Snake.* His discussion begins with Adam and

Eve, who would not take responsibility for their sins. They blamed the snake. Down through the centuries, individuals have constantly blamed other "snakes" for their problems by refusing to take responsibility for their own sense of sinfulness. We always believe that someone or something else has caused our problems. The fault always lies elsewhere.

Ungodliness

We have missed the mark. We are without strength, Paul notes, but we are also ungodly at times as sinners. Sin is not seen much as an immoral act. Sin should not be used in the plural. It is not our sins, but rather our *sin* that is the great, all-pervading problem of our life. To be in the state of sin is to be in the state of separation. Sin has separated us from one another, from one's own true self, or from our God. The great words of our religious tradition cannot be replaced. There are no substitutes for words such as "sin" and "grace."

Sin is that which separates us from ourselves, from God, and from others. Sin is the fragmentation that destroys relationship. Sin, in its widest sense, is not only our individual sins but also our sense of sinfulness—our "God-almightiness." Sin is an attempt to assert our "myness." This is our way of saying: "I want to take control of my life, without any sense of needing God. I am totally in control. I am the master of my fate, the captain of my soul. I do not need others or God."

In the Scriptures there is a clear correlation between baptism and the forgiveness of sins as a matter of death and life. In the early church the connection between baptism and the death and resurrection of Christ was clear to candidates. Those of us who practice believer's baptism have not lost the original symbolism. When a person is led into the baptistery and lowered under the water, death to the old way of sin is symbolized. That person is raised, as Christ was from the grave, to walk as in newness of life with him.

Sin is the reality that leads, the Scriptures declare, to death. Sin, in all of its seriousness, creates death within our authentic self and death in our relationship with other people, and most profoundly it has separated us from God. The Scriptures are very clear about the darkness of sin. "The wages of sin is death" (Rom. 6:23). Sin threatens our sense of life's meaning, and our self-centeredness results in death. Death is the consequence of a meaningless life that has lost its sense of direction and purpose.

I am too old to talk about being innocent, and, if you can read this, so are you. I can remember when I had some sense of innocence. I can remember when I didn't know what drugs or alcoholism was. I can recall a time before I knew what war was, or murder, or death. I can remember when I didn't know what adultery was. All of these were totally unknown to me. I was a child and was completely innocent of such knowledge. But I am too old, and I have committed too many sins not to believe in the reality of sin.

I recall one of the first times in my conscious life when I knew I had done something I really should not have done. I knew what I was doing. I knew I was doing it against my parents' desires. Most of all, I had an aching feeling that I didn't think even God wanted me to do it, but I did it anyway. I do not deny the reality of sin because I know that I am a sinner. I have worked, counseled, and talked with too many other people not to know that we are all sinners. "If we claim to be sinless, we are self-deceived and strangers to the truth" (1 John 1:8 NEB). In this small epistle, John tells us that if we pretend we have no sin or if we attempt to deny our sin, then we make God a liar. God has spoken about the reality of sin within our world. It is here. We cannot pretend to be innocent. When we sin, we sin against ourselves and others and, ultimately, against God.

Rebellion Against God

Paul states, "When we were God's enemies," (v. 10) we had rebelled against God. We chose to turn our back on God and go our own way. God has created the kind of universe in which sin is possible. When we sin, God doesn't reach over and say: "Ah, I saw you do that and I'm gonna get you." We crush ourselves instead against God's laws. God has created a universe in which there are natural laws.

There are also moral and spiritual laws. And when we violate them, we feel the repercussions of our actions. For example, suppose I drink too much and become intoxicated and then get in my automobile and drive down the highway at some breakneck speed without control because I am drunk. Whether I want to or not, the laws of motion and stability will be enforced. If I run into a tree, whether I want to or not, my car will crash and I may be hurt or killed. Or because of my high speed, I may kill other people.

God doesn't will that, but God permits it. God gives us freedom to do his will or to violate it. God gives me the freedom to abuse my body or to make it stronger. God gives me the freedom to try to learn to do good or to do evil. God gives me the freedom to try to live a moral life or to live an immoral life. God does not force me to conform. When I violate the moral and spiritual laws built into the universe, into my life, and into relationships, I often can get hurt. Or I may hurt other people.

Harry Emerson Fosdick said that when he was a young boy his father left the house one Saturday morning and turned to his mother and said: "Tell Harry that he can cut the grass today, if he feels like it." Then he took a few steps and thought for a moment and said: "Tell him that he had better feel like it."

When we disobey God, we harm ourselves. God gives us freedom to live in the world. God is not going to confront us with some giant fly swatter to smack us when we sin. But we hurt ourselves as we break the moral and spiritual laws in the universe.

Though we may receive forgiveness, and hopefully we will, that does not remove all the consequences that may have resulted from some sinful act. When the prodigal son came home, he was forgiven. But his forgiveness would not undo some problem he may have created in the far country. If he became involved with some young woman and she became pregnant, his forgiveness would not undo that act. Or if he was engaged in some fight and he lost a hand, he could receive forgiveness from his father, but his hand would not be restored. God forgives us, but sometimes the consequences of our sinfulness may go on for a long time.

God's Love

Let us now turn the page and look at Paul's description of the amazing love of God in contrast to our sinfulness. In verse 8 Paul writes that God commends, recommends, demonstrates, or proves God's love to us. Proves is a word of logic and is not too satisfying to me. Commends addresses the heart.

There is a great gulf that separates us from God because of God's holiness. God is wholly and holy other. When Moses saw the burning bush and experienced God's presence, he was commanded to take off his shoes because he was in the presence of the holy God. Isaiah saw the holiness of God in the temple in a great vision. God is righteous; we are sinners.

Paul notes in our text that a person might be willing to die for a just person but not for an unworthy person or an undeserving individual (v. 7). But God's love was extended to us even while we were sinners. A person might have hated God, but God still loves that person. Even while I am rebelling against God, God loves me. We may not be deserving of God's love, but God loves us anyway.

Paul states that "Christ died for us" (v. 8). This is a sacrificial death on a cross. Christ died for us while we were sinners. God did not say we had to be good before he would love us. God loves bad children and bad adults, not that he likes for us to do bad things—sin. But Christ loves us even while we are bad and laid down his life for us.

Christ died. That is a fact. He suffered and laid down his life. His death was a sacrifice for you and me. He laid down his life so that you and I might have life. Our Lord paid the price of suffering for our sins. He gave his life to set us free. He delivered us not from the consequences of sin but from sin. The center of sin is self-centeredness. Christ has freed us from the sin of having self at the center and replaced it with God at the center.

If sin is not considered serious business, we make a mockery of the cross. Whatever else we may want to say about the cross, the cross stands in the center of the universe as the great symbol of God taking sin seriously. We will have to decide whether we will make our own atonement by our own efforts, or whether we will accept God's atonement in Christ. The cross stands as God's love that reaches from eternity into time to touch your life and mine and that offers us forgiveness for our sin and a new beginning. Forgiveness is serious business, and so is sinfulness. But God's love is a great love.

Proof of God's Love

The sacrificial death of Christ, Paul states in verse 8 is "proof" of God's love for us. "God demonstrates (proves) his own love toward us, in that while we were sinners, Christ died for us." Rather than "proof," I prefer "commends" or "recommends." This is the way John depicts Jesus when he said, "If I be lifted up, I will draw all persons unto me" (John 12:32). Christ's sacrifice draws persons to God out of that great love.

Twice Paul uses the phrase "much more" (vv. 9, 10) to affirm that the center of our religion is a new kind of life we have experienced in the sacrifice of Christ. We are now "in Christ" or " in the love of God." We are reconciled to God by the death of Christ. "God so loved the world that he gave his only son" (John 3:16). Jesus declared, "He that has seen me has seen the Father" (John 14:9). Christ's life and death demonstrate God's love to us in a unique way.

God's forgiveness allows us to become the authentic persons God has created us to be. God's redemption restores us with the quality of life we were created to have. God reveals to us what we can be through the power of his redeeming love.

The Scriptures declare to us that, although we are sinners who have all sinned and fallen short of the glory of God; nevertheless, God reaches out his loving arms and draws us unto himself and says, "I forgive you." Sin has created a sense of brokenness within us, between God, ourselves, and others.

Sin has separated us from our true and authentic self. We have been distorted by sin, and sin has distorted our relationship with other people. But God, in his forgiveness, offers us an opportunity to build a new bridge to restore our broken relationship with him, to help in the restoration of our relationships with others, and to help pull our broken self together. The word salvation means wholeness or fullness. God brings us back together again.

A pastor had a young man, who at one time had been very faithful in his church attendance, come to see him and express little concern for his wayward path. He gave a lengthy list of sins he had committed, but each time he would say, "But I don't care." "I've done this and that, but I don't care." The pastor asked the young man if he would promise him that he would pray a prayer each night. The prayer was, "Lord, Jesus, you have died upon the cross so that my sins might be forgiven, but I don't care." For several nights, the young man prayed this prayer until finally one night he could not do it. The appeal, the attraction, the commendation of the cross touched his heart and he reached out to accept God's forgiveness.

There may be someone here this morning who has unconfessed sins and has not found forgiveness. These sins may be tearing you down inside. They may be eating at your heart. The gospel is good news. In Jesus Christ you can find redemption, forgiveness, and new life. This is what the gospel is all about. While we were yet sinners, Christ died for us so that we might have life, and have it abundantly.

This morning before you leave this building, I hope you silently will make a confession of your sins—those unacknowledged ones, those you often dare not bring into focus. Seek this morning to find forgiveness and to experience the grace of God. This is what the gospel is about. It is good news that, sinner though you and I are, we can find forgiveness and reconciliation. Come home. The prodigal son wandered off. When he came to himself, he came home to his father. Come home today and find forgiveness, reconciliation, and the wholeness God can give to your life. This salvation is free, but you must be willing to accept it and walk in the environment and companionship with Christ.

> O God, we acknowledge that the sin in our life is often so real. It has pulled us down and separated us from our real self and from those we want to love and most importantly from you. We pray that we can be made whole again through your love and grace. Thank you for loving us, and we come accepting that love we have seen through Jesus Christ, our Lord. Amen.

Part 4
Confronting Our Culture Through
Literature and the Arts:
Preaching and Christian Imagination

Samuel H. Miller, who was former dean of Harvard Divinity School and several decades ago served as pastor of Old Cambridge Baptist Church, was asked once by a theological student where he might attend church in New York City to find spiritual stimulation. Miller replied that he knew of only one or two such churches and could promise that inspiration only if the regular minister were in the pulpit. But he went on to add that he knew of four or five plays where the student would likely experience such stimulation.

Miller's point was apparent. There are many occasions when the pulpit fails to address the deepest needs of men and women, whereas the theatre, contemporary literature, or other forms of the arts may have already expressed the haunting questions of the human heart. The arts in every generation often confront the struggles in human existence before the anguish and questions of the human spirit are translated into theological or philosophical statements. The preacher, then, who ignores modern literature is missing an opportunity to put a finger on the pulsebeat of society. The aches, joys, hopes, failures, longings, and weaknesses of the contemporary Adam and Eve are often most visible not on the pages of theology but on the modern stage or in the pages of fiction.

Contemporary literature probes inside the human soul and exposes the mental and emotional frustrations and illusions within. Theology often can only describe this experience from without. Modern literature opens up the inner thoughts and feelings of a person and gives the reader an opportunity to see inside the mind of another. These writers are, as it was said of Shakespeare, "circumnavigators of the human soul." The preacher reads modern literature not primarily to find illustrations for sermons, but as the repository of the human struggle for existence. To neglect the reading of modern literature may be to close one's mind to the sharpest insights into the theological issues of our time.

Literature and Life

The question for the preacher, "Read any good books lately or seen any stimulating plays?" is more than a casual throw-away inquiry. The modern literature you have read or the current plays you have seen may have revealed more to you about life today than you have sensed in your private study of the Scriptures. Without apology, this literature may have pulsated with the anguish and absurdity many people feel in life: the absence of God; the brokenness of the human spirit; the materialism, secularism, and sensuousness of society; the problems of evil, sin, suffering, and death; and countless other exposures of the walk of modern Adam and Eve.

The preacher who declares he is too busy to read or doesn't want to waste his time reading such "trash" loses an opportunity to engage in what may be the most profound dialogue theology may have with the real world. The deepest needs that members of our congregations feel may be best articulated in the writings of persons unknown and distant to them, yet expressive of their own spirit. The anonymous persons walking the pages and stages of contemporary literature voice the unspoken cries of many persons in our society today.

Reasons for Reading Modern Literature

Why should ministers take time from their busy schedules to read modern literature when there are so many good books on theology and the Bible they never seem able to find time to read? While I encourage you to drink deeply from the finest theology pools you can find, for they are refreshment for a thirsty soul, modern literature offers a medium of communication for the minister with the society around her. As an apologist for the need of a minister to read modern literature, I offer the following reasons why I think a minister, who is serious about theological studies, should likewise be interested in the arts.

Disclose the Reality of the World

Modern literature often discloses the reality of the world in which we live. None of us can be exposed to the entire world. We take in only a small part of the world wherever we live. That small piece of territory becomes the focal point from where we see and hear all the rest of the world. We are often isolated and insulated from much of the rest of the world except through small samples we hear on television or read about in the secular press.

There is much more in the world of which we need to be aware. The reading of modern literature may open that door for us.

C. S. Lewis pointed out what he called six "sub-Christian values in literature":

1. Honor
2. Sexual love
3. Material prosperity
4. Pantheistic contemplation of nature
5. The longing that is awakened by the past, the remote, or the (imagined) supernatural
6. Liberation of impulses

Lewis concluded by noting that his reference was to culture as a "storehouse of the best sub-Christian *values,* not the best sub-Christian *virtues.*" "I mean by this," he continued, "that culture recorded man's striving for those ends which, though not the true end of man (the fruition of God), have nevertheless some degree of similarity to it, and are not so grossly inadequate to the nature of man as to say, physical, pleasure, or money."[1]

Many Christians, even preachers, often want to apologize for reading modern literature. Because of what they consider debased vices of life—the use of profanity and the themes of sex, incest, violence, and immorality—many ministers have thrown modern literature aside and refused to read it. And if they do read it, they are reluctant to expose much of their reading to others. But the value of each book of modern literature must be based on the intention of the author for his writing. Many of the stories in the Old Testament are filled with sex and violence. Do we reject them as being helpful because of this exposure? Obviously we do not. We see a slice of life in the world of that day.

Modern literature attempts likewise to give us a picture, from the author's viewpoint obviously, of what life is like today in some concrete time and setting. At times this may involve scenes of violence, sex, and depravity. But all of this is, unfortunately, part of the human struggle. Denying or ignoring it isolates one from the real world and encourages living in a fantasy land.

Some ministers refuse to read contemporary literature because they hide behind the admonition "to love not the world nor the things in the world." Reading literature does not affirm that the minister loves all the base things of the world, but it does expose him to their reality. The Scriptures are also bold to declare that God sent God's Son into the world because of the great divine love for the world. The Bible reveals the story of God at work in human history—setting Israel free from bondage, leading the Israelites to the promised land, establishing a nation, calling this nation back to righteousness when its citizens strayed, and being present with God's people in exile and restoration. God's ultimate expression of love for the world was "the Word which became flesh." God entered uniquely within history to redeem the world. "There is a very real danger of our drifting into an attitude of contempt for humanity . . . ," Dietrich Bonhoeffer observed. "The only profitable relationship to others—and especially to our weaker brethren—is one of love, which is the will to hold fellowship with them. Even God did not despise humanity, but became Man for man's sake."[2]

The minister's willingness to dialogue with the world through the arts is founded on a theological premise: God's creation of and love for the world. Reading of literature opens us more readily to hear the bad news in the world. There is no denying the reality of sin, evil, and tragedy in the world. Before the good news of the gospel can be proclaimed, there is the bad news that each of us is a sinner. Modern literature often lays bare the utter nakedness of human sin. The warts of human depravity are made visible in the dark corners or public domains of human experience.

Novels such as Clyde Edgerton's *Raney*, Walker Percy's *The Moviegoer*, and Jill McCorkle's *Tending to Virginia* and *Carolina Moon* depict human relationships and remarkable men and women in vivid, provocative, often hilarious, and profound ways. John Killinger's novel, *The Zacchaeus Solution*, which some have compared to a contemporary version of *In His Steps*, shows a modern church dealing with the world's economic downturn. In the novel, church members decide to give half of their savings to assist others. The story unfolds to show the impact this decision has on the church, the community, the nation, and the world. In the process, the church acknowledges the problem of financial desperation and the necessity of the church to take an ethical Christian stance toward it.[3]

The Glass Menagerie by Tennessee Williams is the story of a crippled, lonely girl, Laura, who is surrounded by a neurotically ambitious mother and a brother who wants to help but succeeds only in making matters worse. Her caller, Jim, builds up her hopes at first but shatters them later. Williams depicts the emotions of persons who feel trapped in poverty and urban blight. The play, which many feel has an autobiographical aspect in the son named Tom, who resembles Williams in some ways, focuses on the problem of illusion and reality. Laura escapes from reality by retreating into a world of artificial glass animals, but they too are very fragile.

A play such as this one by Williams exposes human weakness and need—sin. But there is echoed in the play the longing for hope. Listen to the words of Tom, the narrator, as he speaks about the gentleman caller who is, he says, the most realistic character in the play: "Since I have a poet's weakness for symbols, I am using this character also as a symbol; he is the long delayed but always expected something that we live for."[4] Here is the hope of the good news the Christian gospel proclaims.

Raise Awareness of the Conditions of Others

Modern literature not only unveils the world to us, but also this knowledge can make us more aware of the conditions of others. The plunge into the world of modern literature baptizes us in the common, strange, or remarkable experiences of other humans. This baptism into a new or different world enlarges our own awareness of reality and our ability to respond to it. Whether the characters come alive on the pages of Fyodor Dostoevsky, Herman Melville, Albert Camus, Franz Kafka, D. H. Lawrence, Samuel Beckett, William Faulkner, Ernest Hemingway, Saul Bellow, Mark Twain, John Updike, Thomas Wolf, Henry Miller, Richard Wright, James Baldwin, John Grisham, Danielle Steele, Pat Conroy, Dean Koontz, Ken Follett, Dan Brown, Tom Clancy, or others, they mirror sometimes our own hidden needs or longings or awaken our conscience to the deep chambers within someone else's life.

The book *Native Son* by Richard Wright, for example, discloses the hate, resentment, anger, and violence the black man had compressed for centuries. Bigger Thomas is a symbol of the lament in the souls of black people. This book was the beginning of what later came to be called the "black is beautiful" and "black power" philosophy.

No one can read *Native Son* and be unaware of the smoldering violence and longing for full liberation in the hearts of African Americans. You may not be willing to respond, but your awareness has been awakened. Literature can provoke such an awakening. Shelley observes that through imagination, literature provides the means for a person "to put himself in the place of another and of many others; the pains and pleasures of his species must become his own."[5]

Contemporary writers often paint vivid plots that reveal the struggle between the forces of good and evil, sometimes in white-knuckle, blood-curdling, horrifying ways, and at other times with almost surreal and supranational dimensions. The fantasies, science fiction, allegory, myth, legend, fable, or whatever you may want to call J. R. R. Tolkien's *Lord of the Rings*, C. S. Lewis' *The Hobbit* or *The Chronicles of Narnia*, or J. K. Rowling's

Harry Potter books, or Charles Williams' writings all invite the reader or viewer into a sharp contrast with the forces of good and evil. These writings appeal to children, young people, and adults alike. John Killinger's book, *God, the Devil and Harry Potter: A Christian Defense of the Beloved Novels*, offers helpful ways of preaching from the Potter novels. The writings of Dean Koontz, Dan Brown, John Grisham, and others probe this ongoing struggle of good with evil. These imaginative writings could inspire the preacher to prepare a sermon fantasy on a biblical text such as Jonah and the Whale, Noah, or Jesus casting out demons or walking on water. The Book of Revelation could be made to come alive by using one's imagination to project the battle portrayed between the forces of good and evil in its pages.

Address the Questions of Human Existence

The writers of contemporary literature may not only raise our awareness of the real world and make us more sensitive to it, but their writings also may actually address the real questions of human existence long before the theoretical writers pen their theologies or philosophies about these issues.

John Killinger draws an image from Virgil Gheorghiu's novel about how underwater sailors once took white rabbits aboard their vessels to warn them of any dangerous reduction of oxygen. The rabbits died the moment the atmosphere became poisonous. At that moment the sailors knew they had no more than five or six hours left to live. "The artist," said Father Jarrett-Kerr, "is the white rabbit of society; he feels before others the atmospheric changes which will affect us all a little later."[6]

Richard Wright, Ralph Ellison, and others wrote novels about the black man's struggles several generations before James Cone's *Black Theology and Black Power* was heralded as "a truly prophetic book." Albert Camus expressed his philosophy of existentialism through novels such as *The Fall, The Plague*, and *The Stranger* before others began to philosophize about it. Aldous Huxley's *Brave New World,* and Kafka's *The Trail* predate the "death of God" theology by several decades.

The writers of absurd drama, for example, Eugene Ionesco, Samuel Beckett, and Franz Kafka, have raised a metaphysical question about the meaning of life. They testify only to emptiness, absurdity, and meaninglessness. Earlier, Ernest Hemingway and William Faulkner struggled with a similar question about death and the meaning of life. Was not Jürgen Moltmann's masterpiece *Theology of Hope* a resource to the philosophy that had been in the air for generations? "If faith thus depends on hope for its life," he declared, "then the sin of unbelief is manifestly grounded in hopelessness."[7]

In one of his short stories in *Ford County* titled "Funny Boy," John Grisham draws a powerful picture, arising from the dream of a man dying from AIDS, of a rowdy hellfire-and-brimstone preacher in a church revival meeting who invites sinners, as the choir sings, to repent and come forward and surrender all to Jesus. When the man, who is known by people in the community to have AIDS, comes forward and approaches the preacher's outstretched hand, the scene becomes comical as the people rush out of the church through the doors and windows, mothers grasping their children's hands and colliding with each other as they try to avoid the funny man with AIDS. The dream ends before it is known whether the nervous, terror-faced preacher actually takes the "sinner's" hand or not.[8] In this pointed story, Grisham shows how a "Christian" community and church react in a very un-Christlike spirit to a person suffering and dying from a dread disease called AIDS, allowing ignorance, fear, gossip, and prejudice to determine their response to someone in need. Here is authentic preaching through a short story.

Sharpen the Minister's Word Power

Reading modern literature will likewise sharpen the minister's intellectual gifts and enliven his word power. Exposure to good writing should rub off at least some on the reader. By reading carefully crafted novels and plays, the minister is exposed to the power of words to communicate images and pictures of life. Since words are a vital part of our life's blood as a vocation, should we not polish and fine-tune them? How can we not learn from a writer like Annie Dillard, whose wisdom emerges in the excerpts below?

> How confidently I had overlooked all this—rocks, bugs, rain. What else was I missing? I opened books like jars. Here between my hands, here between some book's front and back covers, whose corners poked dents in my palm, was another map to the neighborhood I had explored all my life, and fancied I knew, a map depicting hitherto invisible landmarks. After I learned to see those, I looked around for something else. I never knew where my next revelation was coming from, but I knew it was coming—some hairpin curve, some stray bit of romance or information that would turn my life around in a twinkling.[9] . . .

> For as long as I could remember, I had been transparent to myself, unselfconscious, learning, doing, most of every day. Now I was in my own way; I myself was a dark object I could not ignore. I couldn't remember how to forget myself. I didn't want to think about myself, to reckon myself in, to deal with myself every livelong minute on top of everything else—but swerve as I might, I couldn't avoid it. I was a boulder blocking my own path. I was a dog barking between my own ears, a barking dog who wouldn't hush.[10]

Reading not only opens the mind to pathways that may have never been spread before us, but also teaches us through constant exercise the discipline of working and reworking at thinking thoughts after another and noting how the building blocks of that particular novel, play, or short story were constructed. Novelists such as Hemingway, Kafka, Percy, Koontz, and Brown can teach the preacher the power of symbolism. Faulkner, O'Neill, and Beckett offer a study in different styles. Utilizing the lessons offered by modern writers will eventually have a positive effect upon your preaching.

Nurture the Aesthetic Spirit Within

The reading of contemporary literature can also nurture the aesthetic spirit within us. There is, of course, more to life than having good taste. A person may have good taste and still be a thief or a murderer. But artistic beauty acts as an interpreter of life. Beauty is not our chief end in life's pilgrimage, nor the ethical standard for our decision, but is a faithful companion that enriches our quest. The beauty of words shows order and harmony. The beauty of words is the result of the creative activity of a person seeking to mirror the "thoughts" of God as she sees them." Like Shelley's nightingale, the preacher attempts to sing "sweet songs" and listeners are "entranced by the melody of an unseen musician."[11]

Nourish your thought in the creative companionship of good literature. Your impulses will be refined, and hopefully, your instinct for the sublime will deepen in its appreciation. I believe the beauty of words can point beyond themselves to the beauty within nature and to the God who was revealed in the ultimate beauty in the Living Word. This opens the door to intuition where we can sense the presence of God within.

Scrutinize the Messages

Finally, the Christian minister needs to read modern literature openly to hear the messages being conveyed without being swept under the flood of those messages and losing his own footing. We are affected by what we read just as we are affected by what we eat. Scrutinize the philosophy behind and within the words that communicate the story.

T. S. Eliot warned the Christian reader that no one can read "purely for pleasure." According to Eliot, "It is the literature that we read with the least effort that can have the easiest and most insidious influence upon us."[12] To Eliot, modern literature has been corrupted by "secularism" and denies the primacy of the supernatural over the natural. He continued his argument thus:

> It is our business, as readers of literature, to know what we like. It is our business, as Christians, as well as readers of literature, to know what we ought to like. It is our business as honest men, not to assume that whatever we like is what we ought to like . . . What I believe to be incumbent upon all Christians is the duty of maintaining consciously certain standards and criteria of criticism over and above those applied by the rest of the world; and that by these criteria and standards everything that we read must be tested.[13]

John Killinger in his book, *The Failure of Theology in Modern Literature*, calls the theologian to interpret and editorialize. He attests the diagnostic, therapeutic, and noted values of contemporary writing. He affirms the authors' independence and integrity as writers. But he does believe that the theologian—minister/Christian—should judge modern literature by the standard of the historical content of the Christian faith.[14]

The ultimate test of all reading material for us is judged by the revelation we have in Jesus Christ. In seeking to experience the reality of the world, remember not "to throw the baby out with the bath water." We have tangible Christian values that anchor our faith. Take heed and do not let every new breeze blow you into judging a book solely on the author's own principles and not the higher principle of Christian theology. If we are not careful, we may fall down at the altars of the gods of imagination.

The Arts and the Imagination

All of this discussion about the importance of the minister reading modern literature and being exposed to the arts leads me to attest to the impact of that encounter on the imagination. "Imagination bodies forth the forms of things unknown," wrote Shakespeare, and "gives to airy nothing a local habitation and a name." But the word imagination has not received a good press. We often say condescendingly of a person, "It's all in his imagination" or "She just imagined that" or "He surely has a vivid imagination." When something is hard to accept, we sometimes exclaim: "Imagine that!" The implications are clear; imagination is an escape from reality, a mirrored reflection not the authentic, a fantasy as opposed to the concrete.

But who says this has to be so? There needs to be a healthy concept of Christian imagination. Who says we have to draw only from the left side of the brain? Many of our most insightful sermon ideas seem to come "out of the blue." But rather than appearing out of nothing, maybe they are the product of God's Spirit working quietly within our intuitive self. The second commandment opposed idolatry, not imagination. We can take another lesson here from the Master Teacher.

Phillips' translation of Mark 11:19 states that Christ's teaching had "captured the imagination of the people." Might our imagination be the most focal point of God's whisper to us? Maybe this is what P. T. Forsyth was eluding to in his Lyman Beecher Lectures delivered a hundred years ago when he wrote: "The Christian preacher is not the successor of the Greek orator, but of the Hebrew prophet . . . In so far as the preacher and prophet had an analogue in Greece it was the dramatist . . ."[15]

Henry Ward Beecher, in the first of the Lyman Beecher Lecture series, stated that "the first element on which your preaching will largely depend for power and success, you will perhaps be surprised to learn, is *Imagination,* which I regard as the most important of all the elements that go to make the preacher."[16] He thought that the preacher's imagination was an essential vehicle in communicating the good news drawn from the Scriptures.

J. Barrie Shepherd, in his 2002 Lyman Beecher Lectures, urged the preacher to draw upon a "poetic vision" in striving to declare the mystery of the "mediation of transcendence" that belies the preacher's attempt at explanations of that great mystery."[17] He also asserted that "imagination is the one absolute essential to the preacher. Without it the sermon is Spiritless in the fullest and most theological sense of that word."[18]

George Bernard Shaw wrote the following dialogue about St. Joan of Arc's source of her revelations.

Robert: How do you mean? Voices?
Joan: I hear voices telling me what to do. They come from God.
Robert: They come from your imagination.
Joan: Of course. That is how the messages of God come to us.[19]

The prophetic experiences of Jeremiah, Ezekiel, Elijah, and Daniel seem to testify to similar experiences. Rather than addressing the obviously national dimensions, God seemed to communicate to them through their non-sensuous perception. God's spirit and truth about him are often more grasped or caught than merely taught. The religious imagination is fertile soil for the moving of God's spirit in the lives of people and the chief environment for the preacher to sow his seeds of good news. George Buttrick has called imagination "A preacher's indispensably ally."[20]

A minister draws sermon material from listening to the needs of her congregation, listening to her own heart, and by listening to the messages that arise out of contemporary literature. This literature can provide a rich resource for stimulating the imagination. I offer the following categories as the preacher's occasion to draw on her imagination from the impact of modern literature on her preaching.

The Preacher as Seer

Originally the words seer and prophet were equated. The seer was one who saw into society—apprehended—and spoke "the Word of God" to meet the need or problem he saw. Listen to the prophet Isaiah:

> They are a rebellious people, who say to the seers, "see not";
> and to the prophets, "Prophesy not to us what is right;
> Speak to us smooth things, prophesy illusions." (30:10)

The office of the seer was not to respond to the people by giving them what they wanted to hear—smooth, easy answers—but to probe life with the standards and purposes of God. The ancient prophets were not afraid to draw on their imaginations. Jeremiah often used symbols to portray his message: an almond tree in early bloom, a boiling cauldron, the potter's house, an earthenware jar, two baskets of figs, a yoke, and others. Hosea compared his unfaithful wife to the unfaithfulness of Israel. Amos drew on his imagination and used the images of a basket of overripe fruit and a plumb line to speak about God's judgment on Israel. Through symbols they conveyed a particular truth about God and the world around them.

Today the preacher is also a seer—one who sees, dreams, and has visions. Drawing on his imagination, the preacher is called to see the needs of the congregation and the Word from the Lord. If we can't see, we will not hear our people or speak God's Word. "Eye has not seen, . . . nor ear heard, . . . the things which God has prepared for those who love him. But has revealed to them unto us by his Spirit" (1 Cor. 2:9). Rather than speaking about life after death in this passage, is it not possible that Paul was addressing the way God works in our lives in the present? The preacher sees through the power of God's Holy Spirit illuminating him within.

Drawing on what Paul Tillich called "the principle of correlation," the preacher listens and sees the questions arising out of the reality of the world that have been disclosed through modern literature and then attempts to answer those questions with the message she has seen in God's Word. She is a seer in two worlds—the world of humanity and the realm of the spirit. Look at three examples of some of the questions the preacher can see through the perspective of literature.

The feeling of the absence of God is depicted in Aldous Huxley's futuristic novel, *Brave New World*. Here is a scene where the Savage and the World Controller are examining copies of the Bible and William James' *The Varieties of Religious Experience* and *The Imitation of Christ*. The Savage asks if the World Controller believes there is no God.

> "No," answers the Controller, "I think there quite probably is one . . . But he manifests himself in different ways to different men. In pre-modern times he manifested himself as the being that's described in these books."
>
> "How does he manifest himself now?" asks the Savage.
>
> "Well," says the Controller, "he manifests himself as an absence; as though he weren't there at all."[21]

In one of Hemingway's short stories, "A Clean, Well-Lighted Place," an old man comes each night alone to a bar and sits and drinks until the bartender closes and asks him to leave. In the darkness of the night, he raises a parody of the Hail Mary in the words, "Hail Nada, full of Hada," and the

Lord's Prayer as "Our Nada which art in Nada, Nada be thy name." Nada is the Spanish word for "nothing."[22] Hemingway and Huxley both depicted the absence of God in life long before the "death of God" theologians were writing books about it.

As a seer, the preacher looks into modern literature and senses the fragmentation and insignificance many persons feel today. Who sees the total person and reacts to that individual as she really is? The answer seems to be written in the wind. In many parts of our community the church, businesses, newspapers, salespeople, attorneys, doctors, dentists, and ministers see only fragments of persons. Who sees the total person? The answer seems to be written in the wind.

The literature of the writers of the Theatre of the Absurd depicts life without hope. In their writings, humans are turned into insects and monsters. Their literature denotes the emptiness, absurdity, and meaninglessness of life. Life seems to have no purpose and no exit. Man's existence seems to be like a sick fly caught on a wheel of fate, in motion without direction. Life seems to be going nowhere.

David Karp has an interesting novel titled *One* that depicts a future totalitarian state in which a university professor named Burden is arrested for breaking the law because he perceives himself to be an individual of personal worth. This is heresy. After he is arrested, Burden is put through all kinds of brainwashing techniques to destroy his sense of individuality. The prosecutor decides to prove that human personality can be controlled scientifically. Following his imprisonment and physical and psychological tortures, Burden is only a shadow of his former self, with no memory of his past, his name, his family, or his profession. He is introduced in society as a timid man named Hughes. He is given a minor part in the state, and the prosecutor thinks he has been successful. But then one day a man who kept watch on this experiment discovers that Hughes thinks he is the only Mr. Hughes. Even after all of their brainwashing, this man still senses his individuality. The prosecutor then decides they must kill this man, thereby acknowledging that only death can reduce the human personality from one to zero.[23]

The problem is the same in the emphasis of the novel by Lawrence Sergeant titled *Stowaway*. Toward the end of this story there is a scene on the high seas aboard a vessel called *Liberty Belle*. O'Hara, the first mate, is engaged in conversation with another sailor. O'Hara states that he is determined to make something out of his life. His fellow seaman says, "Oh, what is the use? No man's life really counts for anything. Forget about it." O'Hara's face flushes; a blood vessel begins to throb in his temple. "You are wrong, mister," he responds. "The whole world may not be mine. But the space of it I am in—my part of it—is. It may not be for sure, or for much, or for long. But while I am in it, it'll know me."[24]

As a seer, the preacher notes the pain, struggles, fears, doubts, hope, faith, love, hate, good and evil, life and death, laughter and sorrow that are visible in the world of the arts. A seer not only sees the problems—the bad news—but offers some good news—the gospel. Our preaching has been open to draw from literature to discern the real world. Having sensed it, we respond with the message of hope from the God who loved the world so much he gave his only Son.

The Preacher as Artist

"Art," wrote G. K. Chesterton, "is the signature of man." The preacher is also an artist. She paints pictures or images with words. Through the spoken word, the preacher attempts to evoke a definite perspective about life from her listeners. Language is the brush or chisel the preacher garnishes to color images or carve symbols in the inner chambers of the listener's mind and heart. The sharpness of the preacher's word colors the glow of pictorial figures and beckons the listener to stay alert and follow the train of thought.

Literature has already "invoked reality" in the mind of the preacher. He has felt the heartthrob of life flowing through the pages of authors such as Eugene O'Neill, Thornton Wilder, Archibald MacLeish, Tennessee Williams, Arthur Miller, Edward Albee, Graham Greene, and Saul Bellow. God has manifested his presence in the past and present in burning bushes in various ordinary and unexpected places and continues to disclose his presence through the writings of famous or obscure authors. Whether a writer is explicitly Christian like Frederick Buechner or is struggling with the absence of God like Franz Kafka, both perspectives enrich the preacher's awareness of the real issues of living. Flannery O'Connor spoke to the power of literature this way:

> The basis of art is truth, both in matter and in mode. The person who aims after art in his work aims after truth, in an imaginative sense, no more and no less . . . I'm always highly irritated by people who imply that writing fiction is an escape from reality. It is a plunge into reality and it's very shocking to the system . . . The type of mind that can

understand good fiction is not necessarily the educated mind, but it is at all times the kind of mind that is willing to have its sense of mystery deepened by contact with reality, and its sense of reality deepened by contact with mystery.[25]

The preacher has dipped his brush into the mystery of literature and now attempts to paint pictures for his listeners that are drawn from the culture around him. Henry Mitchell stated this truth forcefully in his Lyman Beecher Lectures at Yale University Divinity School: "If you have an idea that can't be translated into a story or picture, don't use it."[26] Our listeners long for these "handles" or pictorial buckets to hang on to the thought being preached. Mitchell is convinced that the preacher's theological and biblical message will not be received by the whole person until it is translated into moving and graphic art and symbol—word pictures and narrations.[27]

Peter Marshall, the pastor of Washington's historic New York Avenue Presbyterian Church in the mid-1950s, developed his artistic gift well. Listen to his words paint images in your mind in his sermon, "The Saint of the Rank and File":

They wondered if Andrew was in love?

Ah, maybe that was it!
Little did they know how true it was—for indeed he was in love.
He had fallen completely in love with Jesus of Nazareth.
He was in love with a Voice.
    He was in love with a vision
        in love with a Face
            in love with a faith
and every day and every night he dreamed and wondered in his
heart about the things that Christ had said . . .
        "this kingdom of God on earth . . ."

The waves lapping against the boat seemed to be saying over
and over the things he had heard Him say.
    His voice was in the wind.
His face was in the sunlight dancing on the waves.

So, Andrew dreamed and waited.[28]

Likewise, the noted English preacher Frederick W. Robertson preached with a pictorial imagination. His words are alive with figures and images that linger in the mind. Here is a sample from his sermon, "The Irreparable Past":

> Time is the solemn inheritance to which every man is born heir, who has a life-rent of this world—a little section cut out of eternity and given us to do our work in: an eternity before, an eternity behind; and the small stream between, floating swiftly from one into the vast bosom of the other. The man who has felt with all his soul the significance of Time will not be long in learning any lesson that this world has to teach him . . . What will you do before today has sunk into eternity and nothingness again? And now what have we to say with respect to this strange solemn thing—Time? That men do with it through life just what the apostles did for one precious and irreparable hour in the garden of Gethsemane; they go to sleep. Have you ever seen those marble statues in some public square or garden, which art has so fashioned into a perennial fountain that through the lips or through the hands the clear water flows in a perpetual stream, on and on forever; and the marble stands there—passive, cold—making no effort to arrest the gliding water?
>
> It is so that Time flows through the hands of men—swift, never pausing till it has run itself out; and there is the man petrified into a marble sleep, not feeling what it is which is passing away forever.[29]

One of my favorite writers is Loren Eiseley, a naturalist, who has an unusual blend of scientific knowledge and imaginative vision as he explores the mysteries of humanity and nature. His writings appeal both to the mind and the senses. His vivid style is evident in Eiseley's characterization of the past:

> The door to the past is a strange door. It swings open and things pass through it, but they pass in one direction only. No man can return across that threshold, though he can look down still and see the green light waver in the water weeds.[30]

Some of Eiseley's most striking images are drawn in his figures lifted from the ordinary world of nature. But look at the strokes of beauty with which he paints. Feasting on this writer's imaginative gift will nurture any preacher's artistic quest. Here is his observation from one dark night:

> It was cold that autumn evening, and, standing under a suburban street light in a spate of leaves and beginning snow, I was suddenly conscious of some huge and hairy shadows dancing over the pavement. They seemed attached to an odd, globular shape that was magnified above me. There was no mistaking it. I was standing under the shadow of an orb-weaving spider. Gigantically projected against the street, she was about her spinning when everything was going underground. Even her cables were magnified upon the sidewalk and already I was half-entangled in their shadows.
>
> "Good Lord," I thought, "she has found herself a kind of minor sun and is going to upset the course of nature."
>
> I procured a ladder from my yard and climbed up to inspect the situation. There she was, the universe running down around her, warmly arranged among her guy ropes attached to the lamp supports—a great black and yellow embodiment of the life force, not giving up to either frost or stepladders. She ignored me and went on tightening and improving her web.[31]

We are called to proclaim a great gospel. Let's paint the most vivid and memorable sermons we can craft. Preaching itself is an art, and our art can be improved and enriched by modern literature.

The Preacher as Poet

"The Perfect Priest and the Perfect Poet are one," wrote Karl Rahner. The preacher as priest seeks to lead men and women to commune with God; the preacher as poet strives to communicate the mystery of that encounter through symbols, images, and limited vocabulary. Our words can never fully grasp or expound that meeting with the Sublime Other. We can, like the poet, only reflect, suggest, depict, inspire, examine, explore, scrutinize, disclose, stimulate, and challenge. Our words, no matter how eloquent, can never fully expound or explain the wonder of God's good news. Our words, as T. S. Eliot said, "strain, crack, and break" under the load they bear.

An articulate person today speaks about thirty thousand words a day. That's enough words for a good size book. By the close of our lifetime, each one of us will have spoken enough words to fill enough books to stock a good size college library. That's a lot of talk. And for preachers, we may fill up two or three universities with all our talk!

Think of the power of words. If a word is spoken, it is carried by sound waves to the eardrum. If the word is written, it is picked up by the light waves that strike the retina of the eye and convey the message to the brain cells. Words can be powerful, sharp, incisive, and penetrating or they may be dull, lifeless, and abstract.

Words can create powerful images. Images play an important role in our society today. Certain images determine styles, mannerisms, tastes, and preferences. The advertising market is well aware that images and words influence what people buy, eat, and wear, as well as where they go, stay, and play. In Rogers and Hammerstein's musical, *The Flower Drum Song*, a song presents brightly the question, "How will we ever communicate without communication?" Our business is to try to communicate. What would religion be without the words of our faith?

G. K. Chesterton, in *The Ball and the Cross*, describes the struggle of persons to communicate with words in this way:

> "Is not bloodshed a great sin?"
>
> "No," said MacIan, speaking for the first time.
>
> "Well, really, really!" said the peacemaker.
>
> "Murder is a sin," said the immovable Highlander. There is no sin of bloodshed."
>
> "Well, we won't quarrel about a word," said the other, pleasantly.
>
> "Why on earth not?" said MacIan, with a sudden asperity. "Why shouldn't we quarrel about a word? What is the good of words if they aren't important enough to quarrel over? Why do we choose one word more than another if there isn't any difference between them? If you call a woman a chimpanzee instead of an angel, wouldn't there be a quarrel about a word? If you're not going to argue about words, what are you going to argue about? Are you

going to convey your meaning to me by moving your ears? The church and the heresies always used to fight about words, because they are the only things worth fighting about. I say that murder is a sin, and bloodshed is not, and that there is as much difference between those words as there is between the word 'yes' and the word 'no'; or rather more difference, for 'yes' and 'no' at least belong to the same category. Murder is a spiritual incident. Bloodshed is a physical incident. A surgeon commits bloodshed."[32]

Think of the difficulty the preacher wrestles with every week. We have to transmit religious thoughts through words. A blank piece of paper has to be filled with words that mean something and communicate with our hearers. If we have to draw words out of our treasure chest of inspiration each week, let us learn to be a poet and make our words not only stand and walk but also skip, jump, run, and dance with aliveness. Why choose words that limp across our listener's mind and are colorless and dull? Select words that sing and excite the mind.

After hearing Maya Angelou read some of her poetry, Fred Craddock asked her, with such a difficult task to improve the conditions of the black women in America, why she chose the "fragile" weapon of poetry to do such a big job. She looked at him and responded: "Poetry is winged for the heart. Some of you white preacher types just go bruising the tree, but you never chop one down. I chose poetry—it goes to the heart."[33]

One of the most picturesque preachers of our modern era is Gardner Taylor, who served for forty years as pastor of the Concord Baptist Church of Christ in New York City. In a sermon titled "A Storm-Proof Religion," Taylor notes that Goodspeed translated Jesus' words, "Peace, be still" as "Hush." Note his poetical language:

> "Hush." The lightning folded its flame and ran back to its hiding place. "Hush." The winds got still and fled to their homes in the hills. "Hush." And the sea stretched out like a pet before its master. "Hush." And the elements grew calm. The Lord can speak peace to our souls. He says to us, "Hush, do not be disturbed. Do not be troubled. It is I—be not afraid."[34]

Taylor's proclaimed words are couched in simple images that often dance to a poetic rhythm and linger in the mind of the listener or grasp the reader's attention.[35]

The words of Paul Scherer in a Christmas sermon will be hard to forget: "That night of nights when God walked down the stairs of heaven with a baby on his arm." Likewise, Carlyle Marney's words below about the reaction of the disciples linger in the lobby of our mind:

> They did not even then believe in his death, much less his resurrection. And now his death was a brutal fact. It stunned like a blow. It was all they could stand. The wrenching and unrelieved agony of his going so suddenly from them dominated everything. Except for Peter himself, who had a terrible extra burden, for he was horribly, personally, agonizingly shamed—like a beaten dog of some kind he hid under a porch floor unrelievedly ashamed and bereft. And besides, undoubtedly by not someone had come across the body of Judas, so all they could feel was the collapse of everything.[36]

Note also the pictorial image of faith in the words of Nicholas Wolterstorff: "Faith is the footbridge that you don't know will hold you up over the chasm until you are forced to walk out onto it."[37] These images did not come quickly or easily to these preachers. But they were willing to invest the time, study, and preparation essential to imaginative preaching.

For the preacher to work at developing her poetic gifts is to acknowledge her debt to the Scriptures in communicating religious thought. After all, a major part of the Bible is written in the form of poetry. On this list would be Job, Psalms, Proverbs, the Song of Solomon, the creation stories in Genesis, and many sections of the Prophets and other parts of the Bible. Our Lord himself constantly drew on poetic images and metaphors: "The kingdom of heaven is like . . ." "I am the light of the world . . ." "I am the Bread of Life, the good Shepherd, the Way . . ." "Consider the lilies of the field . . ." Many sections of Paul's writings, including 1 Corinthians 13 on love, Ephesians 4 on the unity of the church, Ephesians 6 on the armor of God, and Philippians 2 on Christ's example of humility, ring with poetic beauty.

Much of our preaching is indebted to Aristotelian rhetoric. Maybe it's time we studied Aristotle's *Poetics*, too. "Authentic preaching is in its form more like poetry than scientific or argumentative prose," wrote Charles Rice.[38] The preacher is trying to address the senses along with the rational faculty. Pictures, images, symbols, and story will do this more effectively than abstract prose. Some few preachers have preached sermons written in metered poetry. If you can do that, fine. But few will have that gift, nor will that type of sermon be well received in many churches. We can all develop our poetic imagination, however. P. T. Forsyth has reminded us: "If truth lies at the bottom of a well, poetry is the water that covers and transfigures it, while it refreshes and restores."[39] Contemporary literature and the fine poetry of many persons can teach us how to think and speak pictorially.

In the beautifully moving novel *Cry, the Beloved Country* by Alan Paton, the preacher learns the poet's sensitivity to pain and suffering. The book pulsates with the drama of a father's aching heart and a son's sin. This novelist writes like a poet, and from his pages we draw a lesson about life. Kumalo, a black priest, faces the tragedy of his own son being executed for the murder of a white man. He doesn't know how to face his son's death. Hear this father's poignant cry.

> "Sorrow is better than fear," said Father Vincent doggedly. "Fear is a journey, a terrible journey, but sorrow is at last an arriving."
>
> "And where have I arrived?" asked Kumalo . . .
>
> "No one can comprehend the ways of God," says Father Vincent desperately.
>
> Kumalo looked at him, not bitterly or accusingly or reproachfully. "It seems that God has turned away from me," he said.
>
> "This may seem to happen," said Father Vincent. "But it does not happen, never, never, does it happen!"[40]

Another excellent source, of course, is poetry itself. Poetry from any age can instruct us in the art of communication. The noted professor of anthropology and essayist, Loren Eiseley, continues to be one of my poetic teachers. Listen to these lines from his collection of poems titled, *All the Night Wings*:

> To have tall ears and hemlock-sharpened brain,
> To run from death blue drawn to summer night,
> To prowl the endless alleys of the rain
> Or hop bewildered through the moon's cold light—
> This was the earliest wisdom. This will stay.
> As acorns come again from the bare ground
> So the hurt fox limps back again to play
> And stars return without a ghost of sound.
> This was the earliest wisdom. None can say
> Beyond what galaxies, on what dim coast
> Beaten by breakers, men first learned the way
> That love is, or despair, or which slays most.
> Ignore this protest of a fugitive.
> Say by the heart's unreason that we live.[41]

Coleridge once said there was never a great poet who was not also a philosopher. The poet often reached her conclusions not by rational argument alone, but by a leap of "prepared imagination." Ezra Pound has described poets as "the antennae of the race." Whether we draw on the great masters of the ages such as Shakespeare, Browning, Wordsworth, Coleridge, Byron, Keats, Whitman, Emerson, Tennyson, Milton, Goethe, Whittier, Poe, Longfellow, Frost, and Auden or read lesser-known, contemporary poets, our preaching will be exposed to the visions they have drawn from life around them. We may catch from them some bit of the spark that ignited their fire of enthusiasm.

The Preacher as Storyteller

In a real sense, authentic preaching is storytelling. Much of the Bible is filled with stories about persons and their relationship to God and those around them. The Bible begins with a story about Adam and Eve and progresses with the unfolding stories of Abraham, Jacob, Moses, David, Ruth, the prophets, and others who made up a part of the history of Israel. The New Testament is a story about the gospel story—the good news of God's Incarnate Word and the spreading of that story through part of the first-century world. The preacher seeks to retell various dimensions of that biblical story through the telling of his own shared story. We focus primarily on *the Story*. Our story is a response to *the Story*.

Why are preachers sometimes embarrassed to tell the Story? Charles Rice believes the problem arises from the fact that as Americans we have "all but lost the art of storytelling. We have, perhaps, lost the art because we have lost confidence in the power of the story." He urges the preacher: "Simply tell the story. Tell the story simply."[42]

The preacher needs to learn from our Lord the power of story. Jesus was a master storyteller. Jesus told sixty parables. The parables were his favorite way of teaching. We have heard these stories hundreds of times, but they never lose their powerful impact upon us. Today we can read them again and again, reflect on them, and analyze them, but we can never exhaust them. Their powerful images address our attention and challenge our living.

These remarkable parables of Jesus were not produced in quiet study after prolonged reflection, but they were provoked by situations and confrontations in the life of Jesus that caused him to produce them on the spur of the moment.

When the listener first heard Jesus' parables, he may have thought those stories were directed at someone else. But soon the listener realized in a surprising and unexpected way that he had been drawn into the story. The parables still grasp us today with their profound insights into human nature.

Today we think of these stories as biblical and do not recognize that when Jesus told them, they were really secular or worldly stories. They were drawn out of the common, everyday life of the people of Jesus' time. These stories were not identified as "the language of Canaan," but arose out of the culture and idioms of the ordinary people of the Middle East. Amos Wilder notes this truth in the following quote:

> Jesus, without saying so, by his way of presenting man in the parables, shows that for him man's destiny is at stake in his ordinary creaturely existence, domestic, economic, and social. This is the way God made him. The world is real. Time is real. Man is a toiler and an "acter" and a chooser. The parables give us this kind of humanness and actuality.[43]

The Apostle Paul also drew his images about salvation and atonement from the world around him. Paul used many images to try to explain to his readers how the power of God was disclosed in the cross of Christ. He used an image of justification he took from the law courts. He drew pictures of redemption or emancipation from the slave market, reconciliation from friendship, adoption from family life, propitiation or ransom from the sacrificial system, sanctification from worship practices, and the view of setting a person's account right from the accounting system. Many theologians have built their theological theories around one of these pictures.

The point is that both Jesus and Paul drew on secular images and stories to communicate their message about God. Before persons can respond to the message about God's grace, they have to hear it in areas of their own concern. Jesus and Paul focused the gospel so their listeners heard it addressing their needs. We have to do the same. When the gospel is communicated with understanding, then the hearers have to decide to accept it or reject it.

Modern literature provides a vehicle of communication to contemporary men and women. Thornton Wilder once observed that "the great religious teachers have constantly had recourse to the parable as a means of imparting their deepest intuitions."[44] In his play, *Our Town*, Wilder does not have God appear directly in the play, but the unutterable preciousness of the gift of life is affirmed in this parabolic presentation.

The minister has a limitless storehouse of riches from which to draw stories about life and its meaning. Consider the following literary offerings:

- You can look favorably upon positive Christian novels by such authors as Frederick Beuchner, Will Campbell, Irving Stone, Adela Rogers St. John, Taylor Caldwell, John Killinger, and Marilynne Robinson.

- The fantasy or science fiction writings of C. S. Lewis—namely, *Out of the Silent Planet*, *Perlandra*, *That Hideous Strength*, *The Chronicles of Narnia*, *Till We Have Faces*, *The Great Divorce*, and *The Screwtape Letters*—and Suzanne Collins—such as *The Hunger Games*—can stimulate the imagination and provoke suggestions for preaching in symbolic, mythological, or parabolic ways, especially about the conflict between good and evil.

- Draw freely from secular contemporary works such as Alex Haley's *Roots*, Boris Pasternak's *Doctor Zhivago*, and Solzenitsyn's *The Gulag Archipelago*.

- Modern drama offers a powerful resource for confronting contemporary problems. *My Left Foot* deals with a young man who has cerebral palsy. *Andre's Mother* by Terrence McNally confronts AIDS. *Children of a Lesser God* takes a chapter out of the life of a young woman who is deaf. *The Immigrant* depicts the life of a Russian Jew who migrated to Texas to live.

- *Steel Magnolias, Driving Miss Daisy*, and *The Help* use humor to focus on the problems of relationships, racism, suffering, aging, and death.

- Biography and autobiography provide another area for exploration.

James Cleland preached a sermon titled "Long Day's Journey into Light" in response to O'Neil's play *Long Day's Journey into Night*.[45] John Killinger wrote a Communion sermon, "A Strategy for Survival," based on Piers Paul Read's book, *Alive: The Story of the Andes Survivors*.[46] And Charles Rice developed a sermon, "Herzog: Consider the Lilies," based on the novel by Saul Bellow.[47] When *Jonathan Livingston Seagull* by Richard Bach was popular with students and others, I preached a sermon, "Lessons from a Seagull," based on that short novel and using Isaiah 40:28-31 and Hebrews 11:1-10 as texts. These are only four of many examples where I have built sermons on plays or novels.

The preacher reads modern stories to know life better and to transmit the gospel story more creatively. The use of modern literature is more than decorative or illustrative, though it may be used for that purpose. It is basically a doorway into the mind of modern culture and a doorway into the listener's mind and heart.

I drew on one of Loren Eiseley's stories to introduce one of my sermons. I also took my title for the sermon from this same story. The sermon focused on the sense of meaninglessness that many persons feel today, and the purpose that Christ can offer to each person.

> The place: a commuter train. The time: midnight. Loren Eiseley, an anthropologist, recounts the episode. He boarded a train in New York and felt glad to be leaving the city.
>
> On taking a seat in the smoking compartment, his eyes fell on a gaunt, shabbily dressed man, who was sitting with his eyes closed and his head thrown back on the seat. A paper sack was on the man's lap. The man appeared to be drowsing either from exhaustion or from liquor.
>
> As the train wound its way out of the city, the conductor came into the compartment asking for tickets, and everyone turned to watch the derelict. Opening his eyes slowly and fumbling in his pocket until he pulled out

a roll of bills, he said, in a deathlike croak, "Give me . . . give me a ticket to wherever it is."

The conductor stood stupefied for a moment with the roll of bills in his hand. He mumbled through the list of stations, but once again the man's eyes were closed, and he remained mute. After a moment the price of a ticket to Philadelphia was deducted from the roll of bills, and they were shoved back into the snoozing man's hand. The train sped into the night as the observers of this incident turned back to their newspapers.

"In a single poignant expression," Eiseley notes, "this shabby creature on a midnight express train had personalized the terror of an open-ended universe."

"Give me a ticket to wherever it is." Eiseley has captured in his story a familiar symbol of our situation. We are caught in the current of today's stream of life and simply flow with it, often without any sense of direction or meaning.[48]

At times I have preached a series of sermons on Old Testament heroes of the faith. I would tell their story and attempt to let the listener overhear how the struggles of these persons are also our struggles. I have on occasions delivered a monologue sermon on one of the biblical characters. I would simply tell the story of some figure from within as though it were my story. We can hear our stories in another person's story.

The parables of Jesus can be told as individual stories, or some can be selected and preached in a series. Use your imagination and try to get inside the parable in a fresh way. Here is a modern version of the parable of the great feast told in Luke 14:7-24. I titled this sermon, "The End of Privilege and the Invitation to Unlikely Guests."

> It was a cold February morning. A man stood warming himself over the fire burning in a large trash barrel. You could tell by his tattered and worn clothes that he was a street beggar. Suddenly a well-dressed man came up to the beggar and handed him a card. The vagabond looked at the man as he walked off, and then looked down and read the card:

> You Are Cordially Invited
> To Attend A Banquet
> To Be Held
> In the Home of John Goodfellow
> Prospect, Kentucky
> Friday, February 12
> Cars will pick you up at the Jefferson Street Chapel at 6 P.M.

After reading the card, the beggar continued to watch the well-dressed man as he walked down the street. He noticed that he stopped by a cripple who was selling pencils and handed him a card. He observed that as the man went on down the street further, he stopped by a blind man who was also trying to sell something and gave him one of the cards. He watched the stranger as he continued to walk down the street passing out his cards.

In a few moments the beggar ran up to one of the other persons who had gotten a card and asked: "What do you think about this? Could this be on the level?" "I don't know," the other man responded. "But it's a free meal and I'm going. We can get out of the cold. It may be some kind of trick, but I am going."

Friday night at a few minutes before six o'clock a group of very interesting-looking persons gathered in the lobby of the Jefferson Street Chapel. The group was composed of street walkers, beggars, bums, alcoholics—the rejects of life, or so it would seem.

After a few moments, three large limousines pulled up in front of the chapel. The men had never seen such big cars in their lives. The chauffeur opened the door, and the guests got in. Then they were transported to a house the likes of which they had never seen before.

The cars drove down the winding driveway until they pulled up in front of a large mansion. The door of the house opened, and they were greeted by a friendly host who welcomed them. He led them to a table that had been carefully prepared for the evening meal. As they walked in, they gawked at the lovely house. They had never seen such thick carpet, expensive furnishings, lovely paintings, such everything!

None of them knew the host who sat at the head of the table. Then he said, "Before we eat, let me say the blessing." "Lord," he prayed, "we thank you that we can gather here for this meal. We thank you for these persons who have come to eat. Lord, you know who they are, and you know their names and you know their needs, and I know you care for them and you love them. Bless them and us as we share together in this food. Amen." Then he said, "Dig in!" And they did!

For a while the men and women were busy eating. After a few moments, someone began to ask questions. The blind man asked, "What does the host look like?" Conversation soon began to go around the table. The host didn't have to do much prodding to cut through their thin excuses for not wanting more to eat. When he noticed that someone had cleaned his or her plate, he urged his butler to come in and offer that person more food.

When the guests had finished the meal, they moved over into a room nearby where someone was playing on a piano by a roaring fire burning in the fireplace. They all began to sing old familiar songs. Some of these men and women had not sung songs in years. Finally they began to sing a few familiar hymns such as "Amazing Grace" and "The Old Rugged Cross."

After they finished singing, the host said, "You may wonder why I have invited you here tonight. I asked you to come here because I want you to know that God loves you. I know that what I have done tonight is a small gesture. But it is my way of saying to you that I care for you. I want to give you a New Testament tonight. I have marked some passages in it so that you can read them when you are lonely and hurting and feel that nobody is interested in you. I also want you to know tonight that if you do not have a job and you would like to find one, I will help you get one. If you want help to overcome some kind of problem you may be having—whatever it is in your life— I want you to know that I am willing to offer you support, encouragement, and help with whatever need there is in your life. Now in a few moments a chauffeur will take you back to wherever it is that you will be sleeping tonight. If you don't have a place to sleep, you are welcome to stay here and spend the night with me. I want you to know that I am trying to extend to you something of the love I think God has for you."

As the men and women slowly walked out of the door that night, one gripped the host's hand and said, "You have given me hope. I was thinking of committing suicide, but you have given me hope." A woman said, "I am going to take you up on that offer. I can beat this problem with alcohol. I am going to come back and see if you can't help me find some place that can rid me of this problem." A man walked out and said, "I haven't worked for a long time. Nobody would give me a chance. I am coming back, and I want you to help me get a job." The cars drove off, and soon they were gone.

As far as I know, this story I just told you did not happen. And it is unfortunate, isn't it? Because it would be very Christlike.

Use your imagination and proclaim the Story through modern stories so your listeners will listen and respond.

The Preacher as Humorist

Sometimes one of the most imaginative ways to communicate the gospel message is through humor. This is not an encouragement for the preacher to try to become a comic or clown in the pulpit, but humor can get a message across to the hearer at times when other means would fail.

Again we can look to our Lord for guidance. Sometimes in a humorous vein Jesus drove his message home. Today we miss many of the insights in Jesus' teachings because we can't see or understand the humor in them. Elton Trueblood speaks of these in his book, *The Humor of Christ.*

He indicated that his thought along this line was stimulated one day when he was reading the Bible to his four-year-old son. The passage he was reading happened to be one of the parables of Jesus. When his son heard it for the first time, he burst out laughing. To him, it was humorous. We have heard some of the sayings of Jesus so many times that we miss the humor altogether. Trueblood listed thirty instances of humor he found in the sayings of Jesus. Some of these are obvious even to those of us who have heard the teachings of Jesus many times. Note several of these:

- Jesus once spoke about a man who was concerned about the tiny speck in another's eye and was unaware of the huge log sticking out of his own eye.

- Jesus mentioned a Pharisee who was concerned about a tiny gnat in someone else's soup, but did not notice the camel sitting in his own bowl of soup.

- What man, Jesus asked, would place a lamp under a bed? In that day, a lamp had an open flame.

- Jesus told about a man coming at midnight and asking for three loaves of bread. The latecomer continued to knock at the door, even when the man inside said: "Go away. All of my family is asleep. The cattle are in. Everyone is settled for the night." Nevertheless, he kept on knocking until the sleepy man grew weary with him and went to the door.

- Jesus told about a man who would not come to a feast because he had married a new wife, or had two oxen, and had a new field to plow. In that day, invitations to a feast took top priority, and almost nothing would keep a man away—and certainly not a woman.

I think we have difficulty with some of the sayings of Jesus because we can't see the twinkle in his eye or the grin on his face. Trueblood was convinced that the parable of the unjust steward was said in sarcasm. When Jesus praised a dishonest man, Trueblood believed that Jesus was using this in a sarcastic way to suggest how much more we should do than this man.

I am not attempting to say that Jesus was a comedian. But Jesus knew how to communicate, and he used humor effectively when he talked to people. Children loved to listen to him, and I don't know many children who flock to an adult who is dull and dreary. The common people heard Jesus gladly, and the common people will respond to the preacher who uses humor effectively and selectively.

The preacher should use humor not to gain popularity or to display his humorous side, but to communicate the gospel. Humor is another vehicle to convey the joy and love of God. It is not to be used merely to entertain or to amuse the congregation. Numerous humorous devices are available to us: satire, irony, puns, metaphors, play on words, and the story with a comic theme.

In addition to literature, the comics provide an excellent source for humor. Charles Schultz's "Peanuts" has become so popular in sermons that a book by Robert Short called *The Gospel According to Peanuts* became a best seller. There is no question in my mind that "Peanuts" is a theological commentary on contemporary man and woman. "Pogo," "B.C.," "Kudzu," "Hagar the Horrible," "Ziggy," and "For Better or Worse" are at times more than amusing. They present on occasions a comic slice out of the real world. The message may be only halfway comical, but the point is made. I've taken clippings from many cartoonists as humorous insights into life and faith.

In one of Charles Schultz's comic strips, Lucy, Linus, and Charlie Brown—three of the "Peanuts" children—are lying on their backs on a hillside looking up at the clouds:

Lucy: If you use your imagination, you can see lots of things in the cloud formations . . . What do you think you see, Linus?

Linus: Well, those clouds up there look to me like the map of the British Honduras on the Caribbean. . . that cloud up there looks a little like the profile of Thomas Eakins, the famous painter and sculptor . . . and that group of clouds over there gives me the impression of the stoning of Stephen . . . I can see the Apostle Paul standing there to one side . . .

Lucy: Uh huh . . . that's very good . . . What do *you* see in the clouds, Charlie Brown?

Charlie Brown: Well, I was going to say I saw a ducky and a horsey, but I changed my mind![49]

Persons who are listening recognize their own sense of inadequacy at times and their inability to communicate effectively with each other. We see ourselves in Charlie Brown.

Literature abounds with humorous accounts that confront us where we live every day. Will Campbell's *Brother to a Dragonfly* contains humor and pathos, as does John Updike's *Rabbit Is Rich,* Anne Tyler's *Accidental Tourist* and *Breathing Lessons*, Frederick Buechner's *The Final Beast*, and many plays and biographies.

I draw an example from James Carr's biographical novel, *The Saint of the Wilderness*. This story relates the adventures of an itinerant mountain preacher, Robert Sayers Sheffey, as he traveled and preached through the hills of Virginia and West Virginia. On one occasion he decided to travel to Bluefield by the way of Wolf Creek to South Gap and then across East River Mountain. He had spent the night with a family and was up early riding along Wolf Creek, singing to himself, when suddenly he heard galloping hooves coming toward him. He guided his horse to the shoulder of the road to allow the speeding rider room to pass. Instead of passing him, however, a young rider reined in his horse and engulfed them both in a cloud of dust.

> "My brother, George, got bit by a rattlesnake this mornin'," the young boy cried. "We're afraid he's goin' to die. Pa just now seen you passin' and said for me to overtake you and get you to pray for George."
>
> "Do I know you and your family?" Robert asked him. "Your face is not familiar."
>
> "No, you don't know us, but Pa and Ma both knows of you. Pa said if you'd pray for George, the Lord would let him live."
>
> Robert followed the boy to his home where he saw George lying on the grass in the backyard. The mother, who was attending the lad, would not allow her eyes to meet the inquiring gaze of the preacher.
>
> "Reverend Sheffey," the father said, as he came out of the kitchen, "call upon the Lord so my boy will live."
>
> "Have you ever called upon the Lord's name, my brother?" inquired Robert.
>
> "No, but if you'll do it the Lord will surely hear our prayers. It is said that many things you pray for come to pass even after many years."
>
> "And you have a wife and children, I see. How many? Do they ever call upon the name of the Lord?"
>
> "No, I guess not," the father responded as he hung his head. "There's three boys and us."

Robert always knelt to pray on a sheepskin. "Son," he said to the boy, "would you fetch my sheepskin from my saddle?"

Before his knees were on the sheepskin, the others were already on their knees with their eyes closed. The boy who had been bitten covered his face with his hands.

"O Lord," Robert prayed, "please bring Thy healing to this young man, and Lord in the same breath we thank Thee for snakes and pray that there be many of them. It is because of a snake that this family calls upon Thy holy name today. One of the sons has been bitten, and they call upon Thee. Now, Lord, get the picture: except for the snake they would perhaps never in their lifetimes have turned to Thee. What a blessing this lowly, crawling thing has been! Lord, I want you to send lots of snakes. Send another one to bite the youngest boy here, and send still another to bite this woman who never had her boys kneel by her chair, that they might hear the prayers of their mother. And, Lord, above all things, send a great big rattler, a really large one, to bite the old man so that he may call upon Thy name fervently and much. Amen."[50]

What are the pressures, obstacles, needs, desires, or burdens that eventually drive us to an awareness of our need of God? The mountain preacher saw the absence of any desire for God in the life of this family until they were crushed down by immediate danger. By the power of humor, the author telegraphs a word about life to us.

Discover the way that is most effective for you. Following is one attempt I made to get a different handle on the parable of the chief seats as recorded in Luke 14:7-11. I called this sermon, "Big Shots in the Church." Here is my retake of this parable.

The place: Uptown, USA. The occasion: the Man of the Year awards banquet. The time: the present.

Everybody who was anybody was present for this big night. The persons sitting on the lower level were busy trying to see who was seated at the head table.

There at the head table sat Loretta Lovely; Perry Prosperous; Tom Talkative, a local TV announcer; and the Reverend Peter Pious, pastor of Peach Protestant Church. Harry Hilarity was the M.C. for the night. Hugh Haughty was seated next to Sam Self-righteous and Henrietta High-hat. Next there was Mayor Marvin Moneybags. Governor Kevin Keep the People Confused was on the mayor's right. Judge Jake Justice of *The Rich and Famous* sat next to him. They were followed by Richard Rich, Fred Famous, Rhonda Realtor, Sophia Superficial, Peter Practical, Desmond Deception, Dr. Marvin Medicine, and Mr. Macho Muscles—the famous football player. Filling out the table was General George Gallantry, Preston Patriotic, and Conrad Climb the Corporate Ladder. All of the persons of community worth were there.

The host for this special occasion, Walter Wealthy, looked over the distinguished guests sitting at the head table. He noticed that something wasn't right.

He looked around and finally asked: "Where is Larry Lowly?"

From way back in the cheap seats, a hand went up. "I'm sitting back here."

"Larry, you are the main guest," Mr. Wealthy said. "What are you doing way back there? Come up here to the head table."

Then Mr. Wealthy looked down at the head table and all the dignitaries sitting there. Then he noticed that Ronnie Run Over Everybody to Reach the Top was sitting in one of the chief seats at the banquet table.

"Ronnie," the host exclaimed, "You will have to go down there where Larry was sitting. Larry, you come up here and sit at the main table where Ronnie was."

This tongue-in-cheek story is a humorous attempt to use a method similar to what Jesus employed in his presentation of this parable about persons seeking chief seats at a marriage feast. By the use of this parable, Jesus used humor and whimsical means as he often did to disarm people so he might present a truth to them about God and life. We can attempt in a small way to do the same.

Humor serves as relief from tension and helps relax the listener. Humor cuts through our pretensions and reveals the preacher's humanity. The gospel is good news. *Sursum corda*—"Lift up your hearts!" A merry heart can be an expression of the joy a Christian experiences in the presence of God. Humor is indeed often medicine for the human soul, and also one of the most powerful and seldom-used tools in the craft of preaching.

The Preacher as Creator

God created the world *ex nihilo*—out of nothing. The preacher is faced with this same task on a much more modest scale—though likewise enormously challenging. Facing a blank piece of paper with Sunday coming demands for many preachers what appears to be creating something out of nothing. Fortunately, the preacher is not left completely alone. The preacher has the Bible, the record of God's revelation; the inspiration of the Holy Spirit, who can bring insight out of unfamiliar places and unlikely events; a congregation filled with needs and longings; the experience of his own struggles; the world of nature around him and the culture in which he lives; and the exciting realm of fresh ideas revealed in the world of literature.

No, the preacher does not create out of nothing like the God he worships. We have fruits from the orchards of life all around us from which we can pick. Our creativity is released in the lively imagination we use to "discover" and develop an idea we want to preach. We lean on the power of the unseen presence of God to enable us to become a "seer." Imagination is the touch stone within each preacher where the Word of God confronts the words of an ordinary person and is shaped into the preaching event called the sermon. The one who was created in the image of God passes through the darkness of beginning the search for a word from God each Sunday until the Creator sends light once again. The preacher does live by faith. This faith is also evidenced in his sermon preparation. A deeper faith in the Creator gives creative power to the preacher to begin the process of sermon preparation again. But this is never faith without works. He offers to God the best sermon preparation possible, and then asks God to enable his words to guide others to the Word.

Some of the most creative sermons I have ever heard or read were written and delivered by Jerusha Joshua. "Creative preaching neither distorts truth nor diminishes Scripture's sacredness," Joshua noted. "Rather, creative preaching is spirit-filled artistry whereby the preacher becomes a creative artist—more out of passion than habit—preaching with intentional innovative imagination." "Creative preaching is a process; the creative preacher," she continues, "moved by the creation of his or her sermon, goes deeper, finds and unconsciously tells a story of his or her own." "Putting it emotively," she concludes, "creative preaching is a process through which the heart of the listener is met with the heart of God through the humble creative passion of the preacher."[51]

In *The 2010 Minister's Manual,* Joshua shares four "creative" sermons:

1. "The Pharaoh Who Freaked Out" (Exodus 1:18-22)
2. "The Return of the Prodigal Daughter (Exodus 20)
3. "The Diary of Virginia" (Judges 11:29-40)
4. "Dominic's Messy Christmas" (Luke 2:1-7)

"Dominic's Messy Christmas" is told from the perspective of a donkey named Dominic who lived in the days of the Roman Empire and was a "witness" to the first Christmas. The story is filled with all the reality of the messy conditions of poverty, travel, donkey stalls, and childbirth. With a biblically sound foundation, this narration of the first Christmas is presented in a way the hearer has to listen, filled with an imaginative voice that summons one's attention and filled with information, insights, and details that staggers the mind. Joshua's concluding lines challenge our thoughts on Christmas:

> At Christmas, God meets us *not* "when" we are perfect but rather "in" our deeply flawed and erroneous ways. Christmas is about hope in our fallen estate, grace in our messy state. Christmas disrupts the squeakly-clean, recollected Advent we had planned to make. The light of Christ stirs up the silt in our souls, and sifts us to harsher purity, healing us. For Mariam, Yoseph, and Dominic, Christmas was all about finding the mystery of God's presence in a messy feeding trough. Where will you find God's presence this Christmas?[52]

The creative person remains open to new insight and truth and new approaches. Faith is a pilgrimage that carries us down familiar and at times strange new paths. The best preachers will want to be open to God's spirit and know they have not arrived but are still pilgrims. We are surrounded by mystery, and there is much more yet to be discovered and learned. "To believe that the world is only as you think it is, is stupid," Carlos Castenada quotes his Yaqui Shaman as saying. "The world is a mysterious place. Especially in the twilight."[53]

A creative preacher is willing to take risks, try new approaches, read new books, experiment with different styles or forms, and remain open to God's Spirit. Sometimes it calls for the leap into the unknown, unfamiliar, and uncharted. But think of the thrill of new discoveries and satisfying adventures.

In the concluding passage in Castaneda's *Tales of Power*, Don Juan and Don Genaro take Carlos and Pablito to the top of the mesa. Don Juan points over the edge and says: "There is the door. Beyond, there is an abyss and beyond that abyss is the unknown." Castaneda continues: "Then a strange urge, a force, made me run with him (Pablito) to the northern edge of the mesa. I felt his arm holding me as we jumped, and then I was alone."[54]

In preparing sermons we make that leap into the unknown. We lift up our words to guide persons to the Living Word. At times we feel the strength of the arm of God's presence around us as we prepare and stand to preach and leap into the unknown world before us. Sometimes we tremble at the audacity to stand in a pulpit and declare a word from God. Yet at other times we say with the Apostle Paul, "Woe is me if I preach not the gospel of Jesus Christ."

Notes

[1] C. S. Lewis, "Christianity and Culture," *Christian Reflection* (Grand Rapids: Wm. B. Eerdmans, 1967), 21-22.

[2] Dietrich Bonhoeffer, *Letters and Papers from Prison* (New York: Macmillan Co., 1953), 24-25.

[3] John Killinger, *The Zacchaeus Solution* (Cleveland, TN: Parson's Porch Books, 2010). See some other novels by Killinger to see his style and Christian approach: *Maggie Bowles and the Mystery of the Marigold Turtle* (2011), *Jesse: A Novel* (1993), *The Night Jessie Sang at the Opry* (1996). See also his interpretation of the novels of J. K. Rowling in *God, the Devil & Harry Potter* (2002) and *The Life, Death, and Resurrection of Harry Potter* (2009).

[4] Tennessee Williams, "The Glass Menagerie," in *Twentieth Century Drama*, ed. Ruby Cohn (New York: Random House, 1966), 342.

[5] Percy Bysshe Shelley, "A Defense of Poetry," in *The Complete Works of Percy Bysshe Shelley*, ed. Ingpen and Walter E. Peck, 7, Prose (New York: Gordian Press, 1965), 118.

[6] John Killinger, *The Fragile Presence* (Philadelphia: Fortress Press, 1973), 3. See also William H. Willimon, *Reading with Deeper Eyes: The Love of Literature and the Life of Faith* (Nashville: Upper Room Books, 1998).

[7] Jürgen Moltmann, *Theology of Hope* (New York: Harper & Row, 1967), 22.

[8] John Grisham, *Ford County* (New York: Doubleday, 2009), 297-298.

[9] Annie Dillard, *An American Childhood* (New York: Harper & Row, 1987), 165.

[10] Ibid., 224.

[11] Shelley, "A Defense of Poetry," 116.

¹²T. S. Eliot, "Religion and Literature," in *Religion and Modern Literature*, ed. G. B. Tennyson (Grand Rapids: Wm. B. Eerdmans, 1975), 26-27.

¹³Ibid., 28-29.

¹⁴John Killinger, *The Failure of Theology in Modern Literature* (New York: Abingdon Press, 1963), 36.

¹⁵P. T. Forsyth, *Positive Preaching and the Modern Mind* (London: Independent Press, 1907), 1.

¹⁶Henry Ward Beecher, *The Yale Lectures on Preaching, First Series: Personal Elements in Preaching* (New York: J. B. Ford & Co., 1872), 109.

¹⁷J. Barrie Shepherd, *Whatever Happened to Delight? Preaching the Gospel in Poetry and Parables* (Louisville: Westminster John Knox Press, 2006), 14-15. See also William Brosend, *The Preaching of Jesus: Gospel Proclamation Then and Now* (Louisville: Westminster John Knox Press, 2010), 124-152.

¹⁸Shepherd, 56. See also Thomas H. Troeger, *Imagining a Sermon* (Nashville: Abingdon Press, 1990).

¹⁹George Bernard Shaw, "St. John," in *Drama and Discussion*, ed. Stanley A. Cloyes (New York: Appleton-Century-Crofts, 1967), 362

²⁰George A. Buttrick, *Jesus Came Preaching* (New York: Charles Scribner's Sons, 1931).

²¹Aldous Huxley, *Brave New World* (New York: Harper & Row, 1932), 281.

²²Ernest Hemingway, "A Clean Well-Lighted Place," in *Short Stories* (New York: Charles Scribner's Sons, 1954).

²³David Karp, *One* (New York: Grosset & Dunlap, 1962).

²⁴Lawrence Sergeant Hall, *Stowaway* (Boston: Little, Brown, 1961), 117.

²⁵Flannery O'Connor, "The Nature and Aim of Fiction," in *Mystery and Manners*, ed. Sally and Robert Fitzgerald (New York: Farrar, Straus and Giroux, 1969), 65, 77-79.

²⁶Henry Mitchell, *The Recovery of Preaching* (San Francisco: Harper & Row, 1977), 45.

²⁷Ibid., 47.

²⁸Peter Marshall, *Mr. Jones Meet the Master* (New York: Fleming H. Revell Co., 1950), 52.

²⁹Frederick W. Robertson, "The Irreparable Past," in *Sermons Preached at Brighton* (New York: Harper & Brothers, n. d.), 429.

³⁰Loren Eiseley, *The Immense Journey* (New York: Vintage Books, 1957), 54.

³¹Ibid., 176.

³²G. K. Chesterton, *The Ball and the Cross* (New York: John Lane Co., 1907), 95-96.

³³Fred B. Craddock, *Craddock on the Craft of Preaching*, ed. Lee Sparks and Kathryn Hayes Sparks (St. Louis, Missouri: Chalice Press, 2011), 190.

³⁴Edward L. Taylor, compiler, *The Words of Gardner Taylor: Quintessential Classics, 1980-present*, 3 (Valley Forge: Judson Press, 2000), 180-181.

³⁵See my discussion of his preaching style in "Gardner Calvin Taylor, Poet Laureate of the Pulpit," in William Powell Tuck, *Modern Shapers of Baptist Thought in America* (Richmond: Center for Baptist Studies & Heritage, 2012), 232-253.

³⁶Carlyle Marney, *The Crucible of Redemption* (Nashville: Abingdon Press, 1968), 58

³⁷Nicholas Wolterstorff, *Lament for a Son* (Grand Rapids: Wm.B. Eerdmans, 1987), 76.

³⁸Charles L. Rice, *Interpretation and Imagination* (Philadelphia: Fortress Press, 1970), 56.

³⁹P. T. Forsyth, *Christ on Parmassus* (New York: Hodder and Soughton, n. d.), 238.

⁴⁰Alan Paton, *Cry, The Beloved Country* (New York: Charles Scribner's Sons, 1948), 108.

⁴¹Loren Eiseley, *All the Night Wings* (New York: Times Books, 1979), 47.

⁴²Rice, *Interpretation and Imagination*, 86.

⁴³Amos N. Wilder, *Jesus' Parables and the War of Myths: Essays on Imagination in the Scriptures*, ed. James Breech (Philadelphia: Fortress Press, 1982), 74.

⁴⁴Thornton Wilder, *The Modern Theater*, ed. Robert W. Corrigan (New York: Macmillan Co., 1964), 1185.

⁴⁵James T. Cleland, "Long Day's Journey into Light," in *Best Sermons*, 7, ed. G. Paul Butler (New York: Thomas Y. Crowell Co., 1959), 58-65.

⁴⁶John Killinger, "A Strategy for Survival," in *The Struggle for Meaning*, ed. William Powell Tuck (Valley Forge, PA: Judson Press, 1977), 17-22.

⁴⁷Charles L. Rice, "Herzog: Consider the Lilies," in Rice, *Interpretation and Imagination*, 127-135.

⁴⁸William Powell Tuck, "A Ticket to Wherever It Is," in *The Struggle for Meaning*, 131-141.

⁴⁹Robert L. Short, *The Gospel According to Peanuts* (Richmond: John Knox Press, 1960), 33.

⁵⁰James Carr, *The Saint in the Wilderness* (Radford, VA: Commonwealth Press, Inc., 1974), 317.

⁵¹Jerusha Joshua, "The Creative Art of Homiletics," in *The Minister's Manual, 2010 Edition*, ed. Lee McGlone (San Francisco: Jossy-Bass, 2009), 353.

⁵²Jerusha Joshua, "Dominic's Messy Christmas," in *The Minister's Manual, 2010 Edition*, ed. Lee McGone (San Francisco: 2009), 373.

⁵³Carlos Castaneda, *Journey to Ixtlan* (New York: Simon and Schuster, 1972), 88.

⁵⁴Carlos Castaneda, *Tales of Power* (New York: Simon and Schuster, 1974), 286-287.

Sermon

A Ticket to Wherever It Is
Ecclesiastes 1:14; Matthew 16:24-26

The place: a commuter train. The time: midnight. Loren Eiseley, an anthropologist, recounts the episode. He boarded a train in New York and felt sad to be leaving the city. On taking a seat in the smoking compartment, his eyes fell on a gaunt, shabbily dressed man, who was sitting with his eyes closed and his head thrown back on the seat. A paper sack was on the man's lap. The man appeared to be dozing either from exhaustion or from liquor. As the train wound its way out of the city, the conductor came into the compartment asking for tickets. Everyone turned to watch the derelict. Opening his eyes slowly and fumbling in his pocket until he pulled out a roll of bills, he said, in a deathlike croak, "Give me . . . give me a ticket to wherever it is."

The conductor stood stupefied for a moment with the roll of bills in his hand. He mumbled through the list of stations, but once again the man's eyes were closed and he remained mute. After a moment the price of a ticket to Philadelphia was deducted from the roll of bills, and they were shoved back into the snoozing man's hand. The train sped into the night as the observers of this incident turned back to their newspapers. "In a single poignant expression," Loren Eiseley noted, "this shabby creature on a midnight express train had personalized the terror of an open-ended universe."[1]

Traveling Without a Sense of Direction

"Give me a ticket to wherever it is." Eiseley captured in his story a familiar symbol of our situation. We are caught in the current of today's stream of life and simply flow with it, often without any sense of direction or meaning. Like the microscopic plants in the ocean called "plankton," many today are drifting and wandering. "I think I'll go back to Germany," a young student said to me. He had studied there for three years, and, after only six months in this country, he had decided to go back. "I have felt for so long like an outsider looking in. There are many roads a person can travel on. I'll find mine one day." He, too, is traveling to "wherever it is."

The Trail of Pessimism

The road to "wherever it is" is varied. For some the journey trails off into frustration and pessimism. "What's the point of trying?" the teenager exclaimed. "My parents and teachers never give me a chance; I can't win." "All politicians are crooks," a man observed. "Watergate proves that!" The social worker found a family of eleven living in what used to be a chicken house. "We ain't got nothing," the mother said. "We had to live some place." "You can't escape this ghetto," a youth exclaimed. "We are all trapped here like it was a graveyard."

"Blow-in' in the wind" today are many pessimistic complaints about our country, our cities, world affairs, the economy, the government, the environment, the church, the colleges, young people, old people, and hundreds of other matters. Many feel like the newborn chick, depicted in the cartoon, that pecks its way out of its eggshell, sticks its head out and looks around, and then pulls the broken piece of shell back into place and retreats into the safety of the eggshell. But where is that womb of absolute security, free of difficulties and where every need and wish is satisfied? "Time has expired for them," some say, and they are weary with trying. "Wherever it is" for them is an endless treadmill filled with contradictions, ambiguities, disappointments, and discord.

The Trail of Despair

"Wherever it is" for some ends in despair. Whispers and screams, reminiscent of the Ecclesiastes' preacher, resound from many quarters today. "I have seen everything that is done under the sun; and behold, all is vanity and a striving after wind" (Eccles. 1:14, RSV). Faces, voices, and struggles rush back into my mind, demanding to be heard again and again with a hidden plea for direction out of their darkness. I hear a voice: "What difference would it make if I were not alive?" a young woman asked. "I'm worthless and nobody would miss me." "He walked off and left me and the children for some woman and never looked back," another woman cried. "What do I do now?"

An article I read burns in my memory. The elderly couple sat on the sofa in their living room in a roughhouse in South Philadelphia. They had just been robbed. As they told their story, the cracked and stained wallpaper in the room was illuminated by a single, bare light bulb in a gooseneck lamp. What's so unusual about their story? Are they not just another poor couple getting "ripped off" in a low-income neighborhood? Yes—but more and worse. They are both blind and 104 years old!

A child's voice rises out of the rubble of an undeclared war to pierce an unfeeling world. "I'm nobody's nothing," exclaimed the little boy as he glanced up from where he was sitting on top of a pile of debris in war-torn Saigon. His relatives were all dead. He was alone and unwanted in a city already overflowing with homeless children.

A young man shouted a challenge that went unanswered: "If anyone can convince me that life is worth living," he cried, as he stood on the narrow ledge seventeen stories above Fifth Avenue in New York City, "I won't jump." He jumped.

A Trail of Disturbing Images

The images, unfortunately, could be multiplied endlessly. The number of suicides has greatly increased. Today about 20,000 people commit suicide each year in the United States alone. Around the world that figure swells to 250,000 men and women. Why? "Behold; all is vanity and a striving after wind," the ancient preacher says. Many people seem to find themselves trapped in a dead-end street and see no way to turn. Their yearnings are unfulfilled, their hopes shattered, their dreams punctured, their bodies fatigued, their minds disturbed, their hands empty, their eyes and hearts vacant. The words of a recently disturbing popular song, voiced by a female singer, ask cynically, after describing several pleasant scenes: "Is that all there is?" It is again the cry of meaninglessness. It is purchasing a ticket to "wherever it is."

Disturbing images march across our line of vision daily. Suicide, war, suffering, unemployment, poverty, hunger, drug addiction, alcoholism, pain, and death stare at us from our TV sets, newspapers, magazines, across the street, next door, the hospital bed, the nursing home, the empty kitchen cabinet, the want ads, our front room, our back bedroom. Questions concerning the meaning of life cannot be hidden or ignored. They are here, and they are real. They frighten and haunt us. They bother and confuse us. And sometimes they challenge us. Are we simply caught in the stream of life and being carried by it? Without a sense of direction we have no hope.

In the movie *Bonnie and Clyde,* Bonnie has been enamored by the life of bank robbing and seems to be enjoying it, until one day she reveals a sense of futility about their style of life when she observes: "I thought we were going somewhere, but we are just going."

Traveling with a Sense of Direction

Our going should have some purpose. People are going, nevertheless. Stand on any busy downtown corner or on a subway platform in New York, Chicago, London, Stockholm, Copenhagen, Hong Kong, or even small town U.S.A., and you will observe that people are going. As you observe these people going on any busy square or round, have you ever wondered, along with me: where are they all going, and what are they doing? What are their dreams and problems, joys and sorrows? I have often watched and reflected as they passed on the street, on the train, or on the plane. I wonder if they are curious about me, as well. Are they probing for a direction, too, or are they just going? Do we continue to look at each other day after day, week after week, and do not know or care about each other? Yes, we are busy going, but is our going filled with direction?

Directions, however, are not always easily given or received, understood or followed. Some years ago on Christmas Eve I had struggled for about an hour trying to put together a riding toy for our small son. Noticing the unhappy results and the several nuts and bolts left over, my wife came over, searched through the cardboard box, came up with a yellow sheet of paper, handed it to me, and smilingly teased, "When all else fails, read the directions."

"When all else fails . . ." Why do we wait until we reach that point? I do not know but often we do, in large matters as well as small.

Directions from Jesus

If the ticket to nowhere is dispensed with the stamp "All is vanity and a striving after wind," then the ticket to somewhere is imprinted with the penetrating words of Jesus:

> If any man would come after me, let him deny himself and take up his cross and follow me. For whoever would save his life will lose it, and whoever loses his life for my sake will find it. For what will it profit a man, if he gains the whole world and forfeits his life? Or what shall a man give in return for his life? (Matt. 16:24-26, RSV)

In the words of Jesus, direction is given. They are, however, words that indicate clearly that the "ticket" he issues us is not good if detached.

Many people today suffer a sense of meaninglessness, because they have lost all awareness of absolute transcendence. They refuse to acknowledge any power beyond themselves and defy the believer to prove that God exists. The ancient religious poet was no stranger to this puzzle: "My adversaries taunt me, while they say to me continually, 'Where is your God?'" (Ps. 42:10, RSV). In her childish way, a young girl, as noted in *Children's Letters to God*, expressed the attitude of many cynics when she asked: "Dear God, Are you real? Some people don't believe it. If you are, you better do something quick."[2]

The price that anyone pays for the eclipse of God, however, is to be thrown back on one's own resources. This is an aloneness that none can stand. No wonder it leads to despair and cynicism. Do we decide to "write off" God because there are problems and injustices that defy easy answers?

Commitment and Choices

"Look at the mess the world is in," some observe. "What word do we hear from God about it?" What word would they accept? God has already spoken in his incarnate Word, and, if they will not respond to that word, what word will they hear? Those who have "ears to hear" have heard God's coming in that living Word and have responded to it.

Life requires of us a decision of commitment. We commit ourselves either to the way of despair and cynicism or to the path of faith and hope. Either choice requires commitment. We select faith or non-faith. We choose to believe or to sneer. We turn to hope or despair. We choose, nevertheless. Even our non-choosing is deciding.

Struggle and responsibility are simply a part of the fiber of life. It is still, after all has been said on either side, a leap of trust or non-trust. We can leap into the "slough of despondency" or make a "leap of faith." If we make the leap of faith, we will take up our cross and follow Christ. We have, then, become people of "the way." We also travel this path with awareness, in the words of Dag Hammarskjöld, that "the way chose you—And you must be thankful."[3]

Some years ago when our children were young, my family and I visited King's Dominion, a large amusement park near Richmond, Virginia. Among the many attractions and rides, we decided to take the venture down the giant sliding board. With our sliding sacks in our hands, my wife, seven-year-old son, nine-year-old daughter, and I made the long climb up the steep steps to the top. None of us, however, had anticipated it would be so high! Catherine, my daughter, took her plunge cautiously. Emily, my wife, lunged forward with some reluctance. Bill Powell sat undecidedly until one of the attendants gave him a helpful shove. I caught my breath, leaned forward, and said to myself: "Here we go, I hope." Some others made the climb to the top, saw how high it was, and quickly retreated down the steps, unwilling to risk the slide. They missed the fun and adventure because they would not take the seemingly risky venture.

I wonder how many people do not find the thrill of the adventure of life because they have remained trapped in their own corner of self-sufficiency and have not been willing to make the leap of trust? "What is the end of man?" Calvin asked at the beginning of his catechism. "To know God and love him forever." What is his happiness? The same. We have been created to have fellowship with God, and genuine happiness cannot be realized apart from God. "In him," as Augustine wrote, "we live and move and have our very being." The writer of John noted that the purpose of his Gospel was "that you may believe that Jesus is the Christ, the Son of God, and that believing you may have life in his name" (John 20:31, RSV). Jesus tells us that life in him has direction. It is life filled with meaning and purpose. "I am come," he said, "that they might have life, and that they might have it more abundantly" (John 10:10, KJV).

Faith

Faith provides us with direction. With our lives rooted and grounded in God, we have a sense of inner strength and stability. We are conscious that the universe is not moving madly along without direction but is under the control of a creator who is a loving friend, whom we can know and love.

William James, the famous professor of philosophy at Harvard, wrote to a friend in January, 1868: "All last winter . . . I was on the continual verge of suicide . . ."[4] What was it that brought James out of his mental distress? He noted later that when he had been driven to the edge of the slope, with pessimism at the bottom, and the nightmare of suicide as one of the few options left to him, the final appeal to which he turned was his religious faith.

As Christians we confront our world, not with naïve notions about its conditions, but with inner joy and faith that do not give way to despair. We enter into life with our eyes wide open to the struggles people experience, and our ears are filled to the bursting point with the noise of the world, but we still affirm: "Hallelujah! The Lord God omnipotent reigneth!" With the apostle Paul we declare:

> Yet we who have this spiritual treasure are like common clay pots, to show that the supreme power belongs to God, not to us. We are often troubled, but not crushed; sometimes in doubt, but never in despair; there are many enemies, but we are never without a friend; and though badly hurt at times, we are not destroyed. (2 Cor. 4:7-9 TEV)

Christ's Perspective

Life in Jesus Christ gives us perspective. We often desire to live in an imaginary world, free of struggle and problems, glowing with spectacular events. We sometimes feel that we have been slighted and that someone else has received a better slice of life than we have. We become bogged down in the sameness and routineness of our days and long for something more exciting or dramatic. When suffering or difficulties come our way, we want to cry, "Why me? What have I done to deserve this?"

Some years ago when my daughter fell out of a tree and broke her arm, she looked up from the ground and exclaimed, "I wish this was a bad dream." In times of pain and unpleasantness, we long for escape and relief.

A Higher Vision

Perspective lifts our horizon. It keeps us from being crushed by circumstances or events. If our vision is determined by outward circumstances, then we might easily be defeated by despair. Our vision is lifted beyond the local and immediate conditions when we are aware that we are committed to a God who allows all free will, but who is slowly, decade by decade and century by century, working out his will in the world. We live with the awareness that God does not exempt Christians from all suffering and difficulties, but he assures us of his presence in the midst of our struggles. Tribulation, distress, persecution, famine, nakedness, peril, or sword shall not separate us from the love of God. Paul says in his Roman epistle,

> No, in all these things we are more than conquerors through him who loved us. For I am sure that neither death, nor life, nor angels, nor principalities, nor things present, nor things to come, nor powers, nor height, nor depth, nor anything else in all creation, will be able to separate us from the love of God in Christ Jesus our Lord. (8:37-39 RSV)

This kind of inner assurance enabled Dietrich Bonhoeffer, the German theologian, to walk with courage as the Nazi Gestapo led him to the scaffold. "This is the end," he said to his friends before he left, "for me the beginning of life."[5]

If we seek to get meaning from life only from the comforts and securities of material things, we will be disappointed. The English word for happiness is derived from a root word that means chance. Happiness, according to this approach, will depend on circumstances, the sands of fortune, or just plain luck. If happiness is primarily an external matter, many circumstances can cause it to disappear, such as the death of a loved one, a financial setback, war, natural calamities, accidents, suffering, or disappointments. The Christian's happiness is founded on internal security independent of external circumstances. If our life and happiness are based only on material things, when they are removed, as circumstances often do remove them, then all meaning for living disappears with them. The Christian's security, however, is rooted in the awareness of God's love and providence. It is the "joy" that Jesus said no one can take from you (see John 16:22).

A Reason for Living

When I lived in New Orleans, I had the opportunity of hearing Viktor Frankl, the Austrian psychiatrist who had spent some harrowing years in Auschwitz and other grim, German concentration camps. He spoke of his search for "a will to meaning" in the midst of those horrid conditions of suffering and inhumanity. Out of his agonizing experience he concluded that a person who has a "why" for living can endure almost any "how." One can survive the worst conditions when one's life has purpose. Frankl was convinced that a person finds meaning in life only "to the extent to which he commits himself to something beyond himself, to a cause greater than himself."[6]

In a sense, then, is it not true that a person who commits suicide is one who has become so self-conscious that she cannot see life in any terms beyond her own existence? Despair arises because everything is measured by our own needs and not by what we can do for others. The "why" is gone, and we are crushed. As Christians, we find the "why" to life's meaning beyond our selfish interests when we "lose our lives" in the service of others. As we spend ourselves in service for others, we minister not only to others but also to ourselves.

The Paradoxical Higher Way

Many of the words of Jesus are not easy to understand or apply. They often shatter our pretenses for nominal living and challenge us to a higher way. For many, life's motto for happiness is "safety first," and the old maxim, "self-preservation is nature's first law," becomes the standard for defensive living. Jesus has challenged these assertions and has pointed us in a different direction to affirmative living. He guides us to realize that we find life paradoxically by losing it: "For whoever would save his life will lose it; and whoever loses his life for my sake, he will save it" (Luke 9:24, RSV). The reality of life's meaning, according to Jesus, is found in the dedication to something outside of myself with such intense commitment that I forget about myself. Can this be possible? This is the direction to which Jesus points us.

In the twentieth century, Albert Schweitzer exemplified sacrificial dedication. Although he was acclaimed as a noted philosopher, theologian, organist, musicologist, minister, and professor, he believed something was missing from his life. The void in his life was filled when he prepared himself to go as a medical missionary to Lambarené, Africa. Schweitzer believed he needed to make some acknowledgment to God for the blessings he had received. In his autobiography, he stated that he was stabbed awake one morning with this realization:

> I must not accept this happiness as a matter of course, but must give something in return for it . . . I tried to settle what meaning lay hidden for me in the saying of Jesus: "Whosoever would save his life shall lose it, and whosoever shall lose his life for my sake and the Gospels shall save it." . . . In addition to the outward, I now had inward happiness.[7]

When our lives are directed inwardly, our concerns are selfish and we cannot see beyond our immediate needs or desires. So, we rush from one arena of life to another seeking satisfaction and fulfillment. We long to be fed, groomed, entertained, and protected. We are like the Lock in one of Lewis Carroll's fantasies who ran continually and feverishly looking for something. "Why, whatever is the matter?" someone asked the Lock. "I'm looking," replied the Lock, "for a key to unlock me!"[8] The Lock symbolizes every man and woman. It mirrors our own dilemma. Every one of us longs for someone to come along with the key that will unlock our genuine self and enable us to experience the real meaning of life. Jesus offers us the key to the authentic life in sacrificial living. His paradox provides the key that can unlock our lives. As we follow him, we discover that we save only as we spend ourselves in some cause beyond ourselves; we receive only in giving, and find only by losing.

"The Schweitzers in our world are rare," someone may say. Yes, but Albert Schweitzer does not stand alone. Others, from the age of the apostle Paul to our present era, have marched that sacrificial way. Remember Francis of Assisi, the man of peace and poverty; Florence Nightingale, the founder of the modern nursing movement; William Booth, whose Salvation Army circles the world; Martin Luther, the church reformer; Toyohiko Kagawa, the Japanese social reformer; Tom Dooley, the medical doctor to Southeast Asia; Ann Sullivan Macy, who lifted Helen Keller out of a pit of personal darkness; Martin Luther King, Jr., who dreamed of a new, free society for all people; Mother Theresa who ministered to the poor and hurting of India. The list could go on. They lost themselves in worthy causes beyond themselves. They found the higher way and dared to walk in it.

Seeking Jesus' Way

I have seen others who have walked the paradoxical way of Jesus. They have received little, if any, recognition for their service—no national or world applause. They saw a need and moved to help, in a quiet, unheralded manner. You know their faces in your community.

In my community I can see a retired school principal in her eighties walking to church in the snow to teach a middle-aged black man how to read, as she has taught hundreds before him. I see a man, whose work schedule is demanding, yet who gives many hours each week to the Boys' Club. I see a couple who brings international students into their home and gives them a place where they are loved. I see another couple going week after week to nursing homes and talking, listening, and playing with the patients. I see hundreds of volunteers going to the Gulf Coast to assist victims of hurricane Katrina.

Many others could join this list. They have committed their lives in a quiet manner to the Christ-like way. These are the kind of people who have found the direction of God in ordinary living. These are people who "have bloomed where they were planted" and have not spent time fantasizing about what they could do if . . . They have concluded that the problems of life demand daily attention and are not overcome usually in spectacular ways but by plain hard work. They are aware that they cannot solve all the problems of the world or even in their own community, but they have committed themselves to attacking a problem, a part of a problem, if you like, where they live. They are aware that they may not lift the whole burden of sin and suffering from the back of humanity, but they will get under the load so that others will feel some benefit from their efforts. They work with the knowledge that one does not find a meaningful life, but makes life meaningful. They are aware that they are few, but they labor with the knowledge that throughout history it has always been a few who have engaged in the struggle against the meaningless forces in the world. They work with the awareness that they do not labor alone, but along with God.

Christians link their lives with a cause and a purpose bigger than themselves, "the kingdom of God." They remember the words of their Lord: "Be concerned above everything else with his kingdom and with what he requires, and he will provide you with all these other things" (Matt. 6:33, TEV). No one has all the answers to the questions of suffering, sin, or evil. As we move in the light we already have in the way of Jesus Christ, we find more light, and we can then venture into it. In his light we find direction, and we can walk with the assurance that his way is going somewhere.

Notes

[1] Loren Eiseley, from a university address in J. A. Battle and Robert L. Shannon, eds., *The New Idea in Education* (New York: Harper & Row, 1968), 46-47.

[2] Eric Marshall and Stuart Hample, comps., *Children's Letters to God* (New York: Essandess Special Editions, a division of Simon & Schuster, Inc., 1966), 9.

[3] Dag Hammarskjöld, *Markings* (New York: Alfred A. Knopf, Inc., 1964), 213.

[4] William James, ed., *The Letters of William James,* vol. 1 (Boston: Atlantic Monthly Press, 1920), 129.

[5] Dietrich Bonhoeffer, *Letters and Papers from Prison,* ed. Eberhard Bethge; trans. Reginald H. Fuller (New York: Macmillan Publishing Co., Inc., 1953), 14.

[6] Viktor E. Frankl, "The Will to Meaning," in Paul Tournier et al., *Are You Nobody?* (Richmond: John Knox Press, 1966), 26-27.

[7] Albert Schweitzer, *Out of My Life and Thought,* trans. C. T. Compion (New York: Holt, Rinehart and Winston, Inc., 1961), 85.

[8] Gerald Kennedy, comp., *A Reader's Notebook* (New York: Harper & Row, 1953), 311.

www.ingramcontent.com/pod-product-compliance
Lightning Source LLC
Chambersburg PA
CBHW071707160426
43195CB00012B/1604